As I found myself immersed in these pages, I wished I'd been the one to write this book. It speaks to a part of me that rarely gets expressed so deeply yet longs to do so. I believe that every moment offers glimpses beyond the thin veils of everyday reality. These glimpses mostly elude us, not because they are so obscure but because our busy lives take precedence and blind us. The great gift of this book is that it focuses and holds our attention on those transcendent moments, deepening our appreciation for the Mystery. For me, these pages are reminders of potentials beyond the mind, senses, and obligatory acts of my life—capacities that connect me with the Higher Order where I bask in the true *power of now*.

—Hal Zina Bennett, author of *Writing Spiritual Books*

Joseph Felser's words flow like liquid, and light the pages of his book in a sparkling blend of wisdom and humor, philosophical reflection and personal chronicle. The author weaves a compelling web of dreams, visions, and intriguing synchronicities that bespeak the invisible bonds tying us all to the matrix of nature. His ultimate aim could not be more significant to us at this juncture of our history: to reground our alienated reason in the embodied realities of imagination, feeling, and Mother Earth herself—also known as *Eve*.

—Steven M. Rosen, professor emeritus of City University of New York

Scholar and pilgrim Joseph Felser draws on his own experiences, those of others, and the wisdom literature of the ages to show that the values that connect us to ourselves and to all others can only be found through seeking, finding, and walking one's own path to that place beyond yet within ourselves where we are all one even as we are unique.

—Rhea A. White, director of the Exceptional Human Experience Network and editor-in-chief of *The Journal of the American Society for Psychical Research*

THE WAY BACK TO PARADISE

RESTORING THE BALANCE

BETWEEN

Magic AND *Reason*

JOSEPH M. FELSER, PH.D.

for the evolving human spirit

HAMPTON ROADS
PUBLISHING COMPANY, INC.

Cover design by Tiffany McCord
Cover digital image © 2004 GettyImages/PhotoDisc/Fototeca Storica Nazionale

Lyrics from *St. Stephen* and *Ripple* by Robert Hunter, copyright Ice Nine Publishing
Company. Used with permission.

Excerpts from *The Wind Is My Mother* by Bear Heart and Molly Larkin, copyright ©
1996 by Bear Heart and Molly Larkin. Used by permission of Clarkson Potter/
Publishers, a division of Random House, Inc.

Excerpts from *Ultimate Journey* by Robert Monroe, copyright © 1994 by Robert
Monroe. Used by permission of Doubleday, a division of Random House, Inc.

Hampton Roads Publishing Company, Inc.
1125 Stoney Ridge Road
Charlottesville, VA 22902

434-296-2772
fax: 434-296-5096
e-mail: hrpc@hrpub.com
www.hrpub.com

If you are unable to order this book from your local
bookseller, you may order directly from the publisher.
Call 1-800-766-8009, toll-free.

Library of Congress Cataloging-in-Publication Data

Felser, Joseph M., 1957-
 The way back to paradise : restoring the balance between magic and reason
/ Joseph M. Felser.
  p. cm.
 Includes bibliographical references and index.
 ISBN 1-57174-380-4 (5 1/2 x 8 1/2 tpbk. : alk. paper)
 1. Self-actualization (Psychology)--Miscellanea. 2. Parapsychology. I. Title.
 BF1045.S44F45 2005
 204'.4--dc22
                          2004020591
                  10 9 8 7 6 5 4 3 2 1
       Printed on acid-free paper in the United States

Among the great religious problems of the present is one which has received scant attention, but which is in fact the main problem of our day: the evolution of the religious spirit.

—Carl G. Jung, commentary on "The Secret of the Golden Flower" (1962)

We must look directly at our own experience again—and learn to trust it. We must be our own psychic naturalists, combining reason and intuition. We must refuse to let old theories define our realities for us, limiting and distorting the very scope of our lives.

—Jane Roberts, *The God of Jane: A Psychic Manifesto* (1981)

The Western world must be prepared to analyze religion as a phenomenon that does not necessarily explain the unanswered questions posed by the philosophical mind but that may, in itself, cause such questions to occur to all manner of people in a great variety of situations.

—Vine Deloria Jr., *God Is Red: A Native View of Religion* (1994)

For all those who meet at the fountain
not made by the hands of men

Contents

Acknowledgments

The book that you hold in your hands is very different from the one I began writing almost eight years ago. This is the third or fourth version—truth be told, I've lost count. The project evolved over time, often in surprising and unpredictable ways. New experiences and new questions continually forced me to reexamine what I was doing, how I was doing it, and, most importantly, why I was writing at all. What began life as a strictly academic treatise became, of necessity, a very personal story. Things change.

The one delightful constant in all this is the encouragement and support that I have received from numerous friends along the way. Of course, none of them can (or should) be held responsible for any errors I might have made in these pages. Also, I would not expect any of them to agree with everything I've written here. Above all, however, I'm grateful that each and every one of them joined me for at least a part of my journey. And, to borrow a phrase, what a long, strange trip it's been!

Thanks galore, then, to Suzanne Brown, Rob Butts, Bob Cracknell, Joel Funk, Gina Galate, Michael Grosso, Sam Keen, Paul Newman, Ken Ring, Steve Rosen, Charles Tart, Raymond Van Over, Sheila Reynolds, Sandra Stevens, Rhea White, and Colin Wilson.

I owe a very special debt of gratitude to Hal Zina Bennett. Hal is a superb teacher and coach. Thanks, Hal, for helping me find my authentic voice.

A hearty round of appreciation goes out to all my Virginia friends: Nancy (Scooter) and Joe McMoneagle, and the entire staff of The Monroe Institute (TMI), especially Dr. Darlene Miller, the institute's program director. Bob Monroe was a true visionary.

I owe a special thank you to Frank DeMarco, who was enthusiastic from the start. Thanks also to Richard Leviton, my editor at Hampton Roads, who made a number of helpful suggestions and comments.

I am grateful to my students for sharing their personal stories with me.

Without my wife, Cynthia, it would not have been possible.

And Katahdin, our golden retriever, wisely saw to it that I took frequent breaks for ballplaying and other important spiritual pursuits. Thanks, pup!

Another kind of debt is owed to my father and my (late) mother. Mom, you asked me what it all meant to me. Well, here it is—finally.

My faculty union, the Professional Staff Congress of the City University of New York (PSC-CUNY), provided grants that funded part of the research for chapters 6 and 7.

Prologue

The Hummingbird's Message

Life for the Indian is one of harmony with Nature and the things
which surround him.
—Chief Luther Standing Bear, *My Indian Boyhood* (1988)

A Close Encounter of the Feathered Kind

The fateful encounter took place several summers ago,
when my wife, Cynthia, and I were vacationing on the majestic lake that the native Abenaki tribes of Maine called *Sebago*,
meaning "great stretch of water." At over three hundred feet
deep at its center and eleven miles in length, it is indeed a
great lake—in fact, the deepest and third largest in New
England. Ten thousand years ago, it was part of the Atlantic
Ocean.

Even before I knew this odd bit of natural history, however,
the lake reminded me of the ocean; perhaps it was because of
the close connection I'd felt with the ocean as a child. The lake
and I always seemed to enjoy a mysterious bond, like two secret
conspirators. For example, my dreams always take on a depth
and pristine clarity that match the crystal clear waters of the

lake. It's as if I am gazing into a magic mirror that never fails to reveal the truth.

But this was no dream.

One hot summer afternoon I was lazily paddling about on the lake on an inner tube, soaking up the warm sunshine. The tall pines rustled in the light afternoon breeze. A lone seagull winged its way high overhead in the direction of the marina, probably in quest of a fisherman's tasty cast-offs. Relaxed by the gentle rocking of the waves, my mind began to drift into the peaceful rhythms of its own sweet reverie.

Suddenly, out of the corner of my eye, I noticed something moving near the dock. Turning for a better look, I beheld a tiny figure perched atop the post. As I quietly paddled closer to get a better look, the figure hovered in midair, its rapidly vibrating wings an indistinguishable blur. Slowly descending, it came to rest on the post, its distinctive needlelike bill now fully visible in profile. No more than a few inches in length, its iridescent green-black feathers glistened in the bright sunlight.

A ruby-throated hummingbird!

I had only recently glimpsed my very first "hummer" (as I learned bird aficionados affectionately called them). I marveled at their acrobatic stunts and extraordinary grace. Cynthia bought a special hummingbird feeder with suction cups that we attached to the glass slider in the kitchen. At mealtimes, we enjoyed watching their amusing antics.

But what was this little one doing all the way down here by the water?

Just then, the bird left its perch for the bowed and weathered planks of the wooden gangway. As the waves rolled into shore, gently lifting the gangway, the hummer bobbed up and down, in time with the movements of the gangway, as if it were enjoying a seesaw ride at the park. I could hardly believe my eyes. Moreover, I somehow seemed to sense its enjoyment.

That bird was playing a game.

Knowing that many Native American tribes traditionally view birds as messengers of the spirit, I asked the hummingbird if it had a message for me. Feeling a bit self-conscious, I nonetheless addressed it out loud.

"Do you have any wisdom that you might wish to share?" I asked.

At that, the hummer buzzed away from the dock and headed straight for me, stopping only a yard or so away. Hovering like a miniature helicopter just above the waterline, it darted down to the surface, then up again in the air, three or four times in rapid succession, similar to the game it had been playing with the gangway. Then I watched in amazement as it flew even closer to me, disappearing just beneath my field of vision.

I was stunned. The only place the bird could be was on the other side of the inner tube, only inches from my foot.

As if reading my thoughts, the tiny aerialist revealed itself. It remained suspended above me before settling on the tube itself, close to my right hand. I tried hard not to do anything that might startle the bird. I even kept my breathing regular and calm, as if in meditation.

But the hummer took off once again. For a moment, I thought it was going to fly away. Instead, it flew a short hop into the air, then landed again—this time directly on my left foot. Nestling into the curved webbing of my nylon water shoe, the little bird closed its eyes and made gentle peeping noises, like soft sighs of contentment.

And there, on my foot, my new friend happily remained. We floated along together, bobbing about on the inner tube, enjoying the afternoon breeze and each other's company.

Fifteen minutes or so passed. Then I watched as Cynthia walked down to the lake for her afternoon swim, our golden retriever, Katahdin, cavorting at her side. As she approached the dock, I carefully pointed at my foot and put my finger to my mouth.

Spying my little visitor, Cynthia grabbed Katahdin's collar then bolted back up to the house to get a camera. When she returned with Katahdin in tow, my hummingbird friend was still comfortable on my foot. She snapped a few pictures.

"Woof!" Katahdin was unable to contain himself any longer.

The startled bird zoomed off to perch on a low branch of a nearby pine tree, then briefly circled back toward me before deciding, on second thought, that our big dog was too much for it.

Fortunately, I didn't have to rack my brain to grasp what my winged teacher was trying to tell me. The hummingbird's message was received, loud and clear: Trust.

That bird, not knowing me from Adam, had trusted me with its life. It had recognized me as kin. That was a humbling and awesome experience. In tune with the rhythm of the lake, I had found my own inner rhythm, one that resonated with the greater harmony of the cosmos. I think the hummingbird heard that same song.

Trust.

Trust what? Trust nature, including your own nature. Observe, listen, and pay proper attention—and respect—to both. Then magic will happen, of its own accord.

But what happens if this trust and respect are missing?

Birds of a Different Feather

A few years before the hummingbird incident, Cynthia and I were out one day taking a walk in our new neighborhood, where we'd recently bought a house. Suddenly, Katahdin pulled me toward a certain rhododendron bush near the edge of our property. I could see that something lay underneath, though I couldn't immediately make out what it was.

The mystery object turned out to be a dead bird, a common grackle. We figured that some cat had gotten lucky. Later on, though, we noticed several more dead blackbirds lying about. That must have been one busy cat, I thought. It was very strange.

In the days that followed, however, it became apparent that the real culprit was no agile tabby on the loose. Dead blackbirds by the dozens littered the green suburban landscape, their rotting corpses stinking under the broiling August sun. Worst of all were the dying birds. Flopping about in the gutter, unable to fly, the poor creatures would screech a horrible scream of death. It was agonizing to watch, and alarming. More alarming still was the fact that no one else seemed to notice or care.

One afternoon, I happened to meet the mailman while he was walking his route. With concern in my voice, I asked him if he knew anything about the birds.

"Oh, yeah, that's been happening for years," he stated matter-of-factly.

"For years? And no one knows, or cares to know, why?"

"Nope, I guess not," he replied, in a way that suggested he might be curious.

Hear no evil, see no evil, and speak no evil. A silent spring? Not yet, anyway. Death was certainly noisy (and smelly). Yet still seemingly invisible, at least to the jaundiced eye.

Quietly, without fanfare or public notice, the state environmental department finally came around to investigate. A biologist took soil samples and collected fresh bird corpses in plastic bags. He gave us his card after we happened to see him at work and expressed interest in hearing the results of his laboratory tests.

No one wanted to know the truth (it might affect property values, after all). The culprit turned out to be a ubiquitous and once commonly used pesticide that had been banned since the 1980s when it was found to cause cancer. It had been used to such excess that the beetles it was meant to kill developed immunity to its effects. Yet the chemical remained in the soil and in the bodies of the insects. When the young birds feasted on the beetle larvae each summer, they would poison themselves, destroying their central nervous systems. As they would continue to do for decades to come.

We didn't know it, but we were living on a killing field.

The message of these unfortunate birds was clear: Something is wrong, dead wrong. We humans are at war with nature, including our own inner natures. And for what? Green lawns and greenbacks; to some people, it's all that matters. They are so disconnected from themselves and from nature that they have forgotten the meaning of trust and respect.

On the other hand, there are many well-intentioned seekers who labor under the illusion that connecting to nature (which, after all, is just another name for All That Is) requires a lot of hard work, and special—maybe even privileged—knowledge. They believe that they need priests, gurus, saints, and sages to tell them how it's done, to instruct them in the mysteries. And so they give away their power, opening themselves to manipulation and abuse. Just as blood attracts sharks, so self-mistrust is an open invitation to exploitation.

The truth is, there is no privileged revelation, no hidden knowledge reserved for initiates only or an esoteric elite. Our cosmic connection is always present (hardwired in us by Nature herself) and absolutely inviolable. It is our inalienable birthright. We need only claim it. Or reclaim it, as the case may be. For we are all natural sensitives—psychic from the start, mystically attuned to the larger rhythms of the cosmos since before our physical birth and forever after our physical death. Only we have forgotten.

I know, because a little bird reminded me.

The New Religious Consciousness

The future of what we call religion (or sometimes, to avoid using that troubling word, "spirituality")—our own future, in other words—hinges on remembering what we've been assiduously taught to forget. This will be a difficult, even painful process.

Many of my students ask me if I am religious. They are surprised when I say no.

What is religion, then?

Our English word "religion" originally came from a Latin word (*relegere* or *relictio*) that meant "the careful reading of the great book of nature." The early Christian church, unhappy with this definition (because in its eyes nature was fallen and evil), substituted for it a word that sounded similar to the ear, but which had a very different meaning. This new word (*religare* or *religio*) meant "strict obedience to authority."[1]

After all, if you have nature, who needs authorities?

To move ahead, we must first recover what we have lost. This book is the story of my own quest to recover my natural psychic sensitivity.

Like so many, I was taught to ignore what I knew by my own direct experience, to depend on external authorities (and their answers), and to wage a continuing, futile, and self-destructive war against my own nature. I mistrusted my dreams, hunches, gut feelings, and visions. I doubted that I could be guided by synchronicities (meaningful coincidences) or get my reason and my intuition to work together harmoniously. Most of all, I was distinctly uncomfortable with my own curiosity and embarrassed by my annoying tendency to question established beliefs. Like the biblical Eve, I always felt like an outcast, as if I didn't fit in because I'd done something to offend the gods.

Paradise Regained: Magic and Reason
Together Again, for the First Time

What do you need to know as we pack our bags and prepare to make our way back to paradise? What sort of exotic metaphysical flora and fauna can you expect to see on our expedition? What epistemological assumptions (that is, premises about what we know and how we claim to know it) are best left out of our mental luggage? Why indeed should we bother to undertake this arduous journey? What's in it for us?

As I argue in this book, "paradise" is not the name of a place or a destination (physical or otherwise). Nor does it designate a pure, unchanging state of consciousness, free of conflict or questions.

As I contend in chapter 3, there is no point in indulging our nostalgic longing for a lost—if only imaginary or overly romanticized—past, either in recorded history or before it. For there was no Garden of Eden, and thus no Fall of humanity, no Original Sin. A primordial state of perfect innocence, purity, and simplicity has never existed and will never exist.

Thus the return to paradise does not entail a rejection of the complexities of life or the burdensome complications of self-conscious awareness. Ignorance is not bliss after all, and deliberate, willful ignorance is (or at least ought to be) a crime.

So what, then, is "paradise"? As I explain later in the book, paradise is not a static state of harmony, but an ongoing (and probably never-ending) activity of harmoni*zing* (with emphasis on the *-ing* suffix, indicating, according to my dictionary, an "action, process, or art"). Paradise is not the garden of bliss, but rather, the bliss of gardening. Hence the journey back to paradise is not a regressive or reactionary retreat into some delusional mythological cocoon. Nor does it involve the attempt to realize a Utopian fantasy.

Making our way back to paradise is, however, a "radical" act, in the true and original sense of that oft-maligned term (the Latin *radix* means "root"). Going back to paradise means going down to the root source. What is this living root? What is the flowering plant?

The flowering plant is reason, its living root what I'm calling "magic": experiences of psychic sensitivity that all of us already have, every day of our lives; experiences we'd know we have if we but paid attention to them, for example, precognitive dreams, telepathic communications with humans and other life forms (including animals and nonphysical entities), clairvoyant visions, and synchronicities.

I've had all of these experiences, which I detail throughout the book, and so, I'd be willing to wager, have you. (One huge hurdle to overcome, as we'll see, is that we have been taught to ignore and repress magical experiences, even, or especially, when they're our own.) Paradise, I contend, is the harmonizing of magic and reason.

Right now, we're out of tune—way out. I have a lot more to say about this disharmony in chapter 1, and how we, as a culture, got into this mess in chapter 2. Much of our difficulty stems from what I call "Answerism," a tendency to believe that we have the total picture, which I examine in chapter 3. I explain how I recognized and subsequently tried to mend my own brokenness. The personal stories I share with you will, I hope, make these ideas more clear and understandable.

I show how restoring our balance, or mending the self, means getting back into tune, bringing all our discarded and forgotten parts back into the whole. This "balance" is not, however, a static state of equilibrium; it is a dynamic condition, constantly changing, a dialectical flow, as each new magical experience spurs a new thought, leading to new experience, and so on. You don't stop singing once you learn how. You start, then practice, practice, and more practice.

The harmony of reason and magic may seem to be a tall order. Yet, if the evidence supplied by my magical experiences and philosophical musings (particularly as recounted in my personal stories found in the second half of the book) is any guide, it is not an impossible task.

"My reasoning wants to be faithful to the evidence that aroused it," declared the French existentialist philosopher Albert Camus.[2] This is one of my favorite quotes, for it not only summarizes one of the main conclusions of this book, it also captures my main aspiration in life. We think because we must. We seek truth. But what is the stimulus? Can we own up to it?

As scandalous and inconvenient as it may be to official religion and science alike (for slightly different reasons, as we shall see), reason is a plant that grows—indeed thrives—in the fertile soil of our nonrational experiences of psychic sensitivity.

This sensitivity is what the anthropologist J. G. Frazer called "sympathetic magic." The magician, he wrote in *The Golden Bough* (1890), is one whose "whole being, body and soul" is ever so "acutely sensitive" and "delicately attuned to the harmony of the world."[3] Or, as the esoteric scholar Lewis Spence said, the law of sympathetic magic holds that everything is "secretly linked together by invisible bonds."[4]

These invisible connections are the bonds that vibrate to the psychic touch. In spontaneous cases of telepathy, clairvoyance, synchronicity, and so forth, we are connected to the larger, usually unnoticed patterns of our existence. The psychic is not trivial. It is our personal lifeline to the All.

Why do we ignore these invisible bonds? In part, it is due to our fears, which I examine at length in chapter 5 (and I offer some tips for overcoming these inner blocks). But another major obstacle is the poor, malnourished concept of reason we have inherited from our philosophies—a concept that blinds us to reason's true magical roots.

This is the fault of our western philosophical approach. As an academic philosopher, I know something about this firsthand. One of my key premises is that, since the seventeenth century, we have been operating with essentially two not dissimilar notions of reason (with minor variations on these two basic themes), neither of which is adequate.

From the French philosopher René Descartes (1596–1650), we get the view that reason is a sharp scalpel, slicing and dicing large problems or fields of study into their smallest component parts. In this way, we get down to the basic building blocks of knowledge: what Descartes called "first principles."

Descartes's view is the analytical view of reason, and it matched the search of physicists like Isaac Newton for the atom, the smallest indivisible physical unit. Later philosophers of this analytic bent argued that what we analyze is not reality itself, but only language about reality—words, sentences, propositions, or (with Ludwig Wittgenstein) entire "language games." But the basic idea was the same. Reason is a dissecting tool—a scalpel, a laser—for taking things apart.

From the British philosopher David Hume (1711–1776), we get the view (called "empiricism") that reason is an adding machine, a counting device (abacus, slide rule, computer—take your pick) that totals up the individual impressions of our physical senses and fixes a label thereon: red + round + noise = fire engine.

According to Hume, reason is untrustworthy because it is apt to go out on a precarious limb and draw conclusions not actually warranted by our senses (oops—it's not a fire engine, it's an ambulance). We'd be better off forgetting our theories and ideas (and that most dangerous faculty of imagination; see chapter 1) and sticking to our sense data—but, there we go again, making unwarranted inferences. Alas, we can't help it. We are prisoners of custom and habit, assuming (often wrongly and never with reasonable justification) that the future will be like the past, the unknown like the known.

Although Descartes was an optimist and Hume a skeptic about reason, both believed that, in their own way, they were making reason more rigorously "scientific." But were they? I contend reason is no more a mere adding machine or a logical scalpel than a gardener is her shovel or rake. These are only (some) tools used by reason, and not reason as such. To think otherwise, I suggest, is a fatal mistake.

What, then, is reason?

"Reason," said Joseph Campbell, "has to do with finding the ground of being and the fundamental structuring order of the universe."[5] In other words, as I assume in this book, reason is the faculty of asking ultimate questions, of seeing things as a whole, of making real—not, as Hume thought, spurious—connections.

As the English writer Thomas Carlyle (1795–1881) stated, the true spiritual (or philosophical) hero is one who wonders: "What am I? What is this unfathomable Thing I live in, which men name Universe? What is Life; what is Death? What am I to believe? What am I to do?"[6]

To provoke such deep questioning, one must enjoy deep experiences of a particular kind. Such experiences suggest that all is not as it seems, that there is another, hidden layer of reality. These are the experiences of magic, of nature's invisible bonds. They inspire wonder; wonder begets questioning; and questioning is the soul of reason.

Whether as metaphysics or physics, the human mind strives, either consciously or unconsciously, to express and understand its direct, unmediated experience of these subtle connections. As Joseph Campbell said, the invisible supports and nourishes the visible.[7] There would be no language without telepathy, no prediction without precognition, no discovery without clairvoyance, no inference without dream and vision.

Thus Dr. Willis Harman, past president of the Institute of Noetic Sciences (an alternative think tank that investigates the wider ranges of human potential), has gone so far as to maintain that there is a "secret history of inspiration" that orthodox science and philosophy conceal—even from themselves.[8]

The secret of human inquiry is thus the inquiry of the great but open cosmic secret that spurs on all of our questions and creative insights.

My encounter and communication with the hummingbird was an expression of this magical attunement (an enjoyment of harmony, a taste of paradise), the holocaust of the grackles the result of a denial and rejection of it. In truth, however, there was more magic involved in both episodes than I previously let on. Allow me to explain.

The hummingbird incident occurred not long after I watched a video about the great Swiss psychologist C. G. Jung (with whom I have long had a strong affinity, as I discuss in more detail in chapter 1). The video featured an interview with one of Jung's grandsons, Dieter Baumann (now middle-aged), who recalled an oft-repeated incident about Jung first told to him when he was a child.

When Jung sat outdoors by the lake near his tower retreat at Bollingen, he would easily slip into a state of reverie, "like a Taoist sage in full harmony with both the internal and external worlds," said Baumann. Once, he related, a bird landed on Jung's head and sat there for ten minutes.

When I heard this story, I thought, "Oh, sure, but something *that* magical would never happen to *me*." Then, not long afterward, it did. The universe not only made a liar out of me, it linked me, once again—and in spite of myself—to Jung, someone whose work has meant a great deal to me over the years. Invisible bonds, you see (or don't). My reason had yet another mystery to ponder—more grist for the mill.

In the case of the grackles, magic was also at work in the background. Not long before we discovered the dying birds, I had been brooding about the fact that my mother, who had died of cancer several years before, would never see our new home. I also recalled an incident she'd told me about, many times, that occurred during her first bout with cancer, some twelve years before she succumbed to its recurrence.

She had elected to undergo what was then a highly experimental radiation therapy procedure after her surgery. At the time, this new option was only offered at a Philadelphia hospital. So she hopped the commuter train from suburban New Jersey into Philadelphia, by herself, every day over the course of several weeks, for outpatient treatment. Dressed to the nines and sporting a briefcase, she looked like just another commuter going to work. (It was psychologically beneficial for her to think this way as well.)

One day after the treatment, as she was being driven home from the train station in the taxi, the driver sighed as he came to a stop at an intersection not far from my parents' house. (This intersection is only a couple of miles from the neighborhood where Cynthia and I now live, and where we'd found the poisoned grackles.)

"See that, over there," the driver said, pointing to a brand new housing development. "I used to be a truck driver. We were told to dump stuff—bad stuff, drums full of chemicals—there, when that was just an empty field. It made me sick just to think about it. I had to quit."

My mother went numb. She made some idle remark like, "Oh, my," but said no more. The driver, of course, didn't know of her illness. My mother, of course, hadn't known of the chemicals. Nor did the proud new owners of those nice new suburban homes.

On the surface, my mother's death from cancer and the death of the grackles from pesticides were not connected. However, in a deeper sense, they were part of the same larger pattern—the same war against nature, the same inability to sense those magical invisible bonds connecting everything, the same shortsighted, greedy mentality.

We think we're so clever, that we can manage cause and effect. Like James Bond, we're confident that, at the last possible moment, some technological gadget we pull out of our pocket will save the day. But that's not going to happen. Unless we reestablish the connection with inner and outer nature, unless reason is reacquainted with its magical roots, we will kill ourselves with our sheer cleverness.

One of my main purposes in writing this book is to convince you that nourishing our psychic sensitivity to what the old Native American shamans called "the hoop of life" is not an option, something that we might decide to do at a weekend workshop, if we're so inclined. It is a necessity if we wish to survive as a species on this planet. As I argue throughout the book, those old Indian shamans still have a great deal to teach us—if we're willing to learn.

You might think that this sort of educational project should be the job of religion and spirituality, which acknowledge these subtle, invisible bonds—at least in theory.

In practice, however, traditional religions and even many esoteric spiritual systems seek to cloud our perception of the invisible dimension with distorting fears, illusions, and superstitions. They do this in order to stage-manage and control not only the magic itself, but also the questing intelligence to which our innate psychic sensitivity gives birth. They condemn the psychic as demonic or, at best, as a distraction from "true" spirituality. This distortion is the main topic of chapter 3.

As for science, it, along with its offspring technology, continues to pretend that our reason is utterly self-generating and self-supporting, like a tree growing out of thin air rather than from a seed buried in the rich earth. This idea would truly be magical if the image weren't so laughably absurd. We can repress our sympathy with nature, but we cannot destroy it. Repressed, it exacts its revenge, threatening us with our own doom.

What, then, about my discipline of philosophy? In the darkness of the Christian Middle Ages, philosophy, the ancient "love of wisdom," remained the meek servant of religious faith. In the modern era of the scientific Enlightenment, philosophy courageously proclaimed its independence even as it tacitly exchanged one master for another: science. As the old saw states, "The more things change . . ."

In my years of studying philosophy at both the undergraduate and graduate level, I worked hard at accumulating the various badges of academic honor and achievement. Not to brag, but I earned my share of these: Phi Beta Kappa, Summa cum

Laude, overseas fellowships, and more. I also encountered many fine teachers at the major research universities where I earned my degrees.

To my dismay, however, I discovered that virtually all of my professors were in thrall to one or another version of the old time religion (scientific materialism, Christianity, Marxism). As such, they were either roundly dismissive of, or indifferent to, those personal experiences of the invisible bonds that I could neither disown nor affirm. Those experiences fueled my quest, but I couldn't admit that—at least not openly.

By the late 1970s, when I had begun work on my doctorate, a new "postmodern" movement in philosophy had arisen with its promise of deconstructing all the old shibboleths. On closer inspection, however, most of the proponents of this "new" approach were disillusioned adherents of one of the older, ostensibly discredited, views. Their genial, freewheeling anarchism masked an underlying nihilism comprised of equal parts free-floating anxiety and the sour disappointment of a jilted lover.

To the postmodern mind, you could be or do or say anything because nothing, in the end, is objectively real or significant. It was like being trapped in a conversation with a laughing idiot who treats everything you say as a meaningless joke. Yet whatever they were, I knew my experiences of magic were not mere jokes. Sometimes they were funny, but even the most humorous ones were real and meaningful enough, revelatory of a dimension beyond the visible.

Thus, when the time came to begin my own college teaching career in the late 1980s, I felt deeply conflicted about my approach. On the one hand, I knew that those who undertake a genuine search for wisdom have been touched somehow by nature's secret harmony. On the other hand, to talk openly of this invited ridicule (from the scientists) or, worse yet, distortion and misunderstanding (from the religionists). So even as I taught my subject, I pretended that I didn't live it, thereby obviating the need to confess my sensitivity. No wonder my students were confused. So was I.

Eventually, however, I realized that if I valued my integrity, I had no choice but to risk rejection and misinterpretation. So I began to write and publish on subjects that really interested me (e.g., psi and synchronicity). I also worked hard at confronting my fears (I discuss this in chapter 5) and trying to follow the subtle clues that would bring me closer to my own magical roots (as I explain in chapters 4, 6, and 7).

At the same time, I encouraged my students to reexamine their everyday experiences with an eye to uncovering the secret connections, resonances, and affinities that had hitherto escaped their notice—hidden, as it is said, in plain sight. I was rewarded with many stories similar to my own, some of which I share with you in these pages. The philosophical questions, I knew, would follow as a matter of course. They did (and still do).

"It hurts," a student recently confessed when she realized that her old views were not consistent with what she now felt and thought.

"Ah, good," I replied. "That's a sign you're making progress." Inwardly, I sympathized. I have been there myself.

As a member of the academic establishment, I am perhaps more familiar than most with our decrepit cultural ideologies and the extent of their decay. I have been marinating in them for some time now. Having reached the point of saturation, I made a vow that my reasoning would remain faithful to the evidence that aroused it. If I can get you to consider making a similar vow, and opening yourself, and your reason, to the magic that is all around us, I will have accomplished my main purpose in writing this book.

Why should you care? Why should you read this book?

There are many books out there (both good ones and some not so good) on psychic phenomena. Many of them have been written by people who profess to be, or genuinely are, professional "psychics" whose claims have been tested in laboratories or verified by the results they have obtained in their practical fieldwork. Other volumes have been written by professional parapsychologists, the scientists who have actually done the testing and conducted investigations firsthand. You will find some of these names listed in my bibliography.

But I am neither a professional parapsychologist nor a professional psychic. So what gives? What's special about this book?

Here is where some might be tempted to follow the example of the great German philosopher Friedrich Nietzsche, who wrote books with chapter titles such as, "Why I Am So Wise," "Why I Am So Clever," and "Why I Write Such Good Books." Alas, I've known people much more clever than I. As for wisdom, I love it, and I'm still searching for it, but I'd be the last one to claim that I have it (or am wise). Moreover, since this is my first book, I can't point to my sterling record.

No, the reason why I think this is an important book is not because I'm special, but precisely because I'm not. I'm just a canary stuck in the same coal mine as you—one who's willing to own up to his sensitivity to his surroundings. I'm ready to shout a song of warning at the top of my lungs if need be, even at the risk of looking (or sounding) foolish.

Facing up to our psychic sensitivity and using such experiences to fuel inquiry that will bring about social and cultural change are the personal responsibility of each and every one of us. It is our sacred duty. We are all sensitives, and we can all think, even if we're not professional psychics or philosophers. To shirk our individual responsibility to seek a balance between magic and reason is to invite a disaster from which we may not recover.

If I can do it, so can you. Paradise is only a pain away.

<u>1</u>

"I Fell Asleep Under the Tree"

The diversity and Twinness of the Forked Tree is Natural and gives Power to the Human to endure in every kind of circumstance and challenge. When the Power of either of the two branches of the Great Tree is suppressed or ignored, the Tree will die.

—Hyemeyohsts Storm, *Lightningbolt* (1994)

The Missing Link

Ten years ago my mother lay in a hospital bed, dying of cancer. My father and I kept a constant vigil by her bedside as we struggled to accept the inevitable end. At one point, Mom leaned closer to me. In a conspiratorial stage whisper, she confided that she saw someone standing at the end of her bed.

I looked, but saw only the blank wall and the plastic bin for recycling medical waste. The tone of her voice told me she understood that this someone wasn't "really" there.

"Don't worry," she said, as she patted my hand in reassurance, "it's not Jesus!"

We both laughed at the joke. Even on her deathbed, Mom retained her sense of humor and unflappable composure. Dad and I marveled at her bravery.

"It's Ben Casey," she added weakly.

Doctor Ben Casey, from the old television show. He was a brash but talented neurosurgeon who never gave up on a patient, a super-doc with compassion. Intuitively, I understood why Ben was making his rounds at my mother's bedside. Her own doctor had fled the scene, conveniently slipping out of town to attend a medical conference. He would not return until after she died, early the following morning.

Next to his Hollywood prototype, the flesh and blood doctor was a pale imitation. In spite of my anger, however, I realized that this was not entirely his fault. Something is very wrong when a society's healers can no longer perform their sacred task and their only recourse is to throw up their hands in resignation or hide under the nearest rock. Something much larger than one man's character is amiss.

The situation is analogous to what happened to the American Indians when they were hit with smallpox, influenza, and other hitherto unknown European diseases and plagues. All their tribal shamans could do was shake their heads in disbelief. Healing—the art of making a person whole again—was no longer possible. Balance could not be restored. The world had shattered into broken bits and pieces.

Nearly fifty years ago, in the shadow of Hiroshima and the Holocaust, the English philosopher Bertrand Russell predicted that if the West did not overcome its own cultural and social fragmentation, we would bring ourselves "only nearer to irretrievable disaster."[1] Russell was a man of strict logic and science; his faith lay in reason. Yet he despaired that knowledge alone is not enough. (Surely mere data—our own deity of the hour—is not enough either.) What we need is the wisdom to use the knowledge (and data) properly for humane ends, and to get this wisdom, we must experience the world and ourselves as a whole. We have to be able to *see* the connections between means and ends, just as a great eagle can survey a vast territory from high above in the sky. Not only that, but we have to be able to *feel* the unity of all things. Absent this mystical sense, Russell warned, we will destroy ourselves.

This is an old story. An ancient Greek myth says that when Zeus, the king of the gods, created humans, he grew worried that he did too good a job. Eventually, we might become too powerful and overthrow the gods. So Zeus split us right down the middle, like a ripe cantaloupe (see the speech of Aristophanes in Plato's *Symposium*, sec. 191a). Each of us is only half a self. Sadly, we aren't even aware of our infirmity. We've forgotten what it is like to be whole. Afflicted with a strange longing we cannot even name, we yearn for our lost integrity, our missing other half.

This story is more than a quaint old tale. I see it as a useful metaphor for the dangerous path we have been treading for the past several thousand years in what we proudly call "civilization." Our own jealous gods of religion and science have cut us off from our natural bonds to Earth and Spirit. We have lost touch with both our inner world of dream, imagination, and intuition and the outer world of nature—the animals, plants, and elementary forces that sustain us. Indeed, this is no accident; to become alienated from the one is to become estranged from the other, for they are ultimately one and the same.

Our fate is to feel at once disembodied and dispirited, floating in a nowhere zone. We are detached from everything outside the narrow rut of our increasingly meaningless and empty daily routines of commuting, computing, and consuming. We have been reduced, as the philosopher R. G. Collingwood lamented, to mere "wrecks and fragments."[2]

So what, exactly, is the missing link?

As Bertrand Russell understood, our heart life has not kept pace with the growth of our intellect. We are exceedingly clever but lack the wisdom that comes from feeling a part of life. How else can we explain the collective madness of recent genocides, from Rwanda to Yugoslavia? Daily we commit the unspeakable crime of geocide, murdering entire species of animals, plants, and perhaps even Mother Earth herself. The evidence of our heartlessness lies all around us, from school shootings, terrorist bombings, and "holy" wars to the pathetic dishonesty and corruption of our political, business, and religious "leaders."

It's an awful mess, as anyone can see.

I'm afraid that the only way out of this mess is for each of us to confront our own personal craziness, to experience it and suffer through it, firsthand. Only when I did this could I come to see my own misery as a symptom of a much larger imbalance. Only then was I ready and able to receive the gift of insight: The real connection is never lost.

It all began for me more than twenty years ago, during my first few months of graduate school, when I was slaving away on my doctorate in philosophy. . . .

"So, You Want to Be a Wise Man?"

The cold, grey Chicago autumn was rapidly slipping into an even colder and greyer Chicago winter. Having only recently moved there from the East Coast, the city and the university campus were still new to me, and it all felt strange. I had worked hard in college. While my friends were partying, I was in the library, studying. I had been determined to get into a good graduate school. Now that I was there, I felt ill at ease. Something was wrong, though I could not put my finger on it. I felt like the poor fool who had climbed to the top of the ladder, only to discover that it had been placed against the wrong wall.

One afternoon after class, I stopped by a campus coffee shop located in one of the academic buildings. With its dark wood paneling and carpeted floor, the room resembled my fantasy of the dining room of a private club. Groups of students were congregating around tables and benches, smoking cigarettes and chatting away over steaming mugs of coffee and greasy doughnuts. I saw several familiar faces and went over to say hello.

Someone introduced me to Josh, whom I knew by reputation as a brilliant scholar far along in his graduate studies. Josh was sitting cross-legged on one of the wooden benches. With his curly black beard and half-lotus posture, he looked every inch a combination of Zen master and Hasidic sage. He smiled warmly as we shook hands.

"So, you want to be a wise man?" Josh asked, nodding.

I realized, of course, that he was referring to the literal meaning of "philosophy," the ancient Greek word for "the love of wisdom."

"Yeah, I guess so," I replied.

Josh threw back his head and exploded into hearty laughter.

I joined in, to pretend to my own knowing cynicism—the accepted posture of intellectual sophistication. Yet I had answered truthfully. I wanted something more than a mere degree or an academic position. But I was reluctant to say so. Perhaps I felt naïve. By mocking the idea that we were in pursuit of real wisdom, Josh and I were being astute aspiring professionals. It was all a kind of game. Only this game was no fun.

Not long after the incident with Josh, I was sitting in the class of a world-renowned philosopher. Professor Scott, as I'll call him, combined intellectual precision and rigor with an easygoing manner. His battered brown Volkswagen sported an "I'd Rather Be Sailing" bumper sticker. And you could almost believe it. He was gifted with a rich, soothing baritone voice, not to mention a deft, dry sense of humor. He was a campus star.

On this occasion, someone had asked the professor if he agreed that human beings were basically intelligent "meat machines," as a professor from M.I.T's famed artificial intelligence laboratory had recently suggested. And what if the silicon-based machines could eventually outthink the meat variety? Did that mean they would be superior to humans?

"Hell, give them the vote!" Professor Scott quipped merrily. He leaned back and basked in the boisterous eruption of approving laughter that greeted his clever remark.

A student in the back of the room timidly raised her hand. Helen, as I'll call her, was a shy, quiet person who hardly ever spoke in class. Professor Scott, grinning broadly, nodded in serene acknowledgment of her question. All eyes turned to Helen.

"But *why* would we we want to think like that?" she asked earnestly.

The room grew eerily silent. Time itself seemed to slow down, like when you're in a car accident and it feels as if events are unfolding in super-slow motion inside of a soundproof cocoon.

At last Professor Scott appeared to be saying something. Oddly, his mouth was moving, yet no words were coming out. It took me a moment to realize that he was not winded, but rather, quite uncharacteristically, stuttering.

"Wwwhhhyyy?? Bbbbeeeccccaaauuuse it's TRUE, that's why!!" he spluttered.

Like so many before him, when challenged by a real question, Professor Scott could only retreat into a stubborn affirmation of the unquestionable articles of his (philosophical) creed.

To cast off the solid moorings of accepted answers means departing the security of familiar shores and sailing into uncharted waters, the open sea of questioning. Beliefs are like broken pieces of clamshells and driftwood washed up on the beach. At best, they're the tacky souvenirs of someone else's trip to the seashore, snapshots of yesteryear. People wind up fighting over these worthless trinkets. Answers are possessions, the cause of divided hearts and partial perceptions. They inspire pride, envy, fear, and righteous indignation.

Real questions force us to undertake our own voyage into the wild heart of an undiscovered country. Why should we think of ourselves as mere meat machines? Is the Earth really flat? Is Jesus truly God? Why should I give away all my personal power to a guru? True inquiry is a magical act, directly linking us with the living source. It is what the late physicist-philosopher David Bohm called "the dance of the mind."[3] Our dance partner is reality itself.

Professor Scott, alas, was not a dancer; he was a collector. I could see that on that day in class.

Helen was silent. She asked no more questions (at least not out loud). I, however, began asking myself many questions.

That'll Be Five Senses (Only), Please

I soon came to understand that it was an unquestionable article of faith among my professors that philosophy must be *sci-*

entific. In practice, this meant it was inconceivable that humans might be something more than mere "meat machines" that happen to think. Professor Scott could no more question his belief than the pope could question the unique divinity of Christ. What was an obvious fact to Professor Scott was, in Helen's more fertile imagination, only a mere possibility—and a dismaying one at that.

But according to *scientific* philosophy, it is precisely the fertile (or rather, fevered) imagination that gets us into trouble. It lures us away from "hard fact" and on up into the airy clouds of fantasy and speculation. Ironically, here scientific philosophy agrees with its mortal enemies, the defenders of religion. For example, Saint Augustine (354–430 C.E.), the medieval Catholic thinker, condemned the imagination shorn of dogma as a prostitute that leads the faithful astray.[4] The English writer Edmund Gosse observed that his mother, a strict Protestant fundamentalist, refused to allow any kind of storybook or fictional work into the house out of fear that young Edmund's mind might be stimulated beyond the authoritative bounds of the Bible[5] (just as today's fanatics burn Harry Potter books and crusade to have *The Wizard of Oz* removed from public libraries[6]). No thinking outside the metaphysical box allowed! That is the great bogey of dogmatic religion and science alike.

I discovered that the bible of sorts of the scientific philosophers was a book entitled, appropriately enough, *The Rise of Scientific Philosophy* (1951), by Professor Hans Reichenbach. Professor Reichenbach bemoaned the way that thinkers from Plato to Hegel had been seduced by "an imaginary world of pictures, which can become stronger than the quest for truth."[7] True scientists resist all so-called extralogical motives. They stick to reason, whose job is to process incoming data provided by the five physical senses. Those who believe that mind or consciousness (or "soul" or "spirit") is something apart from measurable brain activity are like the poor deluded rube who took apart his car engine hoping to find the tiny galloping horses. Just as "horsepower" is only a colorful metaphor for engine performance, so "mind power" refers to physiologic brain function.

Reality is what can be seen with our eyes, felt with our fingers, heard with our ears, and so forth.

Most, if not all, my teachers tacitly assumed something like this. Yet I realized that Professor Reichenbach was doing much more than presenting a rarefied philosophical theory of interest to only a handful of academics. In fact, he was articulating some of our basic cultural assumptions, including those that inform our systems of education.

Many years later I read with great interest and empathy New York artist and psychic[8] Ingo Swann's account of his struggles growing up in what he derisively calls "the Age of the Five Senses Only."[9] In the 1970s, Ingo Swann was a pioneer research subject in remote viewing, which is clairvoyance at a distance performed under controlled conditions, whereby an individual can acquire information about a physically distant object, place, or event by means other than the ordinary physical senses.[10]

But even as a child, Ingo knew things that others insisted he could not know. On occasion he had inklings of future events. Also, he could sense what he calls "invisible 'energies' and 'thought-forms' flowing or jumping between people, animals, plants, and even buildings and geophysical objects."[11] To young Ingo, the world was a single, living, breathing form of energy-consciousness.

As time passed, however, Ingo learned that such perceptions were socially awkward. So, little by little, they ceased occurring to him. One such "learning experience" occurred during his Sunday school class when he innocently asked his teacher how it was possible to know the future:

> She held up a Bible and thunderously and fearsomely exclaimed in front of the Sunday school class, and in the best Salem witch-hunt style, that seeing into the future was the work of the devil. "Do you *want* to become a minion of the Devil?" she asked with visible emotion. Indeed, I did not, and I was nearly frightened to death of the possibility—as well as being mortified in front of my Sunday school peers.[12]

Like the young Ingo Swann, I, too, had my share of "unortho-dox" perceptions before they went underground (see chapter 2). I therefore knew from my own experience that the premises of so-called scientific philosophy were false. There are most defi-nitely nonphysical senses. But "empiricism" was a fraud in any case. No one, least of all my teachers, was interested in hearing about my personal experiences. In truth, there was no such thing as the culture of the Five Senses Only. We were not taught to base our reasoned conclusions on our own direct sense experi-ence; we were taught to accept someone else's interpretations of other people's ideas of their sense experiences. In other words, we were being indoctrinated, pure and simple. Think for yourself—only do it just like me. Too much of our educational system is little more than a propaganda machine.

To educate one's senses, it is necessary to exercise them—outdoors. But children are housed all day long inside stuffy classrooms. When I attended primary school, anyone caught dreamily staring out the window at the trees or sky would incur the wrath of the teacher. (I can still hear my fifth-grade teacher, Mrs. Ludlum, screaming at poor Jeffrey Brown at the top of her lungs.) But at least we had recess! Today there is pressure to eliminate recess and make school days longer and more numer-ous. There is no time for our overscheduled, pressured kids to loll around by the local creek catching frogs, as I did with my friend when we were young. The solitude and leisure essential for inner (and outer) development are viewed by the competitive overachiever mentality as a waste of time.

In contrast to the lip service of our own culture, the indige-nous inhabitants of this continent made the proper training and development of the physical (and, of course, the nonphysical) senses a real priority. "We could feel the peace and power of the Great Mystery in the soft grass under our feet and in the blue sky above us," said Chief Luther Standing Bear (1868–1939), a Lakota Sioux Indian.[13] Bear Heart, a contemporary Muskogee Creek Indian shaman, says that one of the first acts of an Indian mother is to take her newborn and introduce the baby to the ele-ments—as his own mother did with him when he was but three days old. Mother Earth, Grandfather Sun, Water and Fire, Moon and Stars—all these became intimately known, and respected and loved, as relatives. Bear Heart reflects:

> I had a sense of belonging as I grew up because of my people's relationship with these elements, and I imagine that's why most of our people related to the environment so easily. We recognized a long time ago that there was life all around us—in the water, in the ground, in the vegetation. Children were introduced to the elements so that as we grew up we were not looking down upon nature or looking up to nature. We felt a part of nature, on the same level. We respected each blade of grass, one leaf on a tree among many other leaves, everything.[14]

You cannot learn how to relate to the elements in Bear Heart's way by studying the periodic table in a classroom. Perhaps that is why I never fail to enter a state of delighted astonishment whenever my wife and I visit Sebago Lake in Maine. To walk through the woods and smell the pines and hear the birds is a tonic. At sunset, when it is so quiet that it feels as though the entire Earth has been covered over in a cozy blanket of silence and tucked in for the evening, I well up with indescribable emotions. I feel as though I have a ringside seat at Creation. Listening to the eerie cry of a loon in the middle of a still night punctuated only by the rhythmic lapping of water at the lake's edge never fails to send shivers down my spine. Sight, smell, touch, taste, hearing—these cannot be reduced to cold formulas or rigid protocols. Nor can they be cultivated and brought to flower by lectures and slides.

Our system of education teaches only the clever manipulation of abstractions and the willy-nilly ingestion of indigestible pseudo-facts provided by authorities both fleshy, and now electronic, with the ubiquitous presence of televisions and computers in every classroom. There is no room in the narrow confines of this cultural prison cell for the full experience of our senses, let alone imagination, inspiration, dreams, feelings, or intuitions.

The "culture of five senses only" turns out to be a culture without any sense at all.

The eminent American philosopher (and veteran psychical researcher) William James (1842–1910) observed long ago that it would be more nutritious to eat a single raisin than to ingest a menu of the most elegantly described gourmet food.[15] Yet we perversely seem to prefer to chew on cardboard rather than taste the food of reality itself. Why is this?

Perhaps it is because we can more easily control and manipulate our cardboard abstractions, whereas raw experience offers something spontaneous and wild. "The Indian tried to fit in with Nature and to understand, not to conquer and rule," Chief Standing Bear lamented.[16] We are grim emperors without clothes, suffering from a severe case of metaphysical malnutrition. Skinny and naked, we starve for a mouthful of real experience.

No wonder, then, that three months into graduate school I was on the verge of a nervous breakdown. Not that I knew it then, but I was just a canary in a leaky coal mine.

How long would it be before I was lying still and silent at the bottom of my cage?

Rabbit Speaks

I stood motionless before the stainless-steel sink in the kitchen. Bright sunlight streamed in through the window, glinting off the silvery metal. Inside the sink I beheld three newborn baby rabbits, their white fur still glistening with the fresh moisture of their mother's womb. I felt joy. Then my attention was drawn to the back door of the kitchen, a "Dutch" or double door. The top portion of the door was wide open. I stood at the half-open door, looking out at a maple tree in the backyard. Beside the tree was a fourth rabbit, a buff-colored adult, sitting up on its hind legs. It was the newborns' mother.

"I fell asleep under the tree."

The words formed in my mind. The mother rabbit was speaking directly to me, mind-to-mind, telepathically. Her tone was sad,

11

mournful. I knew that the tree in question was the old maple, split at its trunk. Half of the tree had been cut down, many years before.

I awoke, bathed in perspiration, my heart pounding wildly. I could not tell if I was exhilarated or frightened (or both). The dream was preternaturally vivid. It had felt every bit as real as everyday waking reality—if not more so. The ancient Taoist sage Chuang Tzu said that he once dreamt happily of being a butterfly. His dream was so powerful that when he awoke, he was not sure whether he was a butterfly dreaming he was a man, or a man who had dreamt that he was a butterfly.

Which was the illusion, and which the reality? Like Tzu, I was ambivalent. The colors in my dream were bright and intense, almost psychedelic in hue—quite different from the monotonous, dull, grey gothic buildings of the university campus. My emotions in the dream had been sharp and strong. By contrast, during the day, I felt virtually nothing, as if I had been anesthetized. The atmosphere in the dream was suffused with an air of ripe expectancy, of incipient revelation. My classes, on the other hand, were uniformly uninspiring, leaving me bored, listless, and impatient—not to mention both irritated with, and envious of, those of my fellow students who could sincerely muster, or at least feign, a degree of ambition.

The dream was an intrusion on my misery. I could not stop thinking about it, even when I wanted to, even when it frightened me. The late science-fiction writer Philip K. Dick once defined reality as "that which, when you stop believing in it, doesn't go away."[17] No matter how much I tried to tell myself, "Look, it was only a dream," it wouldn't go away.

But what did it mean? I had no clue. It was as if I had received a message marked "Urgent!" only to discover on opening the envelope that the note inside was written in incomprehensible hieroglyphics. Furthermore, I had no key, no psychological Rosetta Stone, to help me decode the gibberish. Certainly all my years of schooling had not prepared me to deal with—of all scandalous things—my own dreams! I was frustrated by my own ignorance even as I was haunted by the talking rabbit's cryptic message. Why a talking rabbit, of all silly things? I began to wonder if I was going crazy.

Under the circumstances, I did the only thing that seemed reasonable at the time: I tried to forget about the strange dream and the powerful emotions it aroused. All questions were put on hold. I gritted my teeth and dutifully churned out my term papers.

In the meantime, I had dinner with a woman I'll call Julie. She was an assistant museum curator and also, as it happened, a former Catholic nun. She had left her order after growing frustrated with the authoritarianism and antifeminism of the Church.

After listening intently to my passionate attack on the "meat machine" view of human nature, Julie asked me if I had any contact with the Jung Institute in nearby Evanston. The institute, she explained, was dedicated to the exploration of the ideas of the Swiss psychologist, Carl G. Jung. When I said no, I hadn't, she went and retrieved some literature from the institute and gave it to me.

"You should get in touch with them," Julie stated emphatically.

Trying to appear interested and grateful, I thanked Julie for her suggestion. Inwardly, I cringed. *Jung?* Wasn't he a charlatan? I knew only a little about him. I knew that he believed that all human minds were somehow connected at a deep level, which he referred to as the "collective unconscious." I also knew that these supposed connections manifested as "archetypes," which he alternately spoke of as inborn patterns of behavior, energy systems, or symbolic images appearing universally in the dreams, visions, and fantasies of all people in all times and places. Though I was not sure how to judge these theories, I thought for sure I'd heard somewhere that it was all bunk. (Although my undergraduate mentor had spoken of Freud's work with great respect, he had expressed deep reservations about Jung, whose ideas he criticized as ambiguous and slippery at best. As for my graduate school professors, they mostly ignored maverick thinkers like Jung altogether, except to dismiss them as "mystics"—a pejorative term synonymous with "wooly-minded," "unscientific," and "unphilosophical.") More to the point, I was afraid that any interest I might show in him would ensure the spread of that taint to me. What if my professors found out? For gosh sake, Jung wasn't even a real (professional) philosopher; he was only a mere psychologist!

All this sounds pretty silly to me now. Clearly, I wasn't exactly thinking for myself back then. I was stuck regurgitating secondhand opinions and absolutely terrified of others' opinions of me. So I promptly filed Julie's suggestion in the dead-letter office of my mind, trying my best not to feel like too much of a coward in the bargain.

Jung, at Heart

Perhaps a month later, I was casually browsing in a bookstore when I spied the fat spine of a book with the intriguing title of *Mysteries.* I don't know what made me reach for the book on the shelf. Curiosity, I guess. The author, an Englishman named Colin Wilson, was not then known to me. (Though years later we would correspond, and eventually I would have the privilege of meeting him in the flesh.) As I flipped through the 650 pages of the book, however, I was hooked.

In part, I was only rediscovering many of the topics that had fascinated me as a child. When I was ten years old (in the 1960s) and most of my friends were busy collecting baseball cards, I was reading mass-market paperbacks on topics like telepathy, mediumship, ghosts, and apparitions. Not Mickey Mantle and Roger Maris, but Susy Smith, Raymond Bayless, Hans Holzer, and Nandor Fodor: these were my childhood heroes. Of course, that was before I self-consciously put such books on the forbidden reading list.

But the exciting thing was that the author was conversant with genuinely philosophical ideas. He was a bona fide thinker who took paranormal phenomena seriously, and this was a new concept to me at the time. It was as if I had found the Holy Grail.

I can't say precisely how long it took me to read almost halfway through the book. But eventually I came to a chapter in which the author examines the theories of, yes, C. G. Jung. My attention was riveted by the following section, which describes the genesis of Jung's early formulation of the archetype concept:

In the same year [1906], Jung read an account of the discovery of a cache of "soul stones" near Arlesheim. No details were given about the stones, but Jung suddenly knew that they were oblong, blackish, and had the upper and lower halves painted different shades. At the same time, he recalled a forgotten event of his childhood: he had carved a small wooden figure from the end of a ruler and made a cloak for it. This figure was kept in a pencil box, together with an oblong stone which Jung had painted in two colours, and the box was carefully hidden on a beam in the attic. During school hours, Jung wrote coded messages on tiny pieces of paper and periodically stole up to the attic to place these "scrolls" in the pencil case. It now struck Jung that his little wooden man was like the cloaked figure of Telesphoros, the guardian spirit of convalescence, who is often seen on Greek monuments reading a scroll to Asclepius, the god of healing, and that he had been instinctively performing some primitive rite connected with the release of the creative impulse. (Years later, he saw a similar ritual performed in Africa by natives.) Describing the event later in his auto-biography, Jung tells how "there came to me, for the first time, the conviction that there are archaic psychic components which have entered the individual psyche without any direct line of tradition." He called these "archaic components" archetypes.[18]

I now recalled a forgotten event from my childhood. There had been a small wooden matchbox that I kept in my nightstand drawer. Inside the box was a small oblong stone figure that had an upper and lower half. From a small strip of cardboard, I had fashioned a bed (or throne, as I imagined it) for the stone. Next to the stone, I placed the figure of a tiny spaceman that I had cannibalized from a plastic rocket-ship model. Around the man's shoulders, I placed a cloak that I made for him out of a corner of facial tissue. This setup was the basis of a game of exploration. I imagined that the two strange figures were secretly connected, fast friends. While the special stone never left the box, the little spaceman would go on all sorts of adventures and report back to his superior, the stone.

Just as an individual personality in time might relate to his soul?

Oh, yes, I still had the matchbox, figures and all, in my possession. For some strange reason, I had kept it all those many years. (I have it still.)

Instantly, I realized that Jung was right, after all. We are indeed all connected at some deep level. What's more, it seems that the secret access door to this underground chamber is none other than our old friend, the hated—and feared—imagination.

Play is the key.

The importance of a playful imagination cannot be overemphasized. Many years after this event, I read about Dr. Brian Weiss, a psychiatrist who believes that many psychological problems may be traced to unresolved traumas of past lives. (I discuss my own reincarnational dreams in chapter 2.) Dr. Weiss was giving a workshop when, out of the blue, one of the participants asked him how mediums gather information about the dead. Instead of giving a formal explanation, he spontaneously did a little role-playing.

Playing the starring role of medium, he gave an example of a "reading." He spun a tale involving a young man named Robert who was killed in a car accident, and a leather jacket that the deceased had wanted to be given to a friend named Gary. The questioner seemed satisfied. But after the workshop was over, another woman participant, tearful and visibly distraught, approached Dr. Weiss and asked him where he got his story.

"I made it up," Weiss said.

"No, you didn't," the woman replied. Then she explained that after her twenty-year-old brother Robert had died in a recent car accident, she felt him communicate to her that he wanted his friend Gary to have his favorite leather jacket hanging in the closet.[19]

Simply by pretending, Dr. Weiss had accidentally activated his own innate ability to tap into the collective psyche, where all information is available. The young Carl Jung had done a similar thing and found himself enacting a healing ritual that went back to Stone Age Europe and out to the environs of tribal Africa. Just as I had inadvertently done.

An incredible coincidence, to be sure.

From Colin Wilson, I learned that Jung was obsessed with such coincidences, which he called "synchronicities." Jung began by noting these strange events as they occurred in his own life and in the lives of his patients. The weirdest, most improbable coincidences would typically manifest at very stressful moments in a person's life, at the exact moment when inner change was either possible or even necessary for that person's development.

For example, one day, a female client whose therapy was not going particularly well was telling Jung about a recent dream she had had of a scarab beetle, an ancient Egyptian symbol of rebirth. Jung tried to focus on the woman's story, but became distracted by a persistent scratching noise at his study window. The doctor excused himself and walked over to the window to investigate. As he opened the window, he realized with annoyance that he had inadvertently let in a flying insect.

What struck Jung was that the bug turned out to be a particularly rare type of scarab beetle that should not even have been around Zurich that time of year. When he pointed this out to the woman, she was struck by the preposterousness of the coincidence. What Jung termed her "cold rationalism" suddenly melted like ice cubes on a hot stove. Touched by this magical and wondrous event, she opened to her own inner world, including her feelings. After this, her therapy went well. She was indeed reborn.

Jung cited this episode with the scarab as key to the development of his idea of synchronicity, or meaningful coincidence.

When I read this, I recalled something else. My little stone in the matchbox was not an ordinary stone after all. Actually, it was a gift given to me by a childhood friend.

The gift was a reproduction of an ancient Egyptian scarab, the symbol of rebirth!

I began to feel very peculiar, touched by the uncanny. It was as if, in spite of myself, I were being guided by some mysterious power to the very people and ideas I needed to encounter in order to answer questions I had not yet even consciously formulated. The dinner with Julie, finding a helpful book by "accident," and now this odd business with Jung—it all seemed bizarre. How many more mysteries were there?

And Now for Great Rabbit's Next Trick . . .

I soon picked up a copy of Carl Jung's autobiographical work *Memories, Dreams, Reflections* (1961) to confirm what I had already read and, more importantly, what I now knew by my own experience. As I dug further into Colin Wilson's book, however, I came upon an account of a British Jungian analyst named John Layard. He had treated a patient who had a dream that proved to be a transformative and healing experience at a crucial point in her analysis. The main character of her dream was, of all things, an intelligent and self-sacrificing hare. (Though different in some behavioral and physical respects, hares and rabbits belong to the same biological family of mammals, *Leporidae*—leapers.)

Now my interest was piqued.

Intrigued by this image, John Layard did some investigating.[20] He was astounded to find stories of magical hares and rabbits all over the place, from high culture myths to the popular legends and folklore of peoples in Ancient Egypt, China, Africa, India, modern Europe, and pre-Columbian North America. The Easter bunny, the white rabbit that leads Alice down the hole to Wonderland, and even tales of Br'er Rabbit also seemed to fit this universal archetypal pattern. There were certain common recurring themes among all these stories. The exceedingly prolific hare/rabbit was naturally associated in people's minds with creativity, and also with what Mr. Spock of *Star Trek* fame would call "sudden leaps of logic," that is, the intuitive, mystical, or psychic side of our natures: our innate sensitivity.

How did this association of the rabbit and "magic" come about? Hal Zina Bennett, Ph.D., is a writer, editor, and longtime student of shamanism who has written five books on earth-centered spirituality. In his recent book, *Spirit Animals and the Wheel of Life* (2000), Hal relates an experience he had when he was sixteen years old that set him on his future path as a follower of the natural way. It also may offer an explanation as to how the rabbit came to be thought of as a guide to the mystical side of life.

Hal was out hunting in the woods near his home in rural Michigan with his .22 rifle. He spotted two rabbits and bagged them both with a couple of well-timed shots. While skinning one of the rabbits, he inadvertently nicked his finger. Soon he was suffering from a high fever that would not go away. His distraught parents rushed him to a hospital where he nearly died. Or, perhaps he did.

"That evening," writes Hal, "I had the sensation that I had little, if anything to do with my body any more. In fact, I was certain that I had left it entirely."[21] He was no longer lying in a feverish daze on his hospital bed. Rather, he was outside the building entirely, looking down on the roof from above. He could see everything inside the hospital, including his body on the bed, in perfect detail. He could also see all around him in the landscape, wherever he looked, with the same amazing clarity and detail. There was no pain or fear. He felt wide-awake.

Then, suddenly, Hal was in a strange new environment, where he was confronted with a stark choice:

> I stood at a crossroads, indicated by three paths of light and color. I was standing with my back to the road upon which I'd come. To my right was the road to death, and perhaps a hundred feet away was a tunnel. I was certain that once I entered this space, my life back on Earth would be finished. Though I could not see much beyond the tunnel, what I saw was a very different kind of reality, one that I can only describe as formless and invisible but definitely not Nothingness. What I sensed there moved me deeply, excited me, and part of me longed to move into it, if only to satisfy my curiosity.[22]

19

At that moment, he saw his father sobbing in grief in the hospital room. Feeling sorry for his dad, Hal decided to return to his body instead of taking the path to the afterlife. Subsequently, his fever broke, and he slowly began to recover. His doctors later told him that he'd been in a coma, and that they'd been afraid he might die.

This happened in 1952, more than two decades before the term "near-death experience" (NDE) would be coined and become part of our common cultural currency. However, the out-of-body experience, feelings of bliss, expansion of perception, dark tunnel, the sense of passing to the Other Side, and the decision to return to physical life are all familiar motifs to students of the NDE. Hal would not know to call it that for many years afterward. But it changed his life and sent him on his course of spiritual inquiry.

Moreover, it turned out that the trigger for the entire episode had been the rabbit Hal skinned when he cut his finger, for Hal's doctor informed him that he'd been suffering from tularemia, or rabbit fever, an infection that can be passed from rabbits to humans. In the days before wide-spectrum antibiotics, tularemia was serious, often fatal. If the victim survived, he or she might have a story similar to Hal's to tell, having been brought to the brink of death. The inhabitants of early tribal cultures may have had many such accidental encounters with the Other Side due to hunting infected game, and lived to tell the tale. This may explain, in part, how rabbit acquired its reputation as a mystagogue, a guide to the mysteries.

To the Algonquin Indians of the Great Lakes region (where I was living at the time of my rabbit dream), this mystical creature was called Manabozho or Michabou, Great Rabbit or Great Hare. He was known as a sly trickster, a crafty shape-shifter who could easily change from human to animal form, then back again. The Ojibways said that he was the first Medicine Man, or shaman, and that he was responsible for giving humans their spiritual knowledge. Sometimes cited as the creator of Heaven and Earth, Great Rabbit was usually associated both with the dawn and the moon, the two natural forms of illumination and symbols, respectively, of rebirth and intuitive (lunar) knowledge. Great

Rabbit was the master of the ethereal, nonrational (notice that I don't say *ir*rational) side of humans: creator, psychic, healer, clown, and master shaman. So this was no Bugs Bunny!

Now it finally dawned on me just who, and what, had fallen asleep under the tree.

It was obviously the part of me that had found no place in the culture of logic and "fact." No wonder that the tree under which my telepathic rabbit had fallen asleep (symbolic of lapsing into unconsciousness) was a split maple, half of it cut down. Half of me had been cut out, so I could at least pretend to fit in. But it had never quite worked. Now I understood that. I couldn't pretend any longer. I had to reclaim the rest of me.

I had to wake up—and fast.

There was at least a slim ray of hope. In my dream, the trio of baby rabbits in the sink (womb) held out the promise of rebirth. Something was already waking up, stirring to life once again, not just in the backyard (unconscious), but also in the kitchen. Why there?

As the Jungian analyst Marie-Louise von Franz explained,[23] the kitchen is where food is prepared and cooked. It is the symbolic place of inner transformation, of alchemical transmutation. It's where the heat is: the inner hearth, the fire of love—the passionate heart.

Well, now I knew this. But it was still just intellectual knowing, of course. I was too thoroughly enculturated—too far gone into what the poet Robert Bly calls the sickness of "the rational thing"—to grasp that I had to *do* something with this knowledge. I had to figure out how to forge it into wisdom.

Not that Great Rabbit gave up on me, mind you. But, as the saying goes, before I could get better, I had to get worse. Much worse.

A Sickness unto Health

Rock bottom came for me one afternoon at the university library where I was doing research for a term paper. Suddenly, I began to feel very peculiar. My heart raced uncontrollably and perspiration dripped down my back. I was overcome by feelings of claustrophobia, as if I had to get out of there or—I didn't know what. I was afraid I was either going to have a heart attack or go crazy (whatever that meant). The more I focused on the strange physical sensations I was experiencing, the more frightened I became, until I couldn't stand it one more moment. I panicked.

Hastily gathering together my books and notes, I stuffed them in my briefcase and sprinted down the steps, past the front desk, out into the parking lot. Once outside, I felt somewhat relieved. I could breathe again. I felt as if I had been held down under water. I was still shaken up. Somehow, though, with hands trembling and thoughts racing, I managed to drive several blocks to my apartment, where I felt a bit better.

The panic attacks continued. I kept attending classes but stopped writing term papers. Sometimes I slept, but most nights were one long, sweaty seizure of fear punctuated by fitful lapses into troubled sleep. Finally, after months of this, I went to see a therapist. I figured if I was going to fall, I might want to work with a net.

My therapist listened as I conjured up complaints about my childhood and failed relationships. But it always came back to my writing block. I wanted to quit graduate school, yet I did not want to give "them" the satisfaction. I couldn't quit! That would be a waste. It would haunt me, and I might not finish anything ever again. Reason had its place, after all. But I couldn't just go on like before, either. I was stuck between the proverbial rock and the hard place, feeling more squeezed with each passing day.

Exactly how and when I began to tread the path toward sanity, I am not sure. The panic attacks gradually subsided. Certainly, I began to trust my instincts more. I started taking my books to the small park just down the street from my apartment. After reading a few pages in a desultory fashion, I would sit and enjoy being out of doors. I felt guilty lolling around on the park bench, watching the birds collect crumbs. But it made me feel better, so I continued.

I began to trust my hunches more where people were concerned. At a party, for example, I was introduced to a fellow graduate student. With a handshake and smile, he struck me as someone I would want to avoid. It was as if there had been a red light on his forehead flashing, "Stay away! This one is trouble." In the past, I would not have heeded such warnings. I would have ignored my gut feelings. As it turned out, however, my first impression proved to be accurate. Peter (as I'll call him) was brilliant, a rising academic star. But he was also a cagey opportunist who tended to use people to his advantage. Although I was unable to avoid Peter completely, I wisely sought to minimize my contact with him.

My intuitive sensitivity was slowly returning to life in other small ways as well.

Sometimes at night, lying awake in bed, I would sense baseball-sized spheres of differently colored lights zooming about near the ceiling. I didn't exactly see this with my physical eyes; it was more like an inner mental impression. Whatever these pulsating globes were, they were conscious, intelligent, and aware of me. They felt like old friends checking to make sure I was all right. I found this oddly reassuring.

Another important stride toward health (wholeness) was taken when I heeded my girlfriend's advice and got a couple of cats for company. This made a big difference.

As Hal Zina Bennett notes, there are times when the appearance of animals in our consciousness is a symbolic gesture, telling us something about the state of our psyche—as, for example, in my dream of the telepathic rabbit, which represented a neglected part of my inner self. However, he adds, there are other instances in which one has a transpersonal experience with a living animal presence (in body or spirit). In such cases, the meaning is not symbolic but literal: "The person is convinced that they have communicated with the animal on a profoundly deep level and there is nothing to analyze or interpret."[24]

In other words, learning to appreciate the wisdom and healing power of animals is facilitated by having them around us, or being around them. This was a point taken for granted by indigenous peoples who were surrounded by (and reverent of) the animal kingdom, but it is sometimes lost on modern humans whose encounters with animals are often limited to watching nature programs on television or the occasional trip to a park or zoo. My communication with the cats may not have been as profound as that of some mystics, but we did connect; this I know. (Years after their deaths, I still have vivid dreams of them from time to time. Our reunions are always joyous.) Having them around helped me in several ways.

For one thing, they helped restore my humor, which had largely atrophied. I laughed, especially when I watched them at play. One of their favorite games was to chase each other up and down the hallway in my small apartment. On the hardwood floor, two small cats managed to make quite a ruckus. My girlfriend said that it sounded like a miniature herd of stampeding horses. I felt sorry for the neighbors on the floor below.

They also taught me about affection. The female was a svelte, triangular-faced Siamese with a lilac-grey mask. She was the more loving of the two. There was not a mean bone in her body. If I rolled her on her back and scratched her belly to provoke a reaction, she might start kicking me with her hind legs. But then she would stop suddenly and catch herself, as if she had not meant to play rough. Purring loudly in apology, she would lick my hand. Her unconditional devotion, along with her natural gentleness and sweetness of temperament, was highly therapeutic.

Then there was the male, a somewhat larger, square-headed Siamese with dark, seal-brown markings. He was a clever devil. He made plans. For example, one of his favorite games was to get me out of bed in the morning. He would leap onto the dresser and stand up on his hind legs. With his right paw extended, he would push the picture that hung above the dresser until it banged so loudly against the wall that it would sound as though it were going to come crashing down. I'd yell at him to stop, and he'd look at me, then paw the picture even harder. Finally, I'd get up and pretend to chase him, and he'd have gotten his way. He taught me that animals think. Humans do not have a lock on reasoning things out.

Those cats touched me, and opened me, in many ways. Many

years after they died, I came across the words of the nineteenth-century Pawnee, Eagle Chief (Letakots-Lesa):

> In the beginning of all things, wisdom and knowledge were with the animals, for Tirawa, the One Above, did not speak directly to man. He sent certain animals to tell men that he showed himself through the beasts, and that from them, and from the stars and the sun and the moon should man learn. . . . all things tell of Tirawa.[25]

Feeling this truth in my bones, I wept. I will always be grateful to my furry friends.

Oh, yes. There was a funny little incident with the female cat that I must mention.

One afternoon, when she was still a kitten, I took her to the veterinarian for one of her booster shots. At that early stage in her development, her darker markings had not yet come in fully, so her fur was still a brighter shade of creamy white. While I sat waiting to be called in, a little girl with dark hair came over to me. She pointed at my cat curled up in the rear of my carrier and said something I didn't understand. So I smiled. She giggled. Her father called her back to where he was sitting, and they briefly conversed in what I guessed was Spanish. Then, in heavily accented English, the man addressed me, pointing at my cat cage.

"My daughter, she says you got a *booney* rabbit in there," the father said with what sounded like a trace of suspicion in his voice.

"No, it's not a bunny rabbit," I replied. "It's a cat."

"Well, she says it's a *booney* rabbit," he insisted.

"No, really, it's a cat," I said, feeling somewhat exasperated.

The man just shrugged, while his daughter, forgetting about my rabbit-cat, busied herself with a toy.

From that time forward, the female cat's nickname became "Booner"—as in "booney" rabbit: a little white baby bunny. Just like the ones in the sink, in my dream.

As I said, Great Rabbit had not deserted me. And s/he had a sense of humor.

Well, all of these baby steps toward balance at least got me moving in the right direction. But I knew that if I were to pull myself out of the hole I'd dug, I'd have to confront my past in a new way. There was a part of my childhood that I did not talk about, even with my therapist. It was a secret past, a lost world. To find it again, I would have to journey back there and confront my deepest fears.

And I'd have to do it alone.

2

Child Sacrifice

The Child is father of the Man;
And I could wish my days to be
Bound each to each by natural piety.

—William Wordsworth, "Ode: Intimations of Immortality" from
Recollections of Early Childhood (1807)

Shades of the Prison House . . .

We stood at the bottom of the hill, waiting in tense silence. My heart was pounding so fast and hard it felt like it might explode into a thousand pieces. The night sky hung over us like a thick black blanket. They stood on either side of us, holding flickering torches. I couldn't see their faces. The red-hot fire beneath the earthen ramp at the crest of the hill burned brightly, intense heat radiating from the pit. Fear grabbed me and would not let go, its grip tightening like a vise. And tightened further still, until I began to choke.

I awoke in a panic, screaming and crying. My parents must have rushed in from their bedroom, to see what was the matter. I remember them standing at the end of my crib, after I had calmed down, looking anxiously at me, making sure I was all right.

I was about three years old at the time.

This nightmare is one of my first memories. It recurred for perhaps another year or so—sometimes nightly. And each time it was exactly the same, like a repetitious film loop. I would wake up, heart pounding and bathed in the cold sweat of fear, at exactly the same point. I was just standing there, at the bottom of the ramp, waiting.

Waiting for what?

. . . Begin to Close

Probably because I never talked about the nightmare with anyone, I never tried to think this part through. I suspect my parents believed that my protests about going to bed were just ploys for extra attention. Or else that I was merely a reluctant sleeper, "going through a stage." The truth was, I was indeed reluctant to sleep, but only because of the terrifying dream. I could not explain this to them. Nor did I understand it. I knew only that I was scared to death. Soon, I became afraid of the fear itself.

Then one day, for no apparent reason, the bad dream stopped coming. It was gone. And I forgot all about it. Until, that is, a couple of years ago when I had another unusual dream, followed by a series of coincidences.

I dreamt I was shopping in a busy indoor market in a foreign country, perhaps in Central or South America. There were vegetable and meat stands, and barkers in crowded stalls hawking jewelry and other trinkets. As I roamed through the market, a swarthy, somewhat sinister-looking stranger in a sombrero sidled up to me and whispered something in my ear in what I guessed was Spanish. Not knowing the language, the word made no sense. Yet the dream was vivid, and the whispered word felt like a message. (The market reminded me of a place I had visited many years before in Mexico City.)

A few days later, I was browsing the shelves of my late father-in-law's library when I happened upon a book on the Aztecs. I was casually thumbing through the book when I came to a passage describing a human sacrifice following a victorious battle:

A fire sacrifice was ordained—the most terrible and horrendous sacrifice that can be imagined. A great bonfire was made in a large brazier dug in the ground; this was called the divine hearth. Into this great mass of embers [the five hundred prisoners] were thrown alive. Before they expired, their hearts were torn out of their bodies and offered to the god.[1]

I had been aware that the Aztecs performed such sacrifices. But reading this sent chills down my spine. All at once the flood of memories surrounding my recurring childhood nightmare returned, including the pain and confusion it had caused me. It had never before occurred to me to ask what it was that I had been so terrified of as I stood there waiting at the bottom of the hill. Now I knew, without a doubt: I was waiting to be thrown into that pit of fire. I had been afraid to die. I didn't want to be a sacrifice to feed some angry, vengeful god.

Was this nightmare a memory fragment of some actual, previous earthly existence?

Since I was familiar with the work of the respected parapsychologist Dr. Ian Stevenson, I certainly would not rule this out. For more than forty years, Dr. Stevenson, a professor of psychiatry at the University of Virginia, has been studying early childhood memories that are—to borrow the title of his classic book—at least suggestive of the possibility of reincarnation.[2] Was my childhood dream just such a suggestion?

One of my favorite examples of past-life childhood memories comes from the late writer on science and the paranormal, Michael Talbot. In the introduction to his book *Your Past Lives* (1987), Talbot explained that he always believed in reincarnation because as far back as he could remember, he had memories of former existences, mostly in Asia. As a little boy, he stubbornly refused to call his parents "mother" and "father" until he was five years old, and then he gave in only because his parents were complaining that he was embarrassing them in front of their friends. He explained:

My refusal was not due to any absence of affection on my part. I did not have a mature intellectual understanding of what the tracts of strange memories inside my head meant, but I was vividly aware that I possessed a continuity, a history beyond the child's body in which I found myself. So it did not make sense to me to call the two kind people who were taking care of me my parents. . . . This was not the only precocity that my parents were forced to contend with. They rapidly discovered that they had a child on their hands who insisted upon drinking several cups of strong black tea every day, who preferred sitting cross-legged on the floor to sitting in chairs, and who was fanatically drawn to things Asian.[3]

In a telling afterword to the revised (1992) edition of his *Mysticism and the New Physics* (1981), Talbot noted that this "fanatical attraction to things Asian" went so far as to include a most unlikely spontaneous recitation of Buddhist aphorisms and prayers.[4]

Although my fire-pit dream did not lead me to speak in a foreign language or inspire other inexplicable behavior (as with Talbot), it nonetheless had the "feel" of a real event. Moreover, if the Aztec connection was valid, I could now see that the childhood nightmare fit in with a pattern of dreams that I'd been having over the past ten years. These dreams took place in geographical settings that appeared to be southwestern or western (where I've never visited in physical waking reality), and they all involved Native Americans.

For example, in one such dream I was a dark-skinned migrant farm worker, an American Indian. A bunch of us wearing tattered clothes piled out of an old rusted pickup truck at dawn. Our job was to work the field all day long, from sunup to sundown, digging trenches and turning the rich, dark earth. It was backbreaking work. Every muscle in my body ached. At dusk, as the bright orange sun set, I paused from my labors and leaned on my hoe. Standing silently and watching the sunset, I viewed Mother Nature's marvelous display in awe and reverence. My love for the land, and indeed for all creation, welled up inside me. For a blissful moment, I forgot I was an impoverished farm worker with barely more than the rags on my back to call my own. I felt like a king.

This "dream" had not felt like a dream at all. I could feel the dirt between my fingers and the persistent ache in my back. I sensed this man's passionate love for the earth as well as his connection to his illustrious ancestors, who had lived a far different (free and independent) existence on these same lands, on which he was now but a lowly serf. I *was* this man, yet paradoxically, I was also myself, observing.

In another dream, I am standing atop a high mesa or butte in the blazing hot sun. The air is so thin it is difficult to breathe. The soil is reddish-orange, the cloudless sky a pale blue. My two silent companions are dressed in costumes. Their arms are adorned with feather sleeves, their faces covered by eagle masks. I am wearing an identical costume and mask. In silence, the three of us make a circle, clasping arms at our shoulders. Suddenly, my awareness shifts. I am no longer focused on my companions. Instead, I am more aware of the sky and space around me.

With a thrill, I realize this is because I am floating several feet off the ground. As I levitate, I hear the screech of an eagle, which I assume is flying overhead. But even as I think this, I feel my mouth open and an inhuman cry escape from my throat. Shockingly, it is I who scream with the voice of an eagle. Then I feel myself floating slowly back down to the ground, my feet gently touching the earth. My happy companions surround me, offering hearty congratulations. Words of thanksgiving are exchanged. We stand huddled close together under the burning sun—the brotherhood of the eagle.

Before I had this dream, I had not read about any such ceremonies. I had been vaguely aware that many shamans have claimed to possess abilities to shape-shift, or to turn themselves into animals. I had never known what to make of this claim, except that it might be a valid report of a dream or inner vision.

In my dream, I was a hybrid, an eagle-human. I didn't fly, but

I did levitate. This felt like a physical act, not a vision. I had the woozy sensation of floating several feet above the ground. Also, the sound that emanated from my voice box was not a human sound; it was definitely an animal sound. Although all this had taken place in a "mere" dream, it felt super-real. It was so vivid I never forgot it.

A few months after this dream, I picked up the book *Black Elk Speaks,* the story of the famous Lakota Sioux holy man Black Elk, as told to the Nebraskan poet John Neihardt. In one of the later chapters, Black Elk describes his experience doing the Ghost Dance, the ceremony that led to the massacre of the Sioux by the U.S. cavalry at Wounded Knee.

The Ghost Dance movement originated with a Paiute visionary messiah named Wovoka. Wovoka believed that if enough Indians performed the dance, the unspoiled world as they knew it prior to the arrival of the whites would be restored, and the dead (including the slaughtered buffalo and other animals) would be returned to life.

The first time Black Elk did the Ghost Dance, he said he felt himself "lifted clear off the ground." The following day, during a second ceremony, he said he was dancing with his eyes closed when something peculiar happened:

> Suddenly it seemed that I was swinging off the ground and not touching it any longer. The queer feeling came up from my legs and was in my heart now. It seemed I would glide forward like a swing, and then glide back again in longer and longer swoops.

As Black Elk describes it, what happened next sounds like an out-of-body experience. Tellingly, it is the eagle who inaugurates his ecstatic otherworldly journey:

> I must have fallen down, but I felt as though I had fallen off a swing when it was going forward, and I was floating head first through the air. My arms were stretched out, and all I saw at first was a single eagle

feather in front of me. Then the feather was a spotted eagle dancing on ahead of me with his wings fluttering, and he was making the shrill whistle that is his.[5]

I was astonished. Had I, as the young initiate in my eagle dream, also experienced an out-of-body episode? Could that explain the queasy sensation of physically rising above the Earth? Was this an actual memory of a shamanic ceremony?

In the wake of my discovery about the Aztecs and the revived memory of my early childhood nightmare, I began to consider in earnest whether all these dream experiences meant that I'd lived a previous life (or a series of lives) in the Americas. Like the late psychic Jane Roberts, I have long suspected that most of our traditional ideas of reincarnation are probably distortions of a far more complex reality.[6] Still, I had to admit that this possibility intrigued me. It also raised many questions.

Perhaps I was intuitively tapping into certain memories of the human race (Jung's collective unconscious again). It could be, then, that the fire-pit nightmare of my early years was a memory fragment of some youthful, frightened soldier—a young boy, really—about to meet a horrible death as a sacrifice to a victorious enemy's terrible god.

So which was it: reincarnational memory or psychic perception? Or perhaps a clever psychological insight costumed in a dramatic form? What if it were all three?

Upon the Growing Boy

One problem that comes with trying to pin down an explanation for such experiences (and with exploring inner states in general) is that our mind has a tendency to slip into a simplistic "either/or" pattern. (I do this all the time, even though I know better.) Either something is a literal fact, or else it's a mere psychological symbol. But what if it's not "either/or"? What if it's "both/and"? Why can't we accept that some events (and probably all, if we but knew how to read them aright) straddle our rigid categories of fact versus fiction, and our conventional notions of reality versus fantasy? When I stopped trying to prove (if only to myself) that my fire-pit dream contained a true psychic perception of other times or places, I was able to ask what it might be saying to me if I read it as a story, that is, metaphorically. That's when a whole new vista of meaning and understanding suddenly opened up.

Read in this way, as a literary metaphor, the dream made perfect sense. For the child in me—the self that knew and accepted the reality of magic, of the invisible bonds of nature— had indeed been sacrificed to an angry and vengeful god: the deity we call culture. In the West, this god goes by many names, including Lord Sci-Tech, Father Cap-Mat (for capitalistic materialism), and King Christ-Jehovah-Allah, just to mention a few of His (yes, I do mean to use the masculine pronoun) more familiar aliases. (The gods of the East have different names, but the effect of slavish devotion to them is much the same.)

The author of the book on the Aztecs, one Fray Diego Durán, looked down his nose in cold priestly condescension upon the savagery of the Aztecs. After all, hadn't the biblical tradition turned its back upon the brutality of Moloch (an ancient Caananite deity who demanded the sacrifice of the firstborn) way back when Jehovah spared faithful Abraham the sacrifice of his beloved son, Isaac? (Never mind that Abraham's willingness to do the god-awful deed is praised as a mark of his virtue and fidelity to God.)

The truth of the matter, however, may be far less flattering.

The poet William Wordsworth said that the child comes into this world "trailing clouds of glory." This is usually dismissed as silly Romantic claptrap. Even a cultural critic as vociferous as Joseph Chilton Pearce, who has written movingly about "the magical child"[7] and how our dysfunctional culture inhibits or destroys our psychic relationship to the invisible bonds, dismisses the notion of "a 'natural religion' which would grow unfettered were it allowed."[8] For Pearce, it is essential to have a guru who has achieved "absolute unity"[9] or perfect enlightenment as an external stimulus to and model of development for the child. The ashram is Pearce's answer, and nature requires us to surrender our personal power to the deus ex machina agency of the Hindu guru for her plan to work. (How could there be a state of "absolute" whole-ness or "perfection" for a human being, except as a dangerously naïve delusion? Also, where did this apostolic chain of perfect gurus have its ultimate origin? Is there not an infinite regress?)

But what if this is all wrong? What if guruism is just another symptom of the disease rather than its cure? Is nature so help-less after all? Could Wordsworth's "natural piety" turn out to be the gods' honest truth? What then?

These questions continued to nag at me. It seemed to me self-evident that in ways both large and small we are taught, from a very early age, to suppress and ignore the intuitive gifts that we bring with us—the visions of other times and places, the pull of the invisible bonds. What are we given in their place? The void is filled by the habit of acquisition. First we are taught to acquire knowledge from outside sources only (parents, books, teachers). Later come the endless television commercials prom-ising the bliss of new toys, the trips to the mall, and our full induction into the consumerist order of getting and spending. Then, when we are old enough, we are instructed in the ways to acquire God's good grace by believing certain propositions or performing certain actions (or both).

In sum, instead of a literal physical sacrifice, like the one in my fire-pit dream, what our culture demands as a price of admission is a spiritual sacrifice. Culture, or what we call "civi-lization," presents itself as the dispenser of all glory, the seat of all bliss, the guardian of all value, and the sole purveyor of all truth. As for nature, she's wild and dangerous, brutal and igno-rant—and incompetent to boot. She can't even carry out her own plan without outside help. Whatever you do, don't trust her!

The more I thought about it, the more I realized that I could not separate my questions about inner things from my questions about outer things. The psychic can't be divorced from politics and philosophy; each has serious implications for the others. Self-criticism and cultural criticism are joined because the self is not an isolated entity. No one is an island.

In looking back at what I had been asked to sacrifice in order to feel a sense of belonging, I wondered whether this was indeed an inevitable course of events. Was it a tragicomedy of universal proportions, or was it merely the result of a wrong turn taken in our own Western journey? If the latter, how do we find our way out of the cul-de-sac in which we find ourselves? Where's a good road map when you need one?

To know how to get out, it helps to know how you got into trouble in the first place. You have to retrace your steps to find the first wrong turn. Or else it's hopeless.

Where had I gone wrong? I searched my memory for clues.

Earliest Intimations

What I got was not a memory, but something told to me so often as a child by my mother that it nearly qualifies as one.

When I was a toddler, dressed in the early morning to meet the day, I would ask if I could go outdoors to deliver my greetings. "Hello, birds! Hello, trees! Hello, sky!" I would proclaim in delight.

That, of course, was then—way back then, in the mists of memory. I don't recall how old I was when I stopped talking to the animals; when nature, previously a "thou," became an "it." What happened? When, and why, did I cease to regard the world—my world, that is—as a living world, populated by close friends or at least nodding acquaintances? At what point did I swallow the canard that this world is an inert ball of compacted dust, or a mere artifact created for use (if not abuse) by lordly humans? Or, was my "conversion" only halfhearted at best?

Ask the shadows on the wall. They know.

The Shadow Dancer

Around the time of my recurring fire-pit nightmare, when I was about four, a strange thing happened one night while I lay in bed, tossing and turning, trying very hard not to fall asleep. I did not want to find myself back on that ramp to hell.

After what felt like hours, I threw back the covers and got out of bed. I padded across the hardwood floor to the far side of the small bedroom, where I plopped down on the floor, just beneath the window. The atmosphere of the room felt different somehow—charged. There was a "thickness" all about. It felt like being wrapped in a warm, comforting blanket on a cold, snowy night. Time itself seemed to slow down, like honey poured from a jar. I had no idea what made me decide to get out of bed at just that moment, or why I sat down beneath the window and stared at the wall. Yet I was expectant, as if waiting for something to occur.

Eventually, something did happen. A diminutive shadowy form, no more than six inches high, emerged from behind the oak desk. I could easily make out its shape even in the semidarkened room, a black silhouette against the knotty pine paneling.

It was a female form: a lithe, shapely woman in a short dress—a ballerina.

As I watched, spellbound, the ballerina danced. And danced.

I have no idea how long I watched her perform her graceful ballet. Eventually, I felt very sleepy, my eyelids too heavy to remain open. I padded across the room and climbed back into bed. I quickly fell asleep. And I had no nightmares that night.

What was it? Dream? Waking vision? Apparition? Spontaneous out-of-body episode? Encounter with a nonhuman entity (deva, fairy, sprite)?

Many years later, I would discover through my readings the existence of the astral dancing girls mentioned in a number of esoteric traditions, including the Tibetan Buddhist Dakinis ("sort of space fairies," according to Joseph Campbell[10]), the Hindu Apsara, and the Islamic Houri. While the Apsara and Houri are depicted as little more than delectable cosmic call girls, the Dakini are portrayed in Buddhist mandalas (meditational art) as rather ferocious, frenzied, dervish-like dancing figures wielding sharp knives and drinking blood from skulls. "The inspiration for many of these images," according to Joseph Campbell, "is Kali, the Hindu goddess of [death]. She has been taken over in the Buddha system by these Dakinis, the partners in this dance. Death is being celebrated . . . You are dancing in partnership with Lady Death, and you don't mind."[11]

Perhaps these images are not just symbols of the wrathful (or pleasurable) side of the female (i.e., Nature's) power but, rather, represent and record an actual psychic phenomenon, such as I had experienced. At four years of age, I was far too young to be preoccupied by thoughts of sex or death. Yet my ballerina was a "comfort girl" in the sense that her presence was soothing.

At the time of the experience, however, such mature speculations were obviously way beyond my ken. For years afterward, I thought about her now and then, even before I had the vocabulary to describe what had happened. It was something that I could never fully explain. Nor could I explain it away. Like a Zen koan, the shadow dancer remained a mysterious, tantalizing puzzle I could neither solve nor abandon.

I told no one, of course. Who would have believed a four-year-old anyway?

From time immemorial, the realm of shadows has been associated with the spirits of the dead, the Other World, the night side of nature, or, what Bob Monroe, the famous out-of-body journeyer, succinctly referred to as "There" (as opposed to "Here").

I suspect that my shadow dancer was an emissary from There, and that her purpose was to reassure me that, in spite of my nightmares of fire-pits and human sacrifices, there is nothing to fear, after all. Certainly her immediate effect was calming, a psychological balm. For once, during that tumultuous period, I slept like a baby.

The long-term effect of seeing her was something else. Not reassuring, exactly, more like an inoculation. Philosophical materialism—the belief that only physical matter (regarded as blind, passive, and inert) is real—never crossed my mind. Nor was I ever tempted by the lure of any of the religions and their pat answers (including my own Jewish religion). Somehow I knew that the universe was a lot more interesting and mysterious, and that we don't have to accept any dues-paying creeds to access that mystery. It's free for the asking.

The ballerina made sure I would remember this—and more.

You see, I was born in 1957, the golden age of *Father Knows*

Best and perhaps the high watermark of white male Protestant patriarchy. My preconscious awareness was formed in this atmosphere. This was the year of the Sputnik satellite and the beginning of the great phallic space race. The Red Scare was at its height. Eisenhower was president, Nixon vice president. George Wallace stood in the schoolhouse door. "In God We Trust" was added to our currency and "Under God" to our Pledge of Allegiance at the behest of good, God-fearing Christians (while Thomas Jefferson rolled over in his grave).

This was the bygone era of repression many longingly hope to restore—by persuasion if possible, by force if necessary. Of course, a main feature of this repression was the submission of the female and the (mostly unconscious) fear of her power—especially her spiritual power. Women were supposed to be barefoot and pregnant, and, like little children, best seen and not heard.

As author and musician Layne Redmond explains in her fascinating book *When the Drummers Were Women: A Spiritual History of Rhythm,* this attitude goes back, in part, to the early Christian church and the beginnings of its spiritual monopoly.[12]

From time immemorial, notes Redmond, religious rites were celebrated with orgiastic singing and dancing. Women dancers and drummers often accompanied funeral processions, sometimes even as paid mourners. This little ritual originated in the ancient respect for the power of the shaman's drum, whose rhythm (the heartbeat of Mother Earth herself) produced the trance state that enabled the shaman to travel from Here to There, and to guide the souls of the dead to rebirth. Many shaman-drummers were women.

But then male-dominated Christianity came along and proclaimed exclusive rights to the soul and its proper care, both Here and There. Twice the Church banned female musicians and dancers, first in 300 c.e., and then again in 826 c.e.. As late (or recently) as the thirteenth century, the Church prohibited women who "dance in pagan fashion for their dead and go to the grave with drums, dancing the while,"[13] from attending church services.

Away with the dancers!

Except that nature has this tricky little thing called balance. Whenever things get too much one way, the opposite condition tends to assert itself in order to rectify the imbalance. It's always darkest before the dawn. The Taoists speak of the circular play of Yin (female) and Yang (male), the ancient Greeks of *enantio-dromia* (the transformation of things into their opposites). The Native Americans have their Medicine Wheel, or what some tribes call "the power of the hoop."

Thus by 1961 (when I saw the shadow dancer), the wheel was already beginning to turn, culturally speaking, away from the stale, stiff patriarchy and toward new, more fluid and dynamic forms. To know this, one only had to be sensitive to the signs and portents.

So, call her what you will: Jungian *anima*, feminine consciousness, resurgent goddess, holistic right brain, night side of nature, or just plain Eve. She was to be my guide and guardian. Even when I (temporarily) denied or forgot her, she was there, waiting patiently in the wings to remind me of my quest—and my true self.

The Secret Source

I don't think that I ever consciously decided to keep the shadow dancer my secret. It never occurred to me to tell anyone about her. I'm not sure why. I suppose I thought no one would believe me. Or else that her visit was just too private and personal a thing to share. Yet, paradoxically, beyond the seeming strangeness of the episode, there was something normal and expectable about it. In a funny sort of way, I took it for granted that such things could happen. I assumed that there was more to life than meets the eye, a hidden side to things. And who thinks to mention the obvious?

There were other such experiences I had while growing up, including instances of telepathy or precognition (though I was not yet familiar with those terms). I often knew what others were thinking or feeling, and they didn't have to be right near me for this to work. Once, for example, I was watching a TV show called *The Match Game*. Suddenly, I knew the phrase that the emcee, Gene Rayburn, was going to ask the contestant to complete: "Tomato (blank)," I blurted out loud seconds before he asked. I realized even then that the odds of "guessing" the correct phrase (when it could have been virtually any word in the English language) must have been astronomical.

More often than not, however, this knowledge was not so specific. I just had certain inklings about people, their character and hidden motives. I was especially good at spotting phonies and deceivers. I can't recall any particular episode, but it happened fairly regularly.

When I was eight or nine, I had a peak experience. One summer my parents rented a modest cottage apartment at the New Jersey seashore, where we used to vacation. I absolutely loved the shore. To me, it was a sanctuary, a holy place. The ocean filled me with a sense of mystery and longing I could not even articulate.

We had just made the hour or so trek in my father's Pontiac, packed with boxes, suitcases, and our dog, a nervous toy fox terrier that barked during the entire trip. After we unloaded the car, my mother busied herself unpacking and cleaning. Probably to get us out of her hair, she sent my father and me off to the local variety store, just a few blocks away, to buy a few grocery items, like milk and bread. While Dad got the groceries, I picked out a new rubber ball and a package of strawberry licorice rolls. After paying for our purchases, we began the short stroll back to the apartment.

I walked on ahead of my father. It was a hot, sunny day in late June. The sky was a bright cloudless blue. I opened the brown paper bag to inspect my treasures. I was warmly greeted with the pungent scent of newly cast rubber and the flowery fragrance of the strawberry licorice. I was plunged into a vortex of scents, sounds, and sights, as if all my senses had been switched on high. The smells of the rubber ball and candy mixed with the scent of the creosote-stained telephone poles around me. Though the ocean lay a block to the east, the air reeked—nearly tasted—of salt and fish, seaweed and Sea-and-Ski suntan lotion. My springy flip-flop sandals slapped the soles of my feet with my every step on the blue-grey slate sidewalk in a comfortingly familiar rhythm. I was rapt with joy. The prospect of weeks of summer vacation stretched out before me.

But there was more. I had an awareness, a recognition. Everything around me was alive and conscious, conscious not only of itself but of me as well. This included everything that we usually think of as "mere inanimate objects," including the wooden utility poles.[14] The love I felt for this place was being beamed right back at me. It was as happy to have me there as I was to be there, as if shouting, "Welcome back! Glad to see you!" I was among friends.

This is the hardest part to describe. In the background hovered other, mysterious but welcoming invisible presences. It was like being on the inside of a one-way mirror, observed by eyes that I could not see. On the yonder side of the glass barrier lay something I could hardly imagine. This other reality, like the ocean, was vast and deep. When I stood on the beach, my vision was limited by the horizon. I sensed that this "other side" had no horizon. It gave me goose bumps to think about it.

In truth, none of these impressions were new to me. Together they made up what I might call the unacknowledged atmosphere in which all of my thoughts and perceptions navigated. Yet, in that one supercharged moment, those insights were crystallized in such a way that they could never be completely forgotten, no matter how far away from that physical (or indeed metaphysical) place I would subsequently wander.

I don't know how long this experience lasted. Maybe it was only a minute or so before I settled down from the peak of rapture into ordinary joy, like plunging into the trough of a wave whose foaming crest had just rolled by. At its height, however, I knew what I had experienced was true and valid. Of course, it would be many years before I would attempt to put it into words. At the time, I didn't feel the need to spell it all out. "Of course," I would have said, if I'd bothered to say anything at all.

Odds and Ends

It was around this time that I discovered the term extrasensory perception (ESP), or what parapsychologists would rename *psi*. I devoured paperbacks by popular authors such as Susy Smith, Nandor Fodor, and Hans Holzer. All aspects of the paranormal absorbed my interest: telepathy, precognition, ghosts, poltergeists, UFOs—you name it.

Also, thanks to an aunt who was a chronic insomniac, I discovered late-night talk radio. Long before the advent of Art Bell and company, New York radio had Long John Nebel and Barry Farber, both of whom frequently featured guests like Ivan Sanderson, John Fuller, and other popular paranormalists. More than a few nights I stayed up until the wee hours, with the tinny transistor radio earphone plugged into my ear, fighting sleep, so I could listen to their fascinating conversations.

Oddly, I did not think of myself as an experiencer, only as someone interested in such things. I suppose this was a bit of cognitive dissonance, a necessary bit of self-deception (or self-defense). On an unconscious level, I must have been searching for confirmation, and maybe just for companionship. I did not think of myself as lonely, but I guess I was. I had no one to talk to about the things that mattered most to me, and nowhere else around me did I find anyone speaking about or acknowledging the kinds of experiences I'd had. There were no teachers, no mentors.

This sense of isolation did not change when I began my years of religious instruction. In Hebrew school, which met three or four times a week, I learned all about Jewish history and customs, the ceremonies for the holidays, and that kind of thing. We studied the Hebrew language and read the stories of the Bible (in English) and discussed their meaning. The subjects interested me, but only in a vaguely anthropological sort of way. None of the things I learned there had anything to do with my experiences of what I was calling the Secret Source. The god of the Bible was an interesting bit of history—nothing more.

My opinion was reinforced when I began, on my own, to read the New Testament and study Christianity. Jesus proved to be a fascinating figure, an angry prophet straight out of the Old Testament. I resonated with his demands for social justice. But Christianity gave me the same claustrophobic feeling as Judaism. The notion that the whole universe revolved around the Jews, or "the true Jews" (as the Christians thought of themselves), seemed to me, even then, to be too far-fetched, too parochial to be true. It seemed a neat bit of social engineering, a method of producing group solidarity—but no more. (Actually, the whole idea of a "chosen people" with a special relationship to the Source—whether merited by birth or belief—was morally repugnant to me.)

The biblical religions were too human-centered for my taste. They did not speak to my experiences, most of which had taken place in nature—by the seashore, in parks, my own backyard. A god apart from nature, let alone one against nature, made no sense to me. Moreover, all religions pretended to have all the answers, even when it was clear that they were just faking it (see chapter 3). To me, the universe was so vast and mysterious a place that all the simple explanations—whether religious or scientific—had to be false. I couldn't take them seriously.

The Secret Source thus remained a tantalizing secret, something just beyond my reach, certainly beyond my ken, yet it was something leading me forward in my quest.

Parallel Tracks

My inner life proceeded along two parallel tracks that never intersected. On the one hand lay my haphazard and piecemeal investigations into religion, myth, and what was then called "the occult," stimulated by what I took to be intellectual curiosity. I read whatever interested me, poking around here and there. I loved science fiction and comic books of the superhero variety. On the other hand, I remained saddled with my socially inappropriate, culturally unorthodox sense of reality. It may seem unbelievable that I never put the two together, but that's the way it was.

I certainly didn't then (and still don't to this day) consider myself a mystic or a psychic. The term "psychic" especially tends to distort and obscure the phenomena it is meant to describe and illuminate. It comes from the ancient Greek word *psyche*, which originally meant "breath" or "soul," those being interchangeable. So originally *psyche* was a bridge concept that spanned the physical and nonphysical realities, uniting instinct and intuition. But in the hands of Plato and some later esoteric philosophers, "soul" became something absolutely separate from, and even antagonistic to, the physical body and the earthly realm. Many of the nineteenth-century investigators of phenomena like telepathy, precognition, and ghosts called themselves "psychical researchers." They were infected with a similar, if unstated, metaphysical bias, stemming from their Christian background.

When "scientific" parapsychology displaced the older discipline of psychical research in the early twentieth century and replaced the gathering of anecdotal evidence of exceptional experiences with laboratory experiments (see chapter 3), it also swapped the more technical-sounding *psi* (the twenty-third letter of the Greek alphabet) for the creaky-sounding *psychic*. This was more than a mere name change, however. At least Plato had assumed that everyone has (or is) a soul. Psychical researchers, because they studied the unique experiences of ordinary individuals in the course of everyday life, kept this assumption alive.

But when parapsychologists sought only repeatable events, they needed individuals who could perform repetitively and reliably under controlled conditions. Since relatively few could, or would, do this, it became a tacit operating assumption in parapsychology that, as Ingo Swann notes, *psi* was the product of specially gifted (or psychologically peculiar) individuals.[15] In other words, the psychic "star" system was born. This idea then trickled down into popular consciousness, giving us "psychic celebrities" like John Edward. The psychic star system tends to foster the crippling belief that the rest of us must depend on (and ought to pay homage to) these "stars."

Rather than "psychic," then, I prefer the term "sensitive." As Bear Heart notes, when someone would, for example, foresee the future, Native Americans would just say that they were "sensitive to the things around them, without some fancy label attached."[16] We are all more or less sensitive to our environment. If we weren't, we'd be dead! Most of us are more sensitive to some things and not others. I might be attuned to, say, the presence of oregano in a dish (at one time a mere whiff of it would give me a splitting headache), whereas you might know a day in advance that it's going to rain because your elbow hurts. Mostly it's just a matter of what we choose (or are conditioned) to pay attention to, or where and how we habitually focus our awareness. There are physical and nonphysical environments. But it's all the same sensitivity, just tuned to different stations.

Even some scientific researchers are starting to recognize this. Dr. William Roll, a veteran parapsychologist, is presently undertaking a study of the correlation of allergic and psychic sensitivity.[17] I don't know what will come of this particular study (when I last spoke with Dr. Roll, it was still ongoing), but I think it is a very fruitful area for inquiry.

I say this because as a child I had severe allergies. They were triggered by an event that took place when I was five or six years old. It was my birthday and my mother had surprised me by preparing my favorite dish: lobster. Then, a couple of days later, my aunt invited us over for a special dinner. The main dish was a big secret—yep, lobster! The next day, my body swelled into one giant, red-hot hive, from the folds of my eyelids down to the tips of my toes. My feet were so swollen I couldn't put on my shoes, let alone walk. My mother had to carry me into the doctor's office. I must have resembled the broiled lobsters I had eaten for dinner!

I have often wondered whether this episode had a symbolic component as well.

If, say, you look closely at the bottom of the Rider-Waite Tarot card "The Moon," which belongs to the Major Arcana, you'll notice a lobster emerging from the tidal pool onto dry land. Obviously, the lobster is a creature of the watery depths—the unconscious, the unknown self, the soul, the Source Self, or whatever you wish to call it. When anything first emerges from these depths, it looks alien and strange to us. It may seem primitive or even repulsive, especially if we have been taught to fear what we can't understand. But, like the snake that sheds its skin and the moon that sheds its shadow, the lobster molts, renewing itself.

Thus, as the mythologist Joseph Campbell might say, the lobster—like the snake and the moon—is a symbol of the power of eternal life within the field of time to throw off death and to be reborn.[18] As a water creature, it is directly controlled by the rhythms of the waxing and waning moon, itself symbolic of the feminine (intuitive, right-brain) knowledge. (In his commentary on the Tarot, A. E. Waite, the Victorian occultist and researcher, makes the lobster out to be some sort of diabolical figure; but Waite is just blowing smoke here.[19]) The lobster, as A. T. Mann suggests, *is* this deeper self.[20] That is, it represents our experience of our greater self as we initially encounter it.

So was my severe allergic reaction the result of my inability to deal with this powerful encounter? Did blocked sensitivity to information coming from the nonphysical dimensions lead to an increased (hyper-) sensitivity to certain aspects of my physical environment? The lobster episode may have dramatized this inner conflict in a symbolic way. Yet the lobster was not a mere personal symbol, after all; my physical illness was a medical fact. Nor is this an either/or proposition. We are used to thinking of "mind," "body," and "soul" as names of separate entities rather than as convenient labels we use to distinguish between aspects of a single, unified self. Thus we may overlook the delicate balance (ecology) that exists between what we regard as quite distinct psychic, emotional, and physical sensitivities (like allergies). Probably there is but one primary form of energetic sensitivity that seeks expression in all types of perception, both physical and nonphysical. When one of these pathways is obstructed or overused, the others are affected accordingly, becoming either underactive or overactive.

Because I was sensitive to the social atmosphere around me, I learned early on to obey the various cultural "No Trespassing" signs posted around and about. I picked up on all the cues, subtle and not so subtle. Which only ensured that the two tracks in my inner world would remain on parallel course, not touching or intersecting.

Alas, courageous I was not.

For instance, one day in Hebrew school, a girl in our class, whom I'll call Mandy, asked our teacher, a stocky, fiery-tempered woman, why Christians celebrate the Sabbath on Sunday rather than Saturday, as is the Jewish custom.

The teacher's face turned bright red and her already prodigiously bulging eyes almost seemed to pop out of her head, just like in the old cartoons.

"I'm not here to teach you Christianity!" she bellowed, pounding her plump fist on the desk for added emphasis.

It is probable that the teacher was only covering her own embarrassing ignorance on this matter. Still, we all got the message, loud and clear. Or at least I did. Don't be too curious about other religions, other ways. Don't ask awkward questions.

So I kept my inquiries (and interests) to myself.

There were other, more subtle cues I picked up. Nothing blatant or traumatic, mind you. Just enough to tip my inner "no offense" meter into the red zone.

For example, like most children, when I was maybe four or five years old I had an "invisible friend" named Jerry. Jerry was a good companion and now and then offered friendly advice, though I can't for the life of me remember now what it was or what we talked about or did together. My mother knew of Jerry's existence. One day, while riding in the car, she asked me what he looked like. We happened to be passing a Mobil gas station and I pointed to the trademark symbol, which in those days was a horse with wings—the Greek Pegasus, who carried Zeus's thunderbolts and inspired poets. Except that, like Pegasus, my Jerry was white (rather than red, like the gas station sign).

For some reason, Mom became a bit concerned about my "invisible pals" (I think there was more than one). She consulted a family friend, a nurse with some training in child psychology. Her friend reassured her that I was a normal, if highly imaginative, little boy. Still, I think she was not entirely comforted. This was not her fault. It's just the way it was. Mom wanted me to be "normal" and not to suffer from social stigmas.

Anyway, shortly thereafter, Jerry took off into the sky one

bright afternoon, never to return. And that was that. I pretended otherwise, but inwardly I was sad to see him go.

Communication is a subtle art. I was learning to keep certain things to myself.

Interlude: Mother Earth Remembers Me (Even When I Don't)

Many years later (thirty-five, give or take), I'm wading knee-deep in the water at the edge of the lake. On impulse, I thrust my arm into the water. My hand comes to rest around a particular smooth stone on the lake bed. Bringing it to the surface, I can see that it is a piece of white quartz. Turning it over in the palm of my hand, I admire its odd, triangular shape. Then, blinking my eyes in astonishment, I really see it for the first time: The white stone is unmistakably shaped like the head of a horse in profile, mane and all.

The Lakota writer and teacher Ed McGaa (Eagle Man) calls this a *wotai* (or *wotawae*) stone.[21] It is a special friend: a gift made by Mother Earth for just one person, perhaps tens or even hundreds of thousands of years ago. This is a humbling, yet also uplifting thought. The *wotai* stone connects us with the powers of the universe.

What had been lost so many years before was slowly, but surely, returning.

The Doppelgänger Effect

Don't get me wrong, my childhood was hardly that of a victim of persecution. What happened to me was nobody's fault—not even my own. There's a deeply ingrained cultural mythology at work here, much of it unconscious (see chapter 3). Barriers are erected and trespassers arrested. Well, in a bad situation, you learn to make the best of things. You do what you have to do to get by.

Jung says somewhere that if you don't trust yourself, then you have to expect a neurosis. Or, as Bear Heart warns, "If you let your logic ruin your first instinct, you may pay the consequences."[22] I was training myself to compartmentalize my thoughts and feelings/perceptions, so they would not mix. This leads to self-mistrust. Of course, when you practice keeping things from others, sooner or later you wind up fooling yourself, whether you intend to or not. I deceived myself into thinking that I was okay.

I did not then recognize the symptoms of metaphysical malnutrition. I was hungry for a kind of food that I could not even name. Therefore I began to overeat the foods I could name, especially junk food: candy, potato chips, cookies, soda. Technically, I wasn't obese (at least not yet, anyway). But soon I had to buy "husky boy" clothes, an embarrassing turn that only added to my painful feelings of social isolation and oddness.

One Sunday morning, I accompanied my father on his trip to the local corner store. While he got the Sunday papers, I perused the racks for my favorite comic books. The dingy place reeked of the tantalizing aromas of frying bacon and greasy French fries. Pots of hot, steaming coffee sat on their gleaming stainless-steel Bunn-O-Matics. I took my comics to the register and forked over my allowance money to the cashier.

As I waited for my change, my eyes were drawn to a bulky figure hunched over the lunch counter, greedily stuffing his face with a hamburger. Huge rolls of unsightly flab bulged out of his Ban-Lon knit shirt. Then, as if he'd felt my gaze, the fat boy turned his head in my direction and looked straight into my eyes. Our gazes locked.

Time seemed to stand still. I was no longer aware of the din around me. My jaw dropped open. His eyes widened, showing the incredulity I was feeling. The straight brown hair, the horn-rim glasses, the small mouth: It was me. Or rather, it was a larger version of me. It was like looking into a fun-house mirror. For an incredible instant, I wasn't sure if I was me looking at him or him looking at me. My consciousness flickered in and out like a candle in the breeze, as if I were dreaming while wide-awake.

The cashier handed me my change, and the spell was broken. I followed Dad out of the store, still in a kind of daze.

Though I tried to put the incident out of my mind, it spooked me. From time to time, I would go on a diet and try to lose my excess baggage. Then I'd relapse into my old ways. My weight soared even higher. The scale groaned. When I look at my sixth-grade class picture, I recognize the portly figure with the double chin kneeling in the front row: It's the hamburger boy from the luncheonette, down to the bulging knit shirt. I became him. At least for a while. Eventually, when I was about fourteen, I shed the pounds and kept them off. No special fad diets or pills. I just taught myself to eat healthily. Metaphysically, though, I remained hungry, if still ignorant of my malnourished condition. But I never forgot the hamburger boy incident.

What is a doppelgänger anyway? I first encountered this term in, of all places, a comic book. Even though I recall looking up the word in the dictionary, I failed to make the connection with my own strange encounter.

As was typical of me, back then.

That might not have been entirely my fault, however. The *American Heritage Dictionary* defines doppelgänger as "a ghostly double of a living person, especially one that haunts its fleshy counterpart." But my hamburger boy was anything but a wispy bit of ectoplasm. He appeared as solid as the other patrons at the lunch counter, if anything only more ample in the flesh department. Haunting, yes—ghostly, no.

Actually, it turns out that this is more the rule than the exception. For example, shortly before launching their psychic adventures back in 1964, Jane Roberts, the future channeler of Seth, along with her artist husband, Rob Butts, ducked into a dingy barroom lounge in a seaside hotel located in York Beach, Maine, where they had gone for a much needed change of scenery. Inside the smoky bar they both observed a grumpy-looking older couple, a dour pair of sourpusses, sitting at a nearby table. The pair gave Jane the creeps as she realized that they resembled an older, sadder version of Rob and her.

Even though he was suffering from terrible back spasms at

the time, Rob suddenly grabbed Jane's hand and led her, flabbergasted, onto the dance floor, where they twisted away to a Chubby Checker tune. When Jane looked around for the sourpuss couple, they were gone, as if they'd vanished into thin air. Rob wouldn't stop dancing.

A year or so later, Jane began speaking for Seth, her trance personality. Seth explained that the York Beach couple was a temporary physical materialization of the embittered people Jane and Rob might have become had they not embarked upon a more creative and satisfying part of their lives. Rob intuitively grasped that he was staring down the barrel of his own possible future self—his doppelgänger—when, ignoring his considerable pain, he shocked Jane by dragging her onto the dance floor. It was a symbolic break with the negativity and pessimism that had been dogging them both.

I was in my twenties when I read this account in Roberts's book *The Seth Material.*[23] Despite the obvious similarities with my own encounter with the hamburger boy, even then I wasn't convinced that I'd seen my doppelgänger. After all, why would the mysterious powers of the universe give a hoot about something as trivial as my weight?

The rest of the pieces of the puzzle finally fell into place only a couple of years ago. That was when I met Gloria, a student in one of my philosophy classes. I guessed her to be in her early sixties, though it was hard to tell. She could have been much older. Slim, attractive, and neatly dressed, she gave a very youthful appearance. Her quiet reserve, however, could not mask a kind and gentle nature. Later in the term, Gloria felt comfortable enough to tell me of an unusual encounter she had had as an unhappy teenager:

My [encounter] came in the form of an enlightened conversation with a beautiful lady whom I had never seen before. She appeared before me out of nowhere. She had a wonderful smile, understanding eyes, and great listening ability. The color of her hair, eyes, and skin were of little significance. She was dressed meticulously in the latest fashion. The conversation started with her asking if there was anything troubling me. Being thirteen at the time and slightly overweight, my problem was being a little heavy. Up to that point, I loved and enjoyed eating, especially junk food, and although I did not like being chubby, I did not know how to help myself. I did not like being teased by some kids and was becoming sensitive and self-conscious. But I could not change my eating habits.

[The beautiful lady] listened attentively to my story and after smiling gave me this advice. First, realize all your good qualities inside and out, and that you are in control of your actions. Also, food is a friend, not to be abused or made to create problems. She also advised me to reeducate my way of eating through classes, to read books on nutrition, to develop new eating habits, to join an exercise group, and above all to love myself. She then kissed me on the forehead and disappeared into thin air.

I sat thinking for a while and all of a sudden a light went on in my head and I decided to take positive steps toward following her suggestions. I joined a weight control group which had a gym and diet program and from that day on I took control of my weight. I am still a firm believer in exercise and good eating habits. Through my enthusiasm I have encouraged several friends to join a gym and eat sensibly.

I often think of this "Mystery Lady" and wonder just how much she influenced me, and if eventually I would have gotten willpower or would have seen the light to take action on my own.

Gloria was far too modest to admit to the obvious resemblance between her adult self and her Mystery Lady. But when I heard her story, I sensed that it was her own (possible) future self that had come to counsel her with words of wisdom. Why and how does the universe arrange such things? Clearly, linear time is far from being the absolute one-way arrow our cultural common sense tells us it is. As to the why . . .

The answer to my question was now staring me in the face. My metaphysical double had appeared to me in order to administer a kind of shock therapy, a wake-up call to self-awareness. Like Jane and Rob's sourpuss couple and Gloria's Mystery Lady.

Yet, in a way, this only increased the mystery. If such things can occur on a regular basis, and if the vast powers of the universe are so intimately bound up with our lives—our strivings for greater awareness, self-control, and self-understanding—then why, most of the time, do we feel so cut off from this mystery dimension?

Having examined my own childhood, I began to suspect that I had to look beyond the events I could consciously recall and the surface influences that were obvious to me. I realized I had to explore the deeper, hidden causes of our metaphysical alienation. I had to confront what Joseph Campbell called "the myths we live by."

3

The One Forbidden Thing

In the case of Adam and Eve the announced rule was of a type very popular in fairy tales, known to folklore students as the One Forbidden Thing.
—Joseph Campbell, *The Masks of God: Occidental Mythology* (1976)

Questioning is one of the most vital paths to understanding . . . The question we are always asking ourselves is "who am I," or "who is this living spirit, this fire?"
—Hyemeyohsts Storm, *Seven Arrows* (1972)

Nothing is sacred to the point where it should not be investigated or put under inquiry.
—Robert A. Monroe, *Ultimate Journey* (1994)

Prelude: Some of My Best Friends

While researching this book, I found a yellowed piece of paper tucked away inside an old shoebox. When I was four, evidently I had scribbled out a little rhyme, entitled "Trees." The first and last verse went as follows:

Trees are so very tall,
They make us look so very small. . . .
Some trees grow so very
wide
When I play there
I hide.

Now why, I wondered, had I written this paean to, of all things, trees? And why was I hiding? These questions got me to reminiscing about some old and dear friends. How strange, I thought; I'd almost forgotten about them.

There was a tall, majestic oak that presided over our tiny backyard. It carpeted the ground with acorns each fall, giving off a deliciously nutty aroma. I loved to play under its great sheltering branches. Then there was the delicate dogwood, on whose lower branch I used to swing like Tarzan. But my favorite was a group of spindly white birches that stood in the right-hand corner of our front yard. I would sit amidst the birches, where I played with my plastic soldiers and metal trucks. There was something about those trees that made me feel safe and secure. It was like being watched over by a wise old grandmother or a kindly aunt. I know I talked to those trees, and they talked back.

Our small house stood on the corner of a busy intersection. Cars were always running the stop sign. It would not be unusual to hear crunching fenders or see a car careening onto the neighbor's front lawn. Once a driver was killed. People had come rushing from their houses to help, and there was blood everywhere. Mom told me to go play in another part of the house, away from the front window and the gore.

Eventually, my mother became so concerned about my safety that I was forbidden to play among my favorite birches in the front yard. Given the traffic situation and its attendant dangers, this was reasonable.

And yet . . .

Sometimes we tell ourselves that we have good and perfectly sound reasons for doing what we do. Only it turns out that those reasons may not be the actual causes of our actions. There are secret springs, hidden levers. This is the machinery of cultural conditioning. It grinds away, unnoticed, in the background. All too often it grinds us up in the process, leaving only a useless husk behind.

"Whatever you do, don't go near that tree!" Does this prohibition sound familiar? Can you hear in it the echo of an ancient ban?

Eve's Question, Our Answers

In Genesis, God (Jehovah) tells Adam and Eve that they can eat of the fruit of any tree in the magical Garden save one: the Tree of the Knowledge of Good and Evil. "Touch it," he tells them, "and you will die." That's it. No second chances, no appeals, no three strikes.

Then the serpent comes along and gets Eve going. "Did God say not to eat any of the fruit?" he asks slyly.

"Oh, no," Eve replies. "You've got it all wrong. God said that we can eat of any tree we like, except that tall one, over there, right in the middle of the garden."

"Ah, well," says the snake. "That's because if you eat of that tree your eyes will be opened. You will be like God, knowing good and evil. You will be wise. A philosopher."

Eve wonders: What would it be like to have such wisdom?

So, against Jehovah's emphatic rule, Eve takes some of the fruit and eats. Then she gives some to her husband, Adam, and he eats. And the rest is history.

Well, not exactly. Many claim to believe that this story relates actual, (pre-) historic events. But even if we reject such simpleminded literalism, we might still ask if there's any history in the story. Notice this is a slightly different question. And the answer here is: almost certainly so. The tale of Adam and Eve is undoubtedly a juicy amalgam of fact and fiction, the literal and the metaphoric, the historic and the mystical. The trick is in figuring out which parts are which. We need some sort of key in order to break the code.

The best clue I know of is the one offered by Joseph Campbell.[1] He points out that Eve's creation from the rib of Adam is, after all, a bit of a biological oddity. We all know that, male or female, no one comes into this world except by way of woman. Eve's birth is positively unnatural. Could it be that the subversion of nature is precisely the point?

Eve's name means "the mother of all living." She is Mother Nature, Mother Earth—depicted here as a silly bimbo. The Mistress of the Animals is tricked by one of her own, a lowly serpent. She is ignorant of what her own Tree knows. Following her (womanish!) curiosity and intuition and asking hard questions (especially when it challenges masculine authority) is not the path to wisdom, but rather, the fast lane to hell.

Eden is topsy-turvy, upside down, backward. Just like *Bizarro* Superman, who says "Good-bye" in greeting and "Hello" as he exits. Or, like the Heyokas, the sacred clown-shamans of the Sioux, who walk backward and do all the ceremonies in reverse. The only way to read the Adam and Eve story is standing on one's head, gazing in a mirror.

Sadly, Christianity didn't get the joke and took all this seriously—grimly so. Eve's disobedience and Adam's passive complicity cause the so-called Fall. All of Nature is corrupted. Now the world is rubbish, humanity is rotten, natural processes are evil. Only when Christ returns and the world is destroyed, a new Heaven and Earth created, and the righteous believers saved, will goodness prevail. Nature will be vanquished at last!

Although Hindus and Buddhists don't have the Bible, they have their own versions of this *Bizarro* worldview.[2] To them, life is a hellish merry-go-round ride that never ends, a bottomless can of karmic worms, an unbroken chain of reincarnations or rebirths. Their hope is not to destroy the world, but merely to escape it. Break the circle of existence. Get out! Quit! Jump off the merry-go-round! That's what enlightenment is for.

As the great Groucho Marx said, "Hello, I must be going . . ."

Adam and Eve, of course, had to go; God told them to leave Eden (and then, just as an adamantly unmoved President Gerald Ford, interpreted by a famous headline in the *New York Daily News*, told the beleaguered city in the midst of its financial crisis in 1975: Drop Dead). But what if "God" was only a stiff cardboard stand-in for the wounded Adam? Was the young couple, in fact, forced to move out in shame because Eve had cuckolded her husband with one (or two) of the neighbors?

Silly, you say? Not to Freudian psychologist Bruno Bettelheim, who viewed the saga of Adam and Eve as a cautionary fairy tale about the evils of adultery.[3] "Jehovah," you see, represents the anxious husband of a patriarchal society, where it is very important to ensure that the son who inherits your property is your biological progeny. The ultimate act of creation is, of course, procreation (which is why Genesis is only about genesis). Hardworking husband must tend to his goats on a far-off mountain pasture. What will sexy young wife do while he's away?

This is a test.

Eve, of course, fails—and miserably so. She betrays Jehovah/Adam by dallying with Mr. Snake *and* Mr. Tree! As a good Freudian, Dr. Bettelheim seems to want to treat these as obvious phallic symbols. But, as Joseph Campbell points out somewhere, the snake, considered as a swallowing machine, can also be read as the ultimate female enclosure: the womb. And, as Carl Jung notes, the archetypal tree in myth is just as frequently endowed with the specifically feminine, motherly qualities of nurturing and protection.[4] Of course, as Dr. Freud himself once ruefully observed, sometimes a cigar is just a cigar.

Alas, we must never let the complex facts get in the way of our simple theories!

Yet Dr. Bettelheim was right, of course; the old story is a patriarchal myth, meant to put woman and all she represents in her (subordinate) place. But, being the stalwart Freudian materialist he was, he could only see this in physical (and not metaphysical) terms. He could not see the paradoxical truth that sometimes a tree is just a tree, a snake is just a snake—and yet, at the same time, so much, much more.

Just how much more, you ask?

"Go Find Your Tree"

The ancient Gnostics were partially right: Eve was indeed a hero for snatching the forbidden fruit, but not exactly for the reasons they supposed. For the snake was not a mere (Hermetic) symbol of an inward illumination that would catapult the individual soul into exotic realms of the beyond. (Like the Buddhists, from whom they may well have learned, the Gnostics weren't so hot on this world.) Rather, the snake was a living conduit to an outward experience of kinship with all creation, including and especially the earthly. The snake was the cable and the tree was the port through which the infinite web of life was accessed.

Let me put it this way: What got Eve into trouble was acting as if she could learn something directly from trees and snakes. Yet at one time—and down to this day in so-called primitive cultures—this is not prohibited but expected and encouraged.

Mark St. Pierre is an adjunct professor of sociology and anthropology at Regis University in Steamboat Springs, Colorado. His wife is a full-blooded Sioux (Oglala Lakota). He has lived and studied among the Sioux Indians for twenty years. He notes that there are certain "common threads in the fabric" of all animistic or shamanic tribal cultures. These similarities include "the belief that an ordered spirit world exists, that all in creation, including man, have a soul that lives after death, and that communication with these spirits—plant, animal, and human—provides important information to the living."[5]

This information concerns humans as well as their responsibility to the larger web of life. The Dakota Sioux philosopher Vine Deloria Jr. says that when the Sioux people would gather an herb, such as sage, they would respectfully ask the oldest ("grandfather" or "grandmother") plants which ones they should pick, so as not to deplete the stock by overharvesting the most productive plants. Also, it was an accepted belief among the Sioux that the herbs themselves originally revealed their medicinal uses for humans.[6]

Plants in general and trees in particular are key members of this interspecies communications web. Animist peoples have known this for millennia. Native peoples are well aware that trees function as activators of the spiritual and psychic life, or what I have been calling "sensitivity" (which may explain why their shamans often envision themselves climbing and descending the cosmic Tree in their trance ecstasies). The tribes of the Great Plains, such as the Sioux, Crow, and Cheyenne, held their Sun Dance, in which a felled tree (usually a cottonwood) stood at the center of the circle of dancers, providing the focus for a ritual of communal renewal and personal visionary experience.

Bear Heart, the elderly Muskogee Creek medicine man, singles out the formative role played by the tree in the education of the tribe's young boys and girls:

> To teach our young people how to get in touch with nature and their own intuition, our elders used to take them way out in the woods, blindfolded, and have them sit by a particular tree. "You stay here blindfolded until we come after you. Be with this tree, touch it, hug it, lean against it, stand by it. Learn something from it." After half a day or more, they would bring them back to camp, remove the blindfold, and say, "Go find your tree." After touching a lot of trees, they could find the one they had spent time with. Sometimes they didn't have to touch a lot of trees—those with highly developed intuition could go right to their tree. They seemed to be drawn to it.
>
> That's how we began to connect. It's amazing what you feel from a tree. It can give us energy. When we take long hikes in wooded areas, we often put our fingertips on the ends of the cedar or pine needles. Just standing there touching them, you're going to feel energy come to you. Trees are emitting energy all the time. Every needle of the tree, every leaf, is trying to make the atmosphere

breathable for us. That's why my people have great respect for trees. The trees are our relatives—we call them "tall standing brothers."[7]

You see, those old tree-hugging Indians knew something. They knew that the fruit of the tree is very nourishing after all. Only we have been taught that it is poisonous.

Bungle in the Jungle

Hug a tree?

For some, "Tree hugger!" is hurled as an epithet. After all, the Bible tells us so. Even our secular religion of material progress is happy to quote scripture on this one.

When I was seven, I begged my parents to take me to the 1964 World's Fair in New York. 1964 was probably the high-water mark of our naïve faith in the secular god of Sci-Tech. In 1969, the Apollo astronauts would walk on the moon. But barely a year later, in 1970, the first Earth Day would be held. In 1964, I was still looking toward the future as a magical time of talking robots, space travel, and flying cars.

So we hopped an electric diesel rail car for the short ride to the fairgrounds in Flushing, Queens. The commuter car slowly snaked its way through grimy railroad yards, alongside factories with tall chimneys belching stinking plumes of white and yellow smoke. A half-hour or so later, we arrived at the enormous fairgrounds, packed with visitors.

It was a sweltering June day. We stood in line for over three hours at the General Motors pavilion. This was the famed *Futurama*. Here I would get a glimpse of the marvelous technological future awaiting humanity. I was tingling with anticipation.

As the ride began, our automobile bench seat glided smoothly past amazingly detailed miniature dioramas. Each model scene seemed at least as big as our entire house! There were fantastic cities with superhighways in the sky, moon bases, underwater communities, and, of course, scores of vehicles (General Motors brand, naturally) everywhere.

Soon, alas, our brief ride into The Future was over. Something about that ride bothered me, however. There was one diorama scene in particular that stuck in my mind. It depicted a construction crew mowing down the rain forests in the jungles of South America with gargantuan trucks. The guidebook I'd saved as a souvenir of my visit breathlessly described it thus:

> *Visiting the jungle.* Spectators see a machine that fells towering trees with searing laser light. A road builder, scaled to appear five stories high and longer than three football fields, follows the timber cutter. It levels and grades, leaving a divided, multilane superhighway in its path. The road serves a city that processes the products (lumber, chemicals, and farm commodities) drawn from the tamed jungle.

To most of us civilized exiles of Eden, trees are mere "things" that get in the way of progress. Mow 'em down. Chop 'em up.

Our civilized attitude toward animals is little better. In Genesis, even before Eve's faux pas, humans were put in charge of the animals. Adam gets to name all the animals, which implies a proprietary relationship. Animals are our servants, our slaves, our food. That's it, nothing more. To the seventeenth-century French philosopher René Descartes, the animal was a soulless machine, all body and no consciousness. Poke a cat with a knitting needle and what you get is a simulation of pain, not the real McCoy.

In many of the esoteric traditions of East and West alike, our "spiritual" nature or "higher" self is supposed to overcome our "animal" nature or "lower" self. Guess which one is supposed to be the master, and which the servant?

Our "civilized" idea is that the animal is a creature of pure bodily instinct, a mere automaton. It is the epitome of salacious evil, or at the very least, nihilistically amoral, an efficient killing machine. "The Beast" was the title given to the devil by the author of the New Testament book called Revelation. "Bestial" means bad.

Just recently, I came across a news report about an Israeli fighter jet that dropped a one-ton bomb on a Palestinian terrorist's house, killing him along with fourteen bystanders and demolishing the apartment building. A leading liberal commentator in an Israeli newspaper condemned the act as a descent "down the slippery slope of bestiality."

Oh, really? I thought. How manifestly unfair to the beasts!

A friend of mine recently took a photo safari trip to Kenya. One day, at a watering hole, she observed a group of gazelles nonchalantly taking a drink while a lion strolled by. The gazelles didn't bat an eyelash. Knowing that the gazelle is one of the lion's favorite dishes, my astonished friend asked her guide how this could be.

"Oh, no, ma'am," he said, laughing. "He just eat!"

It is, after all, the self-righteous civilized human, not the wild animal, who kills for justice, to save souls, for revenge, profit, greed, or "just clean fun." Our idea of nature, in fact, has nothing to do with nature, just as our idea of the animal (or, for that matter, of the physical body) has nothing to do with the reality. We are trapped in a decadent set of myths that limit and distort our perception of reality and stifle our innate sensitivity.

Eve took the tree—and, by extension, nature as a whole—as her teacher. For the so-called higher civilizations of West and East alike, this is the One Forbidden Thing.

The Christmas Tree, the Buddhist *(Bodhi)* Tree of Enlightenment, the Kabbalistic Tree of Life of mystical Judaism— all are sanitized symbols, safely sublimated forms of a deeper, wilder, far less manageable truth. The truth is that the tree is no mere symbol. It is a real being, with its own consciousness, its own energy, and its own wisdom to share.

As you will recall, there were two special trees in the garden. After Eve and Adam ate the fruit from the Tree of the Knowledge of Good and Evil, Jehovah cast them out of Eden, lest they eat from the Tree of Eternal Life. We are all in exile, doomed!

However, using our interpretive key (upside down and backward, remember), we know this is a distortion. Eve would have known to eat from the Tree of Eternal Life first, and to view the knowledge she gained from the second tree in the light of what she learned from the first. What do good and evil look like when regarded from the standpoint of eternity?

The tree freely gives itself (its shade, its oxygen, and its subtle energies) to all, without exception. The secret of good and evil is that these are human creations, variable ideas to which nature in her constancy and indiscriminant generosity is sublimely indifferent. The tree reminds us of our unbroken link to nature in her physical and nonphysical aspects, and to the dynamic balance of cosmic forces that we, from our limited perspective, label "good" and "evil." Like the tree, we are deeply rooted in the earth and yet spontaneously seek the light of the sun. Our sensitivity knows no bounds.

Yet there's no contradiction here. We belong to both realms. There is only one world after all. Our immortality, like our mortality, is a free gift of nature. We need not beg, borrow, or steal it from a jealous and vengeful god (or earn it from "selfless" gurus adept at exploiting our fears and insecurities). No one is in exile and all are welcome.

Distant echoes of the primordial wisdom of the tree are occasionally heard in and among us "civilized" folk. For example, in the Taoist *I Ching (Book of Changes)* one can read, "The Earth in its devotion carries all things, good and evil, without exception." The ancient Greek philosopher Heraclitus declared along similar lines, "To God, all things are good, and just and right; but to man, some things are good, and others evil." Even Jesus spoke of God sending rain on the just and unjust alike. (Then again, Jesus supposedly cursed the poor fig tree—a sure sign of patriarchal psychosis.)

This is Eve's tree talking.

But are we listening?

The Pathology of Mythology

One day I was pondering these questions when suddenly I realized something about my telepathic rabbit dream I'd so obviously missed before. I felt like a fool!

Surely the dream tree under which my prolific, intuitive rabbit friend had fallen asleep was no ordinary split maple in the backyard of my childhood home. It was a symbol of the cosmic Tree of Life—the tree of the knowledge of duality and of eternity (for they are really one and the same tree, just as they are one and the same life). Eve's question was thus my own question, her way my own way. Our fates were linked.

There was no turning back now.

How strange, I mused, that our private dreams could mirror the injuries we receive from our public myths. Joseph Campbell talked about what he called "the pathology of mythology," or the ways in which our cultural myths damage our souls and impede our quests. When I first began thinking about how these same myths hinder the development of our sensitivity, I mostly kept my suspicions to myself.

Or so I thought.

One day I was reading a student's term paper. Debbie, as I'll call her, was one of the better students in the class. So I was somewhat taken aback to find her admitting in the conclusion to her paper that she would like to have an open, critical mind. I thought she already had one! However, she confessed, thanks to her eighteen years of religious training, she felt "brainwashed" and incapable of real change.

Brainwashed? I almost fell out of my chair—and not only because I thought more of Debbie than she did of herself. For I had just been going through a file stocked with depressing examples of religious pathology. The manila folder grew fatter by the day, chock-full of news clippings datelined from countries all across the globe (including, of course, our own). Here are a few choice excerpts:

Item: In Massachusetts, a "pro-life" zealot armed with a semiautomatic rifle bursts into two family planning clinics and shoots nurses and receptionists to death in cold blood.

Item: In Florida, another "pro-lifer" is convicted in the shooting murder of a physician who performed abortions at a Pensacola clinic.

Item: In Nevada, two men with ties to radical fundamentalist

Christian groups are arrested by the FBI on suspicion of plotting to release anthrax, a lethal bacteria, a vial of which can wipe out a city the size of Las Vegas.

Item: In California, Christian fundamentalist Randall Terry tells an antiabortion rally dubbed "Love, Life, and Family" that America must become a "Christian Nation" under "Biblical Law." Abortion and contraception will be forbidden, and fathers will be revered as the "Godly leaders" of the family, leaving "the woman in submission, raising kids for the glory of God."

Item: In California, the self-castrated Marshall Herff Applewhite, the son of a Texas preacher and leader of the Heaven's Gate cult, joins his thirty-eight followers in a suicide pact. The Heaven's Gate theology was an eclectic fusion of Christian salvation, UFO lore, and love of computer technology. Applewhite and his Nike-sneaker-clad followers reportedly believed that their souls would be "rescued" from their "earthly vehicles" (physical bodies, that is) by a passing UFO concealed in the tail of the Hale-Bopp comet.

Item: In New York, Islamic fundamentalists are convicted of bombing the World Trade Center and planning to blow up American jetliners full of passengers.

Item: In Iran, Muslim clerics up the bounty on the life of the "blaspheming" author Salman Rushdie to a cool $2.5 million. (The late Ayatollah Khomeini, the fundamentalist ruler of Iran, had originally delivered the death decree, or *fatwa*.) One cleric notes in his weekly sermon that it is the religious duty of Rushdie's closest friends and family to try to kill him first. "Rushdie must die!" he feverishly exclaims. His congregation responds by shouting "Allahu Akbar!" (God is Great.)

Item: In Algeria, Islamic zealots shoot high school girls in the face for not wearing their veils.

Item: In India, fundamentalist Hindus announce their plan to form a political party whose aim will be to make India a Hindu State. Radical Sikhs machine-gun guests at Hindu weddings in the Punjab as part of their plan to establish a Sikh state, called the Land of the Pure.

Item: In Israel, Muslim worshippers are machine-gunned to

death by Jewish fanatics who hail from Brooklyn, New York. A maniacal Jewish fundamentalist assassinates Prime Minister Yitzhak Rabin for trying to make peace with the Palestinians (and for having the audacity to suggest that "The Bible is not a land deed").

Item: In Switzerland and Canada, more than thirty wealthy followers of mystery man Luc Jouret (along with Jouret himself), founder of the Solar Temple cult, commit suicide in a staged pact. Jouret founded the group after breaking away from the Rosicrucians (an elite esoteric group devoted to the transmission of "mystical wisdom").

Item: In Japan, members of the Aum Shinrikyo cult are on trial for releasing sarin, a deadly poison gas, in a crowded Tokyo subway. Aum Shinrikyo is an eclectic fusion of Buddhist and Christian teachings. Its followers, who have been known to parade with masks bearing the image of their guru, Shoko Asahara, in front of their faces, believed that this act of terrorism would bring about the end of the world. Several commuters were killed and many others were injured in the attack. Asahara, who is accused of ordering the attack, is quoted as saying: "I will try to free humanity of its bondage, pain, and despair. Whatever suffering falls upon me I will bear, with holy love, for you all."

Did I hear someone say "brainwashing"?

At first, Debbie's comment upset me. Then I tried to look on the brighter side. After all, I reasoned, if you know (or suspect) that you've been brainwashed, then it hasn't completely taken, has it? There was still hope that she (and those like her) could open to new possibilities, greater realities, and the power of her own natural sensitivity.

Yet how?

But Are You Religious?

One day after class, a student I'll call Monica approached me as I was erasing the blackboard.

"Do you mind if I ask you a personal question, professor?" she asked shyly.

"Sure, go ahead, I'll answer if I can," I replied, wondering what it could be.

"Professor, are you religious?"

There it was again, that dreaded question! Dropped like a fire bomb in the middle of a barn stacked with dry wood. I felt tongue-tied, mentally stammering.

"Well, uh . . ." I mumbled.

Religious? The very word now made me cringe. Yet I certainly was no philosophical materialist. "Atheist," on the other hand, struck me as a homage to an anachronism. The biblical god was history. Why beat a dead horse? Spiritual? Too elitist and condescending. "Psychic" all too often conjured up images of gypsy fortune-tellers with neon signs advertising the mystical wonders of Madame So-and-So at fifty dollars a pop. And while I preferred "sensitive," I knew that to many in our competitively crazed society this word means overemotional, weak-minded, sissified, or even hysterical.

So I just stood there, trying to think of a response.

"Look," Monica said impatiently, "the reason I'm asking is that, well, I was raised Catholic. But I've had experiences lately. Strange experiences," she added hesitantly.

"Well, I've had some pretty strange experiences myself," I admitted with a smile.

"I was in the park the other day," Monica continued in a confidential tone. "I love walking in the park by myself. Suddenly, I got this weird feeling. I glanced over at this bench, not far from where I was standing. There was this old man sitting on the bench. He looked Chinese or something. As I looked over at him, I think he smiled at me. Then he just vanished. I mean, he wasn't there!" she exclaimed.

Monica hesitated again, checking my response. I nodded reassuringly.

"I didn't turn my head or anything," she continued, her voice quavering with emotion. "One second I was looking at him, and then he just disappeared, into thin air. The thing is," she added, "I think I've seen this Chinese guy before. I may have seen him in my dreams. Or maybe it was in the park. I don't know. It's like, he's watching over me. Like we're connected, somehow."

Monica's face relaxed. She seemed relieved. At last she had shared her secret.

"What do you think, professor?" she asked earnestly. "What was he? A ghost? My guardian angel? What?"

Before I could reply, Monica gushed out the rest:

"And there are other weird things. Sometimes stuff in our house will disappear and then just reappear. It's not that it's just missing, you know. We'll look everywhere, all over the house. It's nowhere, absolutely gone. And then, 'poof,' like magic, it's back! Just the other day this happened to my little brother. He had been looking for a picture, a framed snapshot of him with our grandfather, who died recently. He swore he looked everywhere, even in his top dresser drawer. And it wasn't there. It wasn't anywhere. Then, later on, he looked again. And there it was, right in front in his top dresser drawer!

"Professor," she pleaded, pausing to draw a breath. "Tell me, what's it all about?"

I did not want to play the Man of Authority. Not only because I didn't know what it all meant, but also because I felt it was important for Monica to search for her own answers. She knew something unusual was going on. She was paying attention, even though these experiences didn't fit in with anything from her religious background. I thought this was a good omen. Like me, she sensed—though neither of us could find the right words to express it—that it was possible to be religious without religion.

So I told Monica that she must figure out for herself what it all means. I offered to lend her some books and articles on the kinds of phenomena that she described. I reaffirmed my belief that such things do, in fact, happen. She wasn't crazy. Or lying.

Monica thanked me for listening. But as we said our good-byes in the noisy hallway, I sensed her disappointment. I told myself that this was healthy, and that my approach would inspire her to find her own way.

Not long after our conversation, however, Monica dropped my course.

I ran into her later that semester. She apologized for her

departure and reassured me that she had indeed enjoyed the course. She explained that her allergies had been acting up and had caused her to miss too many sessions. I didn't mention our previous conversation, and neither did she.

I felt as if I'd failed Monica. At first I convinced myself that I'd done the right thing, offering her reference materials and some bland words of encouragement. But now I agonized whether I could or should have said (or done) more.

Oddly, I had also failed to notice some obvious similarities between Monica and me—for example, her allergic sensitivities, the peace and contentment she found walking in the park, and her discomfort with conventional religion. None of this rang a bell. It was as if the universe were testing me by sending me another version of myself.

I had to admit that it looked as though I'd flunked.

Something in my basic analysis of the problem had to be lacking, I thought. I was on the right track, but maybe I hadn't traveled far enough along yet. Why would someone like Monica or Debbie get as far as they did, and then just throw in the towel?

"But What Would Be the Answer to the Answer Man?"[8]

The more I thought about it, the more it seemed as if Debbie's reference to "brainwashing" was more than a neat metaphor. This was a real clue.

Remember that old cold-war movie thriller, *The Manchurian Candidate*? In the original version, Angela Lansbury, playing a treacherous spy, casually uttered a code word triggering a posthypnotic suggestion that transformed her son (played by Laurence Harvey), a patriotic American soldier, into Robokiller, a preprogrammed political assassin hot-wired to kill for his Red Chinese controllers. He was operating on automatic pilot but didn't know it.

In the case of Debbie (and Monica), some cultural taboo was being violated and the posthypnotic suggestion was automatically kicking in. Instead of advancing to meet the challenge of new ideas and experiences, they were beating a hasty retreat into familiar dogmas and comfortable mental routines. Where there should have been the exhilaration of a newfound inner freedom, there was only a timid reserve, a closing off instead of an opening up of minds.

Why? What was the secret code word, the mental circuit breaker?

The more I reflected, the more obvious it became. The code word is: Question.

Most of us are addicted to answers and terrified of genuine questions. This is not our fault; this monkey was placed squarely on our backs. It is the single common thread in all of our cultural myths, whether religious, philosophical, or scientific. It's not merely that we're wedded to particular answers, mind you. We're stuck like flies on flypaper to the underlying belief that we can and should be able to obtain all the answers, once and for all. We're prisoners of the grand illusion of a total system of explanation, the vainglorious dream of a final theory of every-thing, the dangerous delusion of the One True Religion. (Even postmodernists who gleefully "deconstruct" systems are all frus-trated system-builders at heart. They maneuver their intellectual bulldozers over sandcastles of ideas with the cold ferocity of a suitor scorned.)

This is the viral DNA embedded in the cells of every ideology, the ultimate "ism."

I now dubbed it "Answerism."

Religious Answerism is often fairly explicit and up-front. For example, as Princeton scholar Elaine Pagels points out, one of the fathers of the early Christian Church, a bishop named Tertullian, insisted that people not be allowed to ask questions, for it is "questions that make people heretics." The Greek word *heretic* means "one who makes a choice." So choosing to ques-tion is definitely on the forbidden list.[9]

Sometimes, though, the prejudice against questions is a tad subtler. I once read a book by a well-known teacher who mod-eled himself on the Hindu gurus he had studied with in India. (In true guru style, his beatific picture adorned almost every page of the book.) He described how he had broken with several of his teachers when he discovered that they were not as purely "selfless" as they pretended to be (surprise, surprise!). In fact, he suggested, they were jealous of him and kept him from developing his abilities. It is very important, he cautioned, to question all such claims of having achieved perfect egolessness. Unless, of course, he added, one finds a *truly* selfless teacher who wouldn't dare dream of exploiting others—a teacher such as (hint, hint!) him. In which case it is very unwise to question what one is told!

I saw that Answerism stifles creativity and promotes violence.

Recalling now my own experience in graduate school, it made sense. I recognized the game that we were being taught to play in lieu of being encouraged to ask genuine questions. I knew why I found that game so distasteful.

That game was war.

The very words we used to describe what we were doing told the story. Like good soldiers fighting to take a strategically located hill, we were supposed to take and hold a fixed (intellectual) "position." Philosophical positions, like their military counterparts, were said to be "defended," "attacked," "defeated," "supported," "abandoned," and "maintained." We were encouraged to find "useful weapons" to be deployed against "adversaries" or "opponents." Assertions were "parried," "hit their target," "forced the issue," or "knocked a massive hole" in an opponent's view, and so forth.

Granted, such verbal jousting paled in comparison with the bloody savagery of religious wars, persecutions, suicides, vendettas, and so on. It was insignificant next to the horrific despoiling of the planet undertaken by the greedy exploiters of Earth's resources (as lovingly documented, for example, at the 1964 *Futurama*). Yet beyond the obvious differences, there was a common psychological and ideological root to all this reflexive violence, whether physical or mental: the Answerist mind-set.

From reading the works of philosopher Thomas Kuhn (who coined the phrase "paradigm shift") and quantum physicist David Bohm, I learned that Answerism holds sway even in science, which prides itself on its open methods of inquiry and the revisable nature of its beliefs. These courageous thinkers showed that while science periodically opens itself to new ideas and experiences that don't fit old paradigms, it quickly closes down again, reestablishing a kind of fundamentalism (what Kuhn called "normal science") that does not permit deep questioning of the new perspective.[10]

So, for example, although Einstein and his relativity theory eventually triumphed over the classical Newtonian picture of the universe, Einstein himself could not, in turn, accept the even more revolutionary implications of the new quantum mechanics. He cut off all communication with Danish physicist Niels Bohr, even snubbing him at a party.[11]

But what did Answerism have to do with Eve?

The Eve story marked the moment in our past when the authority of fixed rules (definitions, interpretations) usurped direct personal experience. There is no fixed formula, no strictly logical procedure, for generating questions. Asking the right question at the right time in the right way is an art, not a science. It takes feeling, imagination, and above all, intuitive sensitivity—the very qualities Eve was prevented from developing when her contact with the web of life was abruptly broken off. After that, we were told by holy texts what our experiences meant—period. (The ones we were permitted to have, that is.)

With the crippling of our ability to question, we fell under the sorcerer's spell. We saw ourselves inhabiting a dead universe—ashes to ashes and dust to dust. A dead world (either "God" was outside it or a nonexistent phantom) can safely be cut up into pieces with abstract ideas—cookie-cutter answers that pretend to be final and complete.

But what if, as the Sioux philosopher Vine Deloria Jr. says (from the perspective of that older, outlawed animist point of view), "the world is constantly creating itself because everything is alive and making choices that determine the future"?[12] Then creation (or evolution) is not something essentially over and done with; it's happening right now, all the time, in ways we can neither predict nor control, nor perhaps even comprehend.

Everything, in other words, is conscious, alive, and free. Creation itself is "heretical"!

So we must keep an open mind and be ready, willing, and able to question—and fundamentally revise—all of what (and how) we think we know about our world. We'd better trust our own experiences, for they can always tell us something fundamentally new and different about ourselves, and about our mysterious (and surprising) world.

Answers are the dregs; questioning is the wine.[13]

Perhaps that is why native peoples did not write texts. Contrary to our prejudice that these were static cultures (the projection of our own rigidity?), they knew to keep their fingers on the pulse of change. This is the heart of questioning. The Indian activist Russell Means recalls that his Grandpa John never finished a teaching story. He always omitted the ending, leaving, say, the lost young hunter struggling to cross the raging creek. This frustrated Russell when he was a boy. But much later, he realized what his Grandpa was doing: "Grandpa John was teaching me the Indian way of thinking, teaching me to use my imagination, to figure things out for myself, to study, and to analyze. He caused my unformed mind to frame questions—and then search out the answers."[14]

For Eve, then, religion is a truly open-ended inquiry. She is unwilling to settle down in any closed (or essentially closed) system of thought. Hers is a quest ignited by curiosity, fueled by intuition, and accelerated by respectful attention to her nonhuman friends in the mineral, plant, and animal kingdoms that she honors along the way.

I knew all this now, but only in an intellectual way. Answerism was definitely out. But what was in? What was the next step? What was I supposed to do?

Loitering at the Doorway of Change

Direction came in the form of three strange "dreams." Only in retrospect, however, did I appreciate this. At the time, I was too close to the forest to see the trees.

Before we were married, Cynthia lived in a condominium that abutted a wilderness preserve, much of it consisting of marshy wetlands. It was a virtual wildlife paradise. We loved to stroll along the edge of the refuge, usually accompanied by Cynthia's dog, a well-behaved, good-natured golden retriever. We would catch glimpses of elegant, ethereal blue herons, high-flying turkey vultures, swift hawks, roly-poly hedgehogs, honking Canadian geese, huge snapping turtles (once we stopped traffic on the access road to allow a mother turtle to get to her nest), and, of course, the ubiquitous deer.

Yet, for all its teeming activity, the place was suffused with a certain primordial quietude. Looking out as far as the eye could see, no human habitation intruded. In fact, the only evidence of human presence was a narrow dirt access road, used mostly by hunters. Perhaps I was just not used to the pure unadulterated wildness of the place, but I sensed that the area was imbued with a peculiar energy. Sometimes when I walked along the path alone in early morning or at dusk, it felt spooky. So I was not too surprised when I later read an item in the local newspaper that told of a reliable eyewitness (an amateur astronomer) who reported seeing strange, unexplained lights flying over the preserve. The paper even labeled it a UFO sighting.

Then there was what I called the Witch's Tree. It was a thick, massive old dead oak that looked like it had been transplanted from the ritual grounds of some ancient Druid cult. Standing out in the middle of an open field, it dominated the surrounding landscape, its bare gnarled branches stretching into the sky like the leathery upraised arms of a mystical priestess performing her supplications to the moon goddess. The only signs of life in the rotting old hulk were the green leaves of the serpentine vines of poison ivy that encircled the tree like a nest of boa constrictors. However, in the dead of winter the naked brown vines were invisible against the decaying brackish bark of the tree. That was the season when the tree looked its creepiest. I imagined (without the slightest bit of evidence to back up my supposition, mind you) that the UFO sighting had been made directly over the tree as the full moon glowed brightly through its spindly branches.

The UFO sighting in the wilderness preserve had not yet occurred, however, when I had three odd "dreams" in close succession. They took place on three separate occasions when I was visiting Cynthia at her condo, which was about a thirty-minute drive up and over rolling mountains from my house. To my way of thinking it was no mere coincidence that I had those dreams when and where I did. For I sensed that the wild energy of that place was somehow speaking to me, and to my concerns. Those dreams, in other words, were messages from Gaia.

The dream sequence unfolded over the course of several weeks in the fall of 1991, when I was hard at work finishing my dissertation. (In March 1992, I would fly back to Chicago to defend my thesis and secure my Ph.D.) By then I had been teaching philosophy for several years as a part-time adjunct instructor at various local colleges in the northern New Jersey area.

Yet despite all of my classroom experience and theoretical learning, I was unsure of the future direction of my work, beset by doubts concerning academia in general and philosophy in particular. Most of all, however, I lacked confidence in myself. How (and what) could I possibly teach, when I knew so little myself? How could I presume to guide others in their quests, when I felt so lost in mine? My students looked to me for answers. But I had no answers—only questions. What was wrong with me?

One night on the edge of sleep, I felt like a disembodied point of consciousness floating in a three-dimensional velvety black void. I slowly became aware of a series of brightly colored forms metamorphosing in front of me. The images were like holograms, fully three-dimensional. Their lucid hues (red, orange, yellow, green) were brilliant, almost psychedelic in intensity, yet semitransparent. Each shape would coalesce, then melt into its successor. Bedazzled by the sheer beauty of the display, the sense of what I was seeing escaped me. Suddenly, I recognized the forms.

They were the skulls of prehistoric humans, only in reverse chronological order: From *Homo sapiens sapiens* (or Cro-Magnon) to the distinctively beetle-browed Neanderthal to a gallery of humanoid ancestors more closely resembling apes. It was evolution in reverse! The strangest part of this hypnagogic vision is that all the while I felt like a student being given a lesson—though by whom, and for what purpose, I did not know. It was a mystery.

The second experience began as a more conventional dream. I dreamed that I was awake in the bedroom, standing by the rear window. Something caused me to open the window—perhaps I heard a noise, or I just knew that I was supposed to do this. I stuck my head out the window that looked onto the edge of the preserve and glanced to the left, down the side of the building. What happened next is indescribable. I didn't so much directly see, as sense, the presence of the brightest, whitest, most intensely brilliant source of light. At first, thinking it was the sun, I flinched, averting my eyes in order not to burn out my retinas. Yet even as I realized that it was not the physical sun, I pulled my head back into the room. I wasn't ready to see it, despite the deep feeling of awe it inspired.

The third experience would probably be classified as a lucid dream, which is defined as a dream in which one is consciously aware that one is dreaming.[15] Yet to me it was no dream—lucid or otherwise.

I found myself standing in the backyard of the condo, on the manicured lawn that gently sloped down toward the reedy underbrush and woods of the preserve just beyond. Realizing that I was dreaming, I was taken aback by the un-dreamlike quality of my vision, which was crisp and clear. Looking about, I was astonished to realize that I could feel everything, including the ground beneath my shoes and my own body, as a physical presence, and yet it was also much more.

Testing my hypothesis, I bent down and gently touched my hand to the ground, finding the earth every bit as solid and real as one might expect. As I stood up, however, I became aware of each blade of grass glowing like a Fourth of July sparkler, radiating light from some hidden source within. The air was suffused with this same sparkling radiance. I also became aware of a strange, far-off sound. It was a gentle tinkling of bells, like wind chimes, only more delicate and ethereal. As I looked to my right, I saw that I was not alone. Sebago, Cynthia's golden retriever, stood nearby, his gaze fixed at the edge of the woods. There I spied the evident object of his canine attention: a rabbit hopping over the boundary line that divided the backyard from the wilds beyond. The dog and I exchanged knowing glances, as if entering into a tacit agreement.

"Let's get the bastard!" I shouted, as I took off after Sebago, who was already galloping off toward the woods in pursuit.

Were these dreams? Visions? Out-of-body visits to parallel worlds? I could not decide. Whatever they were, I sensed they were connected, of a piece.

The "reverse evolution" vision and the "invisible sun" dream seemed to be deliberately juxtaposed, their meanings intertwined. This could only mean there was some sort of guiding intelligence at work—a hidden teacher. Who, or what, was this mysterious guide? I did not know. Moreover, what was the lesson? Here I had more to go on. The parade of skulls took place inside a dark cave; yet the skulls were illumined from within by a brilliant radiance. This light in the darkness did not dim as the present yielded to the distant past. Consciousness, in other words, was always present. I felt a deep bond with those "primitive" humanoids. We were one. They had something to offer: a gift to give.

Also, their inner light was one and the same light whose presence I detected when, in the second dream, I stuck my head out the window of the building (civilization). I glanced to the left, or what is sometimes regarded as the "sinister" direction, not to the "right" (the safe, conventional route). By looking outside the established structures to the heretical, questioning side, I would find the true source—the same source that was present at the dawn of humanity. It was in nature, and in our nature, from the beginning. The left-hand path represented uncharted territory. Yet, like it or not (and it did make me uneasy), that was where I had to go.

The surprising appearance of my old friend, the rabbit, in the third dream told me that I had to be willing to trust my instincts (the dog) to guide me in these new realms. The wily rabbit was leading me from the manicured green lawn of civilization and rational control to the wild woods. This is the mysterious zone that Joseph Campbell termed "the dark forest of the mythological adventure," where there is no way or path. Psychologically, this zone referred to the unconscious; metaphysically, to those nonphysical realms that out-of-body explorer Robert Monroe succinctly dubbed "There."

But something told me that all would not be smooth sailing. Why had I called the rabbit a "bastard," of all things?

A "bastard," of course, is an illegitimate child, an offspring without an officially acknowledged father and, therefore, a somewhat disreputable issue. The meaning now seemed clear: I still doubted my intuitions and instincts. Secretly, my more conventional side ached to disown my own psychic sensitivity. At the very least, I was still afraid to embrace it, fully and openly. I was not ready to trust myself.

The former psychic spy and professional remote viewer Joseph McMoneagle says he knows many people who only loiter by the threshold of the doorways of change, unable to muster the courage to pass through. These people are good at intellectualizing their metaphysics but, according to Joe, manifestly unwilling, in the final analysis, to "give up or alter their extant perception of how or why things work."[16]

In other words, like some forlorn fool straight out of a fairy tale, they are stuck, frozen solid in a kind of suspended animation.

That, alas, was me. I believed. On some level, I knew. Yet I held back. I hesitated. I couldn't bring myself to walk through that door.

No wonder that I was soon to have a visit from Snow White.

4

Fairy Tales Can Come True

Synchronicity takes the coincidence of events in space and time as meaning something other than mere chance, namely, a peculiar interdependence of objective events among themselves as well as with the subjective (psychic) states of the observer or observers.
—Carl G. Jung, foreword to *I Ching, or Book of Changes* (1951)

I thought with delight that the universe or nature gave up its secretiveness once you started paying attention to the small details of living that we've been taught to ignore . . . Nature's seeming secretiveness was actually an invitation to us to really look at its events, innocent of our preconceptions.
—Jane Roberts, *The God of Jane: A Psychic Manifesto* (1981)

Once Upon a Time in Midwinter . . .

So there I was, wandering aimlessly about in the dark forest. For all intents and purposes, I was lost. I'd bravely chased after the wily rabbit. But the rabbit had vanished without a trace (or so I thought), leaving me stranded. It wasn't that I had too much male pride to stop and ask directions; there was no one in sight to ask. What to do? What *could* I do? I muddled along from day to day, waiting for clarity and hoping for direction.

In the meantime, my canine friend (and fellow rabbit hunter), Cynthia's golden retriever, finally succumbed to the thyroid cancer that had begun slowing him down. Sebago had held on for a year after the veterinarians had given him up for dead. But now he was gone. I wondered whether my strange dream had been a forewarning of his imminent passage.

The foul weather didn't help my mood. The winter of 1994 seemed to drag on forever. In the northeast we were hit with a major snowstorm nearly every week. Several times, I had to cancel my classes when I couldn't make it into the college. Then, to top it off, I caught a bad case of the flu and wound up stuck in bed surrounded by piles of dirty Kleenex and cough drops for a good solid week. I knew I was losing my grip on reality when the highlight of my day was watching screaming lowlifes go at each other on Ricki Lake's TV show. The term "cabin fever" didn't even begin to cover it.

The snow continued to pile up. My mound of tissues grew. I was miserable.

My friend the philosopher and paranormalist Michael Grosso notes that "Some dreams give clues to the patterns of our lives—perhaps to the pattern of life itself."[1]

How true! Yet, if we are alert and careful readers of the living book of nature (the original meaning of "religion," remember), we may also detect these patterns during our normal waking experience. The trick (as Socrates said) is to be awake while we are awake, so as not to miss the clues. (Becoming awake during sleep is yet another problem.)

If and Only If Snow Is White

Fortunately, a break occurred in the weather and I was able to return to work. I apologized to my evening class for having missed two sessions (the class only met once a week for three hours). I promised to make up the material.

We began our discussion of Plato's famous early dialogue, the *Euthyphro*. In the piece, Socrates, the philosopher, asks Euthyphro, a priest of ancient Athens, to supply him with a clear and unambiguous definition of the term "piety." No problem! replies Euthyphro, as he is a self-proclaimed expert on all things religious. Of course, the priest fails to deliver and makes an ass out of himself to boot—in public, no less. Euthyphro turns out to be almost as incoherent as the old comedian "Professor" Irwin Corey (remember him?), who would spout ponderous gibberish as if it were the gospel truth.

After summarizing the basic thread of the plot, I opened up the discussion to the class. Eager hands shot up all over the room. The enthusiasm startled yet heartened me. I recognized Leonard, a tall, dark-haired, intense-looking student in the back row.

"Euthyphro is bullshit," Leonard intoned dryly as a number of his classmates guffawed in approval. "I mean, he's just playing with words, like all priests do. Socrates showed that he didn't know what he was talking about. 'Pious' means whatever you want it to mean. Look at all the ways people back up their actions, saying that 'God' ordered them to kill somebody, or start some war. It's a crock."

Now all hell broke loose. The room exploded into a confusing welter of charges and countercharges. "You're an atheist!" someone shouted accusingly. "They just don't want us to have abortions," cried a female student. "Yeah, it's all about sex," muttered another in a cynical tone. Passions swirled and tempers flared. What had I started?

While part of me was happy to see the students so engaged, the rational (professorial) side was a tad fearful of the discussion degenerating into a shouting match and name-calling (shades of Ricki Lake!). It was quickly getting out of hand—and escalating. I had to regain control before pandemonium took over.

"Look," I emphasized, yelling above the din. "Granted there are as many different ideas of what it means to be faithful to the divine as there are ideas of divinity. But suppose there is some sort of true definition of 'piety'—only we don't know, and can't say, what it is. Maybe 'God' isn't just part of a word game people play with themselves. Maybe the divine is real. But whenever we try to pin it down with words, it's like trying to hold on to a fistful of water: The harder you squeeze, the less you have."

In the back of my mind, I flashed on a discussion we'd had in one of my own undergraduate courses years before. It concerned a theory of truth proposed by Polish-American mathematician and philosopher Alfred Tarski. Tarski had argued that "truth" is not just an idle word game but a relationship of correspondence between words (or sentences) and things in the world. Of course, for Tarski these "things" are physical objects— and the divine dimension, whatever it is, is not just another physical thing. So I decided not to bring Tarski into the picture, after all. Hell, I didn't want to complicate matters any further. I just wanted to defuse a bomb!

"Okay," I added. "Let's take our long break." (When all else fails, call time-out.)

The shouting slowly died down. Small groups of students were talking animatedly among themselves. Some went outside for a smoke or to raid the candy and soda machines. I remained behind to collect my thoughts and breathe a sigh of relief.

Just then a petite curly-haired young woman in an arm cast approached my desk. She apologized for her own recent absences and explained that she'd fallen on a patch of ice and broken her right arm. She asked for a syllabus. I rifled through my briefcase and, quite uncharacteristically, couldn't find an extra copy.

"What's your name?" I asked, as I hastily scribbled a note to myself.

"Rhonda Schnee," she replied.

Now my ears pricked up. "Oh, 'Schnee,' that's German for 'snow,' isn't it?"

"Yes," acknowledged Rhonda. She looked surprised (but pleased). But I didn't tell her that I didn't know any German. I only knew this because of a book I'd read some fifteen years earlier, in which Alfred Tarski's theory was discussed with the example, "The German sentence 'Schnee ist weiss' is true if and only if snow is white."

Now that's odd, I mused—a most peculiar set of coincidences. The snowstorms, the (unmentioned) snow example, and now Ms. Snow, in the flesh, having fallen in the snow. But as the second half of class commenced, my mind turned back to Plato and anxious thoughts of how I was going to cram in the rest of the dialogue in half a session.

Later that evening, I was in bed reading a book when I came across the name of the late Helen Wambach, a California psychologist who had become interested in reincarnation. Dr. Wambach had even used past-life regression as a therapeutic tool in her regular practice. She had also been one of the first researchers to use hypnosis in order to progress volunteers forward in time to the future (or rather, to several, quite different possible alternative futures). This all sounded very familiar.

Instantly, I jumped out of bed and retrieved the cassette tape I'd been playing in the car on my way home from the college. It was a radio interview with Michael Talbot, the science writer and paranormal researcher. I rewound the tape and listened. Sure enough, the interviewer mentioned Dr. Wambach, along with her collaborator, who coauthored the book on their joint study (published after her untimely death), *Mass Dreams of the Future.* But neither Talbot nor the interviewer could recall the man's name.

Now I remembered that somewhere on my library shelves there lay a copy of Wambach's book, as yet unread. Quickly scanning the shelves, I excitedly pulled out my pristine copy of *Mass Dreams of the Future* and glanced at the cover.

The name of Dr. Wambach's collaborator and coauthor was Chet Snow.

There it was again!

I felt a familiar chill run down my spine. This was uncanny. I wasn't making it up. I had an eerie feeling, as if it had all somehow been stage-managed from behind the scenes. If I'd been less attentive, I might have missed the clues.

But why snow? Did the universe have a sense of humor? Was I the butt of an in-joke I didn't get? I felt out of the loop. Maybe there was more to it than synchronicity. What was the point of having my nose rubbed in snow?

The Snow Begins to Pile Up

A month or so later I was glancing through a New Age magazine when I came across an interview with a person described by the author as a respected researcher and editor in the parapsychology field. My excitement mounted as I read the piece.

The researcher seemed to be echoing many of my concerns as she confessed her dissatisfaction with the narrow, technical approach of conventional parapsychology, with its fetish for repeatable results in the laboratory. She proposed instead that everyone pay attention to their own "Exceptional Human Experiences" (or EHEs)—seemingly isolated episodes in our lives that stand out by their apparent violation of the rules of common sense, the laws of nature, or what society deems possible. But instead of treating them as bizarre if interesting accidents or one-time events in a dead past, the researcher was advocating that we regard them as living seeds of transformation, to be nurtured by the quality of awareness we bring to them. She insisted that if we looked at our lives from the standpoint of these "random" episodes, we would see an emerging intelligible pattern.

Excited to discover a kindred spirit, I immediately sat down and wrote the parapsychologist a letter. I included a brief mention of my most recent "snow" coincidences, as I thought this might arouse her interest. When several months passed without receiving a reply, however, I grew embarrassed at my earlier enthusiasm. Despite all of my academic bona fides, I must have sounded like a loon, going on like that about my experiences.

"Oh, well," I sighed. At least my *ideas* weren't so nutty, after all. Here was a reputable researcher saying the same things I had been thinking.

In the meantime, as spring arrived and the winter ice pack finally began to melt, I received Ms. Schnee's term paper. It started out as an interesting discussion of death and the Western belief in an afterlife. But she grabbed my attention when she confessed that her own initial skepticism about such possibilities had recently been shattered by a series of unusual (exceptional?) experiences. (Mind you, I had not yet discussed my own unusual beliefs or experiences in class. I was far too timid back then to do this.)

It seems that a friend of Rhonda's had developed a talent for spirit (or so-called automatic) writing. That's when someone purportedly makes contact with the dead and allows them to communicate in writing by using the body of the medium or channel. Rhonda's friend had contacted some spirits and received information that she could not have known by ordinary methods. Much to the pair's considerable surprise, the information subsequently checked out. That gave them confidence.

One day the friend's father walked in as she and Rhonda were holding a session. He laughed in their faces when they explained what they were doing. He taunted them and accused them of making the whole thing up. Then he decided to "test" them by giving them a question to ask his dead mother. Only he and Mom knew the answer. When the correct answer was returned, he stood there, dumbstruck.

Rhonda was so impressed by these demonstrations that she began to do spirit writing, obtaining results that were, on the whole, equally impressive. As a result, her ideas about life and death, and what is possible, were greatly transformed. It was just the sort of process that the parapsychologist in the magazine had been talking about.

Rhonda's story encouraged me to focus on the EHEs of so-called ordinary people—including, of course, my own. Here was a case in point, in which a person's openness to her own experience had expanded her outlook, her sense of self and reality. It was possible to overcome social and cultural conditioning—even ridicule by authorities. It was possible for people to expand their perspective, simply by paying attention to what was going on around them. No one had to settle for "brainwashing"!

A week or so later, I was perusing the shelves of a local bookstore when I picked up a copy of Ralph Blum's *Book of Runes*. As a rule, I'm not a fan of divination systems. Some people swear by the Tarot or *I Ching*, though I could never understand the attraction. But, on a whim, I decided to give the runes a try. I bought a set.

The first rune that I drew was supposed to represent the general overview of my situation. It turned out to be *Isa:* ice, or freezing. Whoa! The runes now had my full attention. Ralph Blum called the rune I had drawn *(Isa)* "Standstill":

> The winter of the spiritual life is upon you . . . Be patient, for this is the period of gestation that precedes a rebirth . . . In your solitude, exercise caution and do not stubbornly persist in attempting to work your will . . . Trust your own process, and watch for signs of spring.[2]

Suddenly, I realized how dense I'd been! For some reason, it hadn't occurred to me to treat "winter" or "snow" (or the color white) as a poet might; in other words, as a metaphor. From that angle, I had indeed been frozen solid, my process stilled. Inevitably, however, comes the thaw: Ice melts and water begins to flow again. The cosmic law of the seasons is akin to the psychological law of our innermost being. Nature is nature, after all. According to the Native American medicine wheel, snow is associated with the power of the north. As the Sioux writer Ed McGaa (Eagle Man) says: "The cold north has Mother Earth rest beneath the white mantle of snow. She sleeps and gathers up her strength for the bounty of springtime. When the snows melt, the earth is made clean."[3]

All this made good sense to me. So there was meaning in these odd coincidences, after all. I had just missed it before. These were indeed synchronicities.

Yet were these just metaphors describing my inner condition? Or were they outer signposts as well, pointing me in new, perhaps unsuspected, directions?

Signs of Spring in Winter, Signs of Winter in Spring

Then one warm June day I went to the mailbox and found a letter from the parapsychologist! She apologized for the delay and agreed that we were on the same wavelength (I'd sent along copies of some of my papers). She also encouraged me to write up my experiences with the snow/white synchronicities. If I did, she promised to consider publishing the piece in her new journal, *Exceptional Human Experience,* of which she served as editor-in-chief.

Alas, nothing came of my efforts to write the article. I would make a few notes, then give up in frustration. I told myself that the episode was too convoluted to explain. Mostly, though, I felt uncomfortable talking about my experiences. After all, I was trained in the academy. I wrote philosophy papers in which I dissected someone else's theories. Making my own inner experiences the centerpiece of the discussion ran counter to everything I had been taught. It was indecent—gauche, even.

So, you see, I generously gave myself heaps of excuses not to write that paper!

But the parapsychologist kept after me, urging me on. She said that the act of focusing my attention on the experience was part of the experience itself, and that it would provide me with fresh insights into its meaning. Also, she casually let drop a remark regarding something to which, until that point, I had been oblivious.

The parapsychologist gently reminded me that her name was Rhea *White.*

That was it! It was like water breaking through a dam. Everything flowed easily and smoothly after that. I wrote the paper in no time, in a frenzy of inspiration.

I now felt certain that Rhea herself (or rather, our connecting) was part of the meaning of the whole episode. She had also suggested that I look up a good friend of hers who taught in the psychology department at the college. She described him in glowing terms as "a most highly evolved" individual. He was an open-minded psychologist interested in parapsychology and philosophy. His name was Steve Rosen.

Steve and I hit it off instantly. Our friendship was cemented when we discovered that we'd spent our respective childhood summers in the same seaside town on the New Jersey shore. We also had much in common at the level of ideas, including a willingness to question conventional ideas, especially as they limit inquiry into the paranormal.

At our second meeting, Steve gave me a copy of a short article he'd written for Rhea's journal. In it he described an unusual experience that he'd had many years before in graduate school. In retrospect, he felt sure that this episode marked a decisive turning point in his career and, in fact, in his development. Before then, he'd been a conventional experimental psychologist, not seriously unhappy with the reigning paradigm of rat-in-a-box behaviorism and mechanistic materialism.

Later that night, I read Steve's paper, which included the following:

> At the time when I was still working on my doctorate in psychology, I was lying in bed one night, my wife reading beside me. I was half awake, half asleep, and went into a spontaneous reverie and saw myself moving along on a sled through the snow. I had the feeling that the snow was very soft, comforting, enveloping, and I was gliding very smoothly—no bumps—just the flow. There was something very serene about it.
>
> And then the sled began to rise into the air. It started to lift off, and as that happened, I felt a tremendous intensity building up within myself. It was directly correlated with the elevation of the sled. The intense feeling built up to the point where I sensed that every cell of my body was on the verge of exploding with ecstasy. It was a joyous and painful experience—painful in a joyous kind of way. The intensity of it became so excruciating that with an effort of will I had to shut it down.[4]

I could hardly believe my eyes: snow again.

Steve smiled warmly when I pointed out the snow connection at a subsequent meeting. He hadn't noticed it before. He also elaborated on his written report, noting that after this episode he was visited by a powerful series of revelatory insights. It was only much later that he connected these insights with the ecstatic sled vision. But it was this inspiration that led him to view reality (and himself) in radically new ways. It also sparked his new fascination with quantum physics, mathematics, cosmology, and parapsychology.

Steve may have shut down the ecstatic sled experience, but it had nevertheless opened him up in surprising and unexpected ways. It was an EHE.

Gone was the old scientistic dismissal of the intangible and immeasurable. Gone was the depressing view of the cosmos as a meaningless accident, a burlesque clown circus of separate bodies (matter-in-motion) haphazardly bumping and grinding up against each other in dead empty space against the background of the dour tune of entropy.

In its place was a spectacular vision of the cosmos as a dynamic process, or, in Steve's words, "just the flow." But an intelligent and all-embracing flow that could somehow find equal room for such polar opposites as joy and pain, spirit and matter, intellect and intuition, language and silence, and, above all, oneness and separateness.

Steve could no longer accept the Western view that breaks down all living wholes into isolated mechanical parts (atoms and subatomic particles). But neither could he endorse those Eastern mystics for whom only pure, absolute consciousness is real, and all diversity—the entire realm of physical bodies and individual personality—mere illusion *(maya)*.

According to the twentieth-century Hindu sage Sri Aurobindo, for example, "Even the highest individual perfection, even the [most] blissful cosmic condition, is no better than a supreme ignorance. All that is individual, all that is cosmic, has to be austerely renounced by the seeker of Absolute Truth."[5] All is indeed One—but not just one. It is many, too. As above, so below. But as below, so above! The flow of influence runs both ways, from the invisible to the visible, and from the visible to the invisible. "Earthly" is not second best.

Or, to borrow a familiar image: The ocean is not the mere sum of its drops. But neither do the drops simply dissolve, without residue or remainder, into the ocean.

Steve became obsessed with finding images that could express, or at least suggest, this flowing yet paradoxical wholeness he had intuited. (His quest reminded me of the quixotic Richard Dreyfuss character in *Close Encounters of the Third Kind* when he kept trying to model the vision of Devil's Tower that had been implanted in his mind.) Steve fastened on the mindbending art of M. C. Escher, and also on the Möbius strip, a bizarre mathematical curiosity with unique properties (it's a cylindrical ring that has been given a half-twist, rendering it at once single- and double-sided).

During this period Steve also "accidentally" discovered the work of the world-renowned physicist David Bohm, who had independently arrived at ideas strikingly similar to his own. (This was the early 1980s—when I, too, "accidentally" stumbled upon Bohm's work.) He and Bohm struck up a correspondence that evolved into a deep dialogue.[6] Steve later visited the famous physicist in England where they continued their collaboration.

Yet the initial trigger for all this had been Steve's (aborted) vision of the snow ride.

I kept returning to his poignant account of that experience. His description of it as "very serene" reminded me that *Isa* is not just a frozen zone, a time of waiting, standstill, or dormancy. Winter works its own, special brand of magic. After all, what can match the stark glistening beauty of a new snowfall as it covers the landscape with its clean white blanket? The recent snowstorms had annoyed me as a "responsible adult" because they made travel difficult and complicated practical life. But these were the very qualities I most prized as a child. I relished escaping from school for a day—guilt free. I loved how quiet it got when no cars were zooming down the street, and all you could hear was the rhythmic *crunch, crunch* as you trudged through the drifts. Everyone had to slow down and take it easy, instead of rushing around. So peaceful.

Steve had also described the snow as "very soft, comforting, and enveloping." These are typically feminine traits. They suggest nurturing and caring. But what about the ecstatic, expansive energy that had nearly blown Steve's mental circuits—perhaps the very energy that subsequently fueled his insights into the nature of reality?

At the time of his vision, Steve knew nothing about the kundalini energy that, according to the Tantric traditions of yoga, lies dormant, coiled up like a little (female) serpent, at the base of the spine in the first, or root, chakra, one of the seven subtle energy centers. Much later he speculated that the episode might have been a spontaneous awakening of kundalini that he aborted. Even so, it had proven to be a major boon.

It dawned on me that snow/white and Eve were fast friends. Rhea had sent me some of her earlier published essays and unpublished papers. I began to comb through them in search of evidence that I might use to test my new hypothesis.

Snowstorm

Young Rhea White dreamed of playing professional golf on the women's circuit. She yearned to be a champion. Carefully and methodically honing her skills, she played in statewide matches, at one point even making it to the quarterfinals of the New York State Women's Golf Championship. She was well on her way to realizing her dream.

Then came an experience for which she didn't even have the words. At least, not until decades later, in the 1970s, when philosopher and physician Dr. Raymond Moody Jr. would coin the term: near-death experience (NDE).[7] Rhea remembers it this way:

> My near-death experience occurred when I was a junior in college and had driven my 1936 Ford from Penn State to Syracuse University to pick up a friend whose car was being repaired. He was to be my guest at a big weekend at Penn State. A terrible driving snowstorm developed. Visibility was almost nil as we started back south. There is a long hill as one leaves Syracuse, and try as I might, I could not get to the top. I was not the only one. Both sides of the road were lined with stranded cars. My

friend asked me if I'd like him to try, and although my father had told me never to let anyone else drive my car, I answered fatefully, "Well, we'll never get there with me driving!" So we switched. My friend Stu was a very good dancer; he had a light touch on the gas pedal. He got us over the hill and we continued, going about fifteen miles an hour. Then, out of the swirling snow ahead came a coal truck. As it approached it began to skid toward us.

The next thing I knew I was up in space, or so it seemed, as if looking down on the Eastern seaboard, pin-pointing State College, PA, which steadily receded as I rose higher. As I relinquished my fixation that we had to get there in time for the festivities, it dawned on me that this being pulled away from Earth was what it was like to die. Obviously not being able to do anything about it, I relaxed, as if leaning back into space, and then I felt the "everlasting arms" encircling and cushioning me from behind. Then it was as if a voice said to me, "Nothing that ever lived could possibly die," as if by definition. I felt a sense of living stillness, peace, wonder, pure aliveness— and then I woke up on the hood of my car, in pain, unable to move, with the sound of the metal of the car tinkling as it settled, my head turned so that I could see cars creeping along the slippery road with people inside craning their necks to look at us. . . . Stu was killed instantly when the truck totaled the car, entering on the driver's side. . . . I had eleven fractures and was in and out of a drugged state for days, but when I was con-scious, I could sense this singing stillness. It was what I had felt when I thought I was dying. It combined a sense of deep peace and a kind of poised expectancy, as when a child wakes up on his or her birthday. And as the days went on, I could feel myself healing, my bones knitting. This was an exceptional experience in itself, because somehow I felt I was aware of this gentle fizz of healing energy like ginger ale in my bone cells.[8]

Believe it or not, it took me a few more readings before I noticed it: snow again.

That did it. Now I was sure I was on the right track. I had to understand what had happened to Rhea. How did she get from her NDE to an EHE?

After her recovery, Rhea was able to resume her golfing activities. But her heart was no longer in it. The dream of becoming a professional athlete had mysteriously faded. In its place was an insatiable hunger for knowledge. She was consumed by a desire to read through the world's spiritual literature. Although she didn't think of it in this way at the time, she needed to figure out exactly what had happened to her when she was dead, yet not dead. She could not yet even talk about her experience. Yet it drove her to pore through every dusty tome she could get her hands on. She eagerly read hundreds of books, on all sorts of topics: religion, philosophy, mysticism, psychology, psychiatry, and psychical research. She also began to meditate.

Then Rhea discovered that the creaky old psychical research of the nineteenth century was busy transforming itself into the streamlined, more intellectually respectable, twentieth-century discipline of parapsychology. Philosophers, classical scholars, and other humanists who specialized in collecting anecdotes of people's strange experiences and speculated about the nature of consciousness had dominated nineteenth-century psychical research.

But the new "hard" science of parapsychology hoped to provide definitive, verifiable, statistical proof in the laboratory of the reality of such phenomena as telepathy, precognition, and psychokinesis (direct movement of matter by mind). Speculation and storytelling were out; the white lab coats and clipboards of social scientists and physicists were in. The pioneering dean of this new movement was one Dr. Joseph Banks Rhine, a respected psychology professor at Duke University.

Something clicked. Rhea made her way to Duke. Apprenticing herself to Dr. Rhine, she learned his methods and became an assistant in his laboratory. That was more than forty years ago. It marked the beginning of Rhea's lengthy career as a parapsychologist.

All was not well in parapsychologyville, however. Over time Rhea would grow disillusioned with her chosen profession. To an outside observer, it was easy to see why. Rhea was like a sky-rocket fueled by a burning desire to understand her extraordinary journey beyond death. For all the good it did joining up with Team Rhine, she might as well have become a short-order cook in a greasy spoon or a bean counter in an accounting agency. She was bound to walk away dissatisfied.

In this respect, Rhea might be compared with the late writer Susy Smith, who wrote more than thirty books on the paranormal. (When I was eight years old and my friends were collecting baseball cards, I faithfully toted around a dog-eared paperback I'd bought off a drugstore rack—Susy Smith's *ESP.*) Back when she was a newspaper reporter and columnist, Susy began communicating with the spirits of the dead, including her own deceased mother. Making her way to the Rhine laboratory at Duke, she was warmly greeted by "this imposing group of academicians." But when she explained that her interest was in the issue of the survival of bodily death, she was politely told that real scientists could not get into the messy business of "ghost-chasing." Instead, they gave her the keys to the library. "What I stirred up at Duke was a lot of complete indifference," Susy confessed.[9]

Susy Smith's story of her reception at Duke's famed parapsychology laboratory hit a nerve, and not just because she'd been one of my childhood heroes. Her outsider status at Duke closely matched the trajectory of Rhea's career, the story of which I'd pieced together from the numerous essays (her unpublished and published papers) she'd sent me and the correspondence we'd exchanged over time. It wasn't just that official parapsychology proved to be too timid in the face of the big questions concerning immortality and death, or that it looked down on "merely anecdotal" evidence for psi as scientifically irrelevant. There was more to it than that.

I was angry. I identified with both Rhea and Susy. I found myself cheering them on. Having been guided by synchronicity to Rhea's work, I knew I had to understand my emotional reaction. What was it all about?

When I was younger, maybe nine or ten years old, one of my prize possessions was a book entitled *Great Men of Science* (or something to that effect). My parents had given it to me as a present, and I'd read it from cover to cover many times. It told the stories of courageous individuals, such as Galileo and the Curies (an occasional woman slipped into the male club), who stood up for knowledge in the face of ignorance and superstition. This, at least, was the familiar myth.

In reality, however, I came to see that science as an ideology and as an institution is concerned with shifting power from the individual to itself. It wants to cancel out the individual, and thus as part of its agenda promotes self-mistrust and a lack of self-confidence in our private judgments about our personal experiences. (In this respect, science is little different from the Christian churches, which use the doctrine of Original Sin to the same end.) Nor is this an accident. It goes to the heart of the scientific enterprise.

When the German philosopher Arthur Schopenhauer (1788–1860) said that "in history we see the mind occupied with quite individual things for their own sake,"[10] he was not being complimentary toward history. In Schopenhauer's time, natural science was becoming the new path to truth (and technological power). Science seeks to discover general principles, the universal laws of nature, in order to predict and control that nature. It loves rules. History, on the other hand, adores exceptions. It wants to understand the causes and effects of singular events, like a war, or a stock market crash. Science has abstract mathematical formulas. History, like a grandma or grandpa, tells stories. How trustworthy are these stories? "Clio, the Muse of History," said Schopenhauer, "is as thoroughly infected with lies as a streetwalker is with syphilis."[11]

What Schopenhauer says about the unreliability of history as a discipline also applies to the human faculty of memory. This is key. Our individual life stories are as unreliable as Clio's, says science. If you want truth, you won't get it by asking the individual to introspect (or retrospect). Don't tell them to reflect or write their biography. Give them a personality test. People lie, but statistics don't. The wide sample cancels out the vagaries of individual distortions. In other words, the outside experts know you better than you know yourself. In fact, they know better, period. You are thus no longer your own authority. Left alone, you are prey to your own bizarre irrationality. Reason is the organ of sanity, of consensus.

Now I understood why I felt a kinship with Rhea and Susy. They were standing up for their own experiences. It was they who were like the characters of my childhood book that celebrated the great heroes of science. Unlike the old style of hero worshippers, however, they were encouraging everyone else to be heroic in their own way, too, and not simply to look up to them.

Don't get me wrong. I'm not against the true spirit of scientific inquiry. Indeed, quite the reverse. The Latin origin of our English word "experiment" is *experientia,* which means to try or test for oneself. That's exactly what we must do.

Yet that's exactly what we're discouraged from doing by institutionalized official science (including much of parapsychology), which operates like a secular priesthood, bestowing its selective blessing of "reality" only on phenomena that can be replicated in the laboratory and statistically measured. Like the medieval church, modern science sees itself as the exclusive custodian of Truth. The sacred language of science is not Latin, but numbers. "Indeed," writes the renowned remote viewer Ingo Swann (one of the most "tested" psychics ever), "it is quite understood that parapsychologists adapted to quantitative statistics with a vengeance." This move was based, says Swann, "on the political assumption that doing so would permit the full acceptance of parapsychologists into the ranks of the mainstream-funded modern sciences themselves."[12] In other words, if you want recognition and funding, it pays to be holier than thou.

The rub is that the unique and unrepeatable events of our daily lives—including the "paranormal" ones—do not unfold within the parameters of controlled conditions. We should not ignore or dismiss these events simply because they cannot receive the priest's blessing. To allow the institutions of science (even those of parapsychology) to define reality for us alienates us from our own natural sensitivity and inner critical authority.

This does not mean that we are debarred from understanding psychic phenomena. Indigenous peoples may not have had science, but they knew an awful lot about nature, in both its physical and nonphysical forms. Why? Because they paid close attention to what happened in and around them. Like them, we have to go to the phenomena.

This, in effect, was what the older psychical researchers had done. The famous Harvard professor William James (one of the founders of psychical research) was both a medical doctor and a psychologist. But primarily he was a philosopher—what used to be called a man or woman "of letters." He belonged to what C. P. Snow famously called "the literary culture" of readers, as opposed to "the scientific culture" of number crunchers.[13]

James sat patiently for hundreds of hours with trance mediums gathering data on the after-death survival question. He read through volumes of reports containing anecdotal evidence of ghosts, apparitions, and out-of-body experiences. He even made his own bizarre dream experiences the subject of a brilliant essay ("A Suggestion about Mysticism") in which he offered incisive speculations about the nature of consciousness. In short, James was entirely comfortable with what he called life's "buzzing, blooming confusion"—the sometimes bewildering variety of experiences that make up our lives. He felt that a true philosopher must take nature as it comes—wild and spontaneous.

Sadly, the number crunchers won out. As we have seen, even humanistic fields like philosophy were cannibalized by the quantitative-analytical mentality. It began in James's own day, with the birth of modern advertising agencies in the last decades of the nineteenth century.[14] Around 1910 or so came the rise of modern market research techniques that were used to target specific consumer groups. Following the First World War, the brand new social sciences—psychology in particular—had their heyday. More influential than even Freud and Jung with their concept of the unconscious (the submerged fears that advertisers sought to exploit) was the pioneering work of Professor J. B.

Watson, who published his groundbreaking paper on behaviorism in 1913.[15]

To Watson, human beings were mere automatons whose responses could be conditioned by the right stimuli. Consciousness and introspection (not to mention spirit or soul) were myths; the observable behavior of the physical organism was the only reality. With the arrival of new mass audience outlets in the 1920s and 1930s—the cinema and radio—the mass hypnosis of the mass media was no longer a pipe dream, but a fast-approaching reality. Watson's behaviorism, in cahoots with Madison Avenue, reduced the human being to a programmable lab rat, a guinea pig worthy of study and manipulation—a statistic.

In this atmosphere, what could not be quantified or expressed in terms of mathematical equations was deemed irrelevant. Phenomena that could not be replicated at will within the highly controlled conditions of a scientific experiment were not considered real, or worthy of study. "Nature" meant only what could be predicted and controlled—and, of course, exploited (economically or otherwise). This was true even for a subject as esoteric as ESP, which of course always struggled to pass muster with the "hard" sciences like physics. Any psi effect that could not be studied and repeatedly duplicated in the confines of the laboratory was "merely anecdotal," "subjective," "soft"—in a word (the kiss of intellectual death), "unscientific."

William James insisted that people's inward experiences as they unfold in the (messy) course of their lives are as much a fact of reality as anything else. By the 1930s, though, James was considered a dinosaur. The old literary culture, which saw context and story as essential to meaning, was in full-scale retreat. Scientists might be inspired by their own exceptional experiences, but they had better keep that under their hats. Inspiration itself was not scientific. It could be a source of shame and embarrassment.

Yet what if this new method were all wrong for the phenomenon—like trying to examine a snowflake on a hot stove? What if it promised only misunderstanding rather than understanding?

What if the very point of an anomalous event were lost when it was not seen from the perspective of the experiencer, as an episode in his own life story? What if we had to develop a talent for listening to these experiences speak to us in their unique terms, rather than trying to fit them into the narrow artificial boxes of our cookie-cutter categories, our prefabricated concepts, and our controlled experiments?

I think that these were the sort of questions that finally drove Rhea away from orthodox parapsychology. They were my questions, too.

I began to grasp why she called these EHEs (she had already identified several hundred different types, from apparitions to xenoglossy) catalysts for change, or "seed" experiences. For if we water them with our careful attention, and give them the bright sunlight of whatever understanding we can muster, they will grow and blossom in the rich soil of our lives. Rhea was convinced (as am I) that everyone has had at least one such experience. All we have to do is look at our life.

While I was writing this chapter, I happened to mention near-death experiences in one of my classes. A young woman came up to me after class. She told me that she had just recalled a weird event that had slipped her mind. It had happened when her daughter was born, about eighteen months before. She had suffered complications from the birth and had hemorrhaged. But as she lay comatose in her bed, close to death, she felt herself get up and walk to the neonatal unit. There she lovingly beheld her newborn baby, sick with a fever. Only no one else seemed to know! Instantly, she awoke in her bed, crying and pleading with her father to go check on her baby. Her father then asked the nurses to check on his granddaughter. It turned out the baby was sick, just as my student had known. She thanked me for reminding her of this forgotten out-of-body experience.

So instead of emphasizing regularities or what can be controlled and predicted, we should focus on those tantalizingly odd and unbelievable, often unforgettable, frequently disturbing or even frightening episodes that we would otherwise tend to write off, dismiss, or deny. We should treat them as invitations to further inquiry. Once we see our lives from this "underside" perspective, we will have a different life story to tell. Attending to our EHEs will act as a trigger for self-transformation, for finding and making hitherto unsuspected connections. New meanings and new experiences will emerge in due course. Hence Rhea's constant refrain: Write your EHE autobiography!

Now I understood why she had been pushing me to write that synchronicity piece. It was an act of respect, a means of paying homage to nature and her invisible bonds—the magical threads that wind their way through, inside, around, and beyond us. These EHEs were not simply messages sent from the grander universe to us; they were living tendrils straight from the Source. Grabbing one was like taking a lifeline meant to connect us to the All.

Snow-Blind

One day out of the blue I mentioned something about my snow/white synchronicities in an email to a friend named Suzanne, a psychology Ph.D. and a keen sensitive.

"Oh, yeah," she replied, "the Snow White archetype is *really* powerful."

Snow White?

This is where it gets embarrassing. You see, I had always written the phrase "snow-white," or "snow/white," but never, ever *Snow White*. It never occurred to me that I was dealing with a famous character out of a fairy tale. Or rather, that she was dealing with me. That yet another cultural myth was alive and well and messing with my life (even if it was for my benefit) had been the furthest thing from my mind.

So I dusted off my edition of *The Complete Grimm's Fairy Tales*.[16] I read Joseph Campbell's scholarly commentary. I poked around here and there. I took a look at the extensive work on fairy tales done by Marie-Louise von Franz, a longtime student and colleague of C. G. Jung. I also read the poet Robert Bly's book on the Iron Hans fairy tale.[17] I won't bore you with the details. It wasn't that methodical in any case. I just followed my nose wherever it led. I'll share a few thoughts, and leave it at that. (The experts can pick it apart as they like.)

First, a few preliminaries:

1. *Walt Disney was not the first to "Disneyfy" these stories by cutting out "offensive" details.* The Brothers Grimm themselves bowdlerized the oral stories they collected and wrote them as they saw fit. Sometimes these details matter.

For example, in the 1819 Grimm's edition, Snow White's mother dies after giving birth and it is the evil stepmother who tries to murder her stepdaughter out of jealousy. This is the way most of us know the tale. But in the earlier 1812 edition, there was no stepmother: the murderous queen is Snow White's own biological mother. This was too shocking for the tender ears of good German burghers! So the Grimms fudged the text.

However, the original scenario makes it much clearer that the villainous queen and the super-naïve, ultra-pure Snow White are strictly symbolic figures. After all, one could rationalize that her stepmother in disguise might fool a young seven-year-old girl. But how likely is it that a daughter would fail to recognize her own mother—three times, no less? The sheer preposterousness of it jolts you into another level of awareness. Take away the absurdities, and you inadvertently remove the cues that guide the reader toward a deeper understanding and appreciation of the story's true meaning.

So, from here on in, I'll just assume that you've tossed your Disney video and at least familiarized yourself with a decent translation of the 1812 edition of Grimm. That way I can skip the tedious process of retelling the story and cut to the meaty parts.

2. *No one knows how old these stories are, who wrote them, and why.* Joseph Campbell insists that fairy tales are fragments of high culture myths that have degenerated. Robert Bly, on the other hand, believes that the origins of these oral tales may go back thousands of years, to the animist prehistory of Europe, well before the agricultural revolution and the arrival of "higher" civilizations. Who is right?

My suspicion is that stories like Snow White were created during the transition period between prehistoric animism and the birth of "higher" civilization. The ancient shamanic ways were being replaced (and repressed) by new myths and new, more complex and hierarchically structured societies. The people who made up what we call fairy tales experienced this transition as a tragic, terrible loss and were aware of the dangers involved. Fairy tales warn of these dangers and offer help to those who mourn the loss.

3. *This conjecture agrees with an intriguing suggestion offered by Marie-Louise von Franz, perhaps the greatest student of fairy tales ever.* In *An Introduction to the Interpretation of Fairy Tales*, she suggests that the origin of most fairy stories is an actual "supernatural or para-psychological experience" (in other words, someone's EHE). She cites an anecdote about some unfortunate events that befell a nineteenth-century Swiss family:

> The family still lives in Chur, the capital of Graubünden. The great-grandfather of the people who are still living had had a mill in some lonely village in the Alps and one evening he had gone out to shoot a fox. When he took aim the animal lifted its paw and said: "Don't shoot me!", then disappeared. The miller went home, rather shaken because speaking foxes were not part of his everyday experience. There he found the mill-water racing autonomously around the wheel. He shouted, asking who had put the mill into motion. Nobody had done it. Two days later he died. In spiritualistic or para-psychological records this is a typical story. All over the world such things sometimes happen before someone dies: instruments behave as if alive, clocks stop as if they are part of the dying owner, and various queer things occur.[18]

As we have already seen, to an individual living in an animistic culture, talking animals, helpful trees, and living, conscious tools imbued with their own distinctive personality (say, a prized bow or axe) are *not* so out of the ordinary. Such events were only perceived as unusual or *super*natural as animistic attitudes became forbidden fruit, for theological and social reasons.

In line with Dr. von Franz's hypothesis, certain events were especially memorable and served as the core around which popular tales were spun because they (unconsciously) reminded people of what they had lost, or were in the process of losing. This catastrophe occurred as people found themselves trapped inside a culture that ridiculed and despised their innate sensitivity—the same sensitivity we all possess and can exercise, if we but know of its existence and grasp the rules of its use.

Perhaps by now you've already guessed the real identities of Snow White and the evil Queen. So without further ado:

Snow White is none other than our lost intuition, despised, feared, and abandoned. Exiled and left for dead in a dark wood, sentenced to hard labor in the mining camp of the dwarves deep in the bowels of the Earth, and finally thrust into the cold storage of a deep, dreamless sleep of suspended animation, poor Snow has been through the mill.

As for the villainous Queen Mother, she, of course, is Eve. Forced by the new culture to dismember herself and cast away her curiosity and sensitivity, she has become a cold, cruel, calculating machine, capable of the cruelest trickery and deceit. Looking into the mirror of reflection, the waking rational ego sees, and loves, only itself in its imagined splendid isolation. Reason cut off from the depths of heart and soul has become a devouring monster of self-regard, a cannibalistic banshee out to eat her own dearest child: the spontaneous, vulnerable part of herself that she can no longer accept.

In the meantime, Snow White has not developed; indeed, she has regressed. When cut off from the rest of the personality, our intuitive sensitivity atrophies like an unused limb. (Compare this with the classical Greek myth of Narcissus and Echo. Narcissus, gazing into the magic mirror of the pond, is enamored only with himself. Echo has lost the power of significant speech and can only parrot back what has been said to her.) Naïve Snow White no longer "recognizes" her own mother, just as the queen no longer recognizes Snow White as her own and longs to extinguish every vestige of the ghost that haunts her.

After eating Mother Eve's poisoned apple, Snow White falls into a coma and is presumed dead by the dwarves, who lovingly place her miraculously intact body in a glass-topped bier. She is rescued by "a King's son"—a Prince—who, after glancing at the sleeping beauty, cannot part with her. "I cannot live without seeing Snow White," he declares. By accident (as if there were any such thing), as the bier is being transported by the prince's servants, they stumble over a tree stump, and the bit of poison apple lodged in Snow White's throat is dislodged. The spell is broken, and she awakens from her enforced slumber.

The meaning of this seems clear: Any real change must come from within; it cannot be imposed from the outside. The young prince, though part of the rationalistic male patriarchy (the king), represents a new creative impulse for reform—a masculine willingness to embrace nature and her magical side. The tree stump (like the tree stump in my hare dream) signifies intuitive growth that had been cut short. Where you stumble, there you will find your treasure. The psychic impulse is reawakened, and the personality is healed—or at least on the mend.

Snow White is thus the basic program guide for recovering our whole self.

These were my conjectures, at any rate, when I received some support from an unexpected source: John Layard's book on the hare/rabbit, which I hadn't opened in years. Something made me look there. I noticed a section entitled "Association with Whiteness and Snow," where I read: "Whiteness—usually described as 'silveriness'—is also commonly connected with the moon," that is, lunar knowledge or the "pure light" of psychic sensitivity. And, most telling of all, among the Algonquin Indians the Great Hare was said to have a close relative: "my brother, the snow."[19]

So my old rabbit friend hadn't abandoned me, after all. Merely changed costumes!

I thought back to my dream of many years before. The rabbit had mournfully told me that it had fallen asleep under the tree. Now I knew for sure that this was the same "sleep" experienced by the disowned and despised Snow White.

I now knew what I had to do. I not only had to write my own EHE autobiography. I also had to get my students to pay attention to their own EHEs. Anyway, I owed it to Snow White, Eve, and the rabbit. We had to help others wake up.

Espresso for the Soul

I would not be disappointed. Rhea's hypothesis turned out to be valid. As soon as I started talking openly about my own EHEs and encouraging others to do likewise, the accounts from my students poured in. Here are three fairly typical ones (the titles, and editing, are mine):

"The Girl Who Fell Down and Visited Heaven"

"Elaine" is an eighteen-year-old college freshman majoring in liberal arts.

When she was eleven, she attended a family barbecue. Elaine was running around in the backyard playing a chasing game with some of her cousins when she fell against the side of a brick wall and hit her head. During the time that her mother was pouring water on her face and frantically trying to revive her, Elaine experienced what she later called "heaven." She was filled with an incredible sense of peace and contentment unlike anything she had ever experienced before or since. "I remember feeling so at ease with myself," Elaine recalls. "Everything was perfect! There were no problems to think about or solve; there was nothing to worry about! Just a blissful feeling of total freedom."

Elaine doesn't think that the experience of "visiting heaven" changed her or her outlook on life in any way, but she admits that she's not so sure. Recently, she was at work when she had the sudden impulse to stand by the window (which she never does). On the street below she watched as an elderly woman slowly crossed the intersection. In her mind's eye, Elaine saw a white car hit the old woman. Seconds later, she was horrified when a white car turning the corner ran into the elderly woman. She is not comfortable having such premonitions.

"Seeing Things"

"Nicole" is thirty-eight and works part-time in a home decorating center. She is a full-time student majoring in travel and tourism.

When she was about seventeen or eighteen, she spent the weekend at a friend's house. In the middle of the night, she turned over on her back when something at the foot of her friend's bed caught her attention. At first she couldn't make out the form. Then she realized that it was the figure of a dark-skinned man dressed in a white suit. He just stood at the foot of her friend's bed, staring straight at Nicole. Nicole admits that she was not sure whether she was completely awake, or in the twilight state between sleeping and waking. She observed the man and seemed to know what he was thinking. He was surprised that Nicole could see him. She wondered whether he had lived in the house before and had come back to "visit." Finally, she became angry that he kept staring at her. Annoyed, she rolled over onto her stomach and fell asleep. At no time during the experience did she feel afraid, though she was surprised by her lack of fear.

The next morning, Nicole told her friend's mother and her friend about the apparition. The mother matter-of-factly responded, "I didn't know you could see ghosts." Evidently, the man in the white suit was a regular "guest" in the house.

Since then, Nicole has premonitions and often knows beforehand when someone close to her is going to die. "I think I can sense things around me," says Nicole. "Sometimes I sense people around me that might have the same insight."

Nicole admits that her unusual experiences have forced her to ask herself difficult but important questions. "Now when these things happen," Nicole says frankly, "I ask myself, Who am I? Am I an old soul from long ago living in my body that doesn't want to go to the other side? What am I? A partly gifted person who has special powers and does not know how to use them? Will these powers be helpful or harmful? Why am I here?"

"A Field Trip to the Other Side"

"Kaito" is in his early twenties. He came to this country from a small village in Japan to study English.

When he was twelve, Kaito went on a field trip with his class to a park in Yokohama to celebrate their graduation from elementary school. While playing with his schoolmates, Kaito suddenly had a strong desire to visit the sole kiosk in the park. As he approached the front of the kiosk, Kaito says that he "felt something very strange." Then, as he circled around to the left of the building, he was overcome by feelings of dread. "I felt I should not have come to this place," Kaito recalls. "I felt something terrible happened at this corner." This was followed by sensations of physical pressure all about his body, as if something were attempting to invade his organism. Kaito fled the area and went back to join his friends. By the end of the day, he had completely forgotten about the unpleasant incident. As far as he was concerned, he had had "a nice trip."

"Coincidentally," several days later one of Kaito's teachers lent him a book on social problems in Japan. The title of the book was *Yokohama Street Life*. The author of the book described his experience taking on the life of a homeless person in order to get an inside view of what it was really like to be homeless in Japan. Several of the homeless people he interviewed told him about an incident that had happened in the 1970s, when a street gang killed a homeless man and dumped his body in a trash can next to a kiosk in a city park.

It was the same park, the same kiosk—indeed, the same spot on the side of the building—where Kaito had been assaulted by horrible feelings of terror and dread, and the sense of being pressured physically by an external force.

When he realized this, Kaito remembers, "I felt awful." But such things are no longer unusual in his life. "I hated this kind of weird ability," he admits. "But I feel responsible now. Not so many people can feel this kind of thing. My mother also has this kind of weird ability. So I just let this kind of experience happen to me."

I noticed that what at first seems like a bizarre, one-time event (visiting heaven, seeing a ghost, experiencing the anguish of a murder victim's final terrifying moments) turns out to be the opening act in an ongoing show. Strange coincidences follow; further abilities manifest; and, most important, questions mount (even if they are temporarily shoved aside). Important, philosophical-type questions. There's a definite ripple effect.

Could these gentle ripples be joining together to form a great tidal wave of change?

Well, what's to prevent it? True, I knew from my own experience that the trail might suddenly grow cold, and that one could easily get discouraged, or even bored, during dry spells. And then there was the fear factor. Social fears, to be sure, like the fear of being considered odd, crazy, or just plain antisocial. But there was something else, too, something much deeper and darker. There was a bogey I had not yet faced.

I began to suspect that these EHE accounts might only amount to whistling past the graveyard. Unless I could confront my deepest fears, I began to suspect that the "tidal wave of change" might only be so much wishful thinking.

I had to face the goblin.

5

The Goblin Factor

gob•lin (gôb' lĭn) n. A grotesque, elfin creature of folklore, thought to work mischief or evil. [Middle English *gobelin*, from Norman French *gobelin*, name of a ghost that supposedly haunted the town of Évreux in the twelfth century.]
—*The American Heritage Dictionary* (1996)

The geography of the inner world has vacant places, and here and there monsters and metaphors.
—Eileen Garrett, *Many Voices: The Autobiography of a Medium* (1969)

Fear is the great barrier to human growth.
—Robert A. Monroe, *Ultimate Journey* (1994)

The Only Thing We Have to Fear?

What is your greatest fear?

Most psychologists (along with Woody Allen) would probably insist that, whether you consciously know it or not, your ultimate fear is death. According to these experts, all of our furious activity, from shopping and lovemaking to novel-writing and higher mathematics, is little more than a vain attempt to stave off our feelings of doom and gloom as we cower helplessly before the inevitable visit of the Grim Reaper.

Perhaps the experts are right, but I doubt it. Extinction is not the bogey.

It's expansion.

Every semester I treat my students to one of the worst arguments ever advanced by a great philosopher (and believe me, there have been some howlers). It occurs in a dialogue of Plato, where Socrates argues that it's unwise to fear death. Listen to this:

If you fear something, says Socrates, this implies that you know it is bad. But, after all, no one knows about death—the mysterious "undiscovered country," as Shakespeare would say. Death might turn out to be the ultimate joy ride (as numerous near-death experiencers have indeed attested). So there's nothing to be afraid of, right?

It hardly ever takes more than a few moments for the students to spot the flaw in the argument. I call on someone. "Yeah, but it's only natural to be afraid of what you don't know," the lucky winner will invariably opine. "Uncertainty is hell."

If so, it's not just dying that scares the bejesus out of us: it's living. After all, if we're being honest with ourselves (as Socrates counsels), we will confess that the universe is a great unknown. As the physicist David Bohm was fond of saying, reality is always something other, and more, than what we think it is. Native American tribes enshrined this realization in their description of the ultimate as Great Mystery. Each of us, as a microcosm of this macrocosm, likewise represents a great unknown. If we're afraid of mystery, then we're afraid of ourselves. We're afraid of the cosmos. We're afraid of life.

What terrifies us, I suspect, is the prospect of losing the security of what we think we know in order to explore the infinitely vast, uncharted possibilities of what William James, in that elegantly agnostic phrase of his, dubbed the "More." To embrace a larger vision is sheer agony. There's hell to pay—maybe literally.

Writer's Block, Goblins Score

At the time I was grappling with my own goblins of fear, however, I had no idea who or what they were. I was fighting in the dark against unknown phantoms—and losing the battle.

I was writing a book on contract for a reputable publisher. After I'd turned in a few sample chapters, my editor called to congratulate me. She was so pleased with my work, she said, that she'd been moved to read long excerpts out loud to her son. It was exactly the kind of book she'd been hoping to acquire, she gushed, and it was already hers.

The editor's high praise sent me strolling in the clouds. But it wasn't long before I fell down to Earth with a thud. Day after day I sat before my computer, unable to write a single word, my mind frozen, a total blank. I had come down with a painful case of writer's block.

After missing several deadlines, I turned in pages I would have preferred to burn. My previously effusive editor now turned coldly silent. After a brief exchange of tartly worded faxes and awkward phone calls, we agreed to cancel my contract. The project was officially dead, and I was left to ponder the wreckage.

With nothing else to do, I had plenty of time to mope. What had gone wrong?

But Where's the Rest of Me?

Like a detective trying to solve a murder mystery, I scoured the crime scene for clues, hoping to break the case wide open. At least I had a corpse: my book. The murder weapon was a bit trickier. On the surface, of course, it was my bad case of writer's block that had doomed the project, naturally making me the chief suspect. Yet the question was, why had I frozen up? Was the blockage the cause of my problem, or the effect of an even deeper one?

The obvious answer is that it was the cause. I'd tied myself in a tortured knot of self-consciousness for fear of disappointing my editor's high expectations. Yet what if that deep freeze were only a secondary symptom—the kind of shock and numbness one experiences *after* a death. In that case, the real murder was an inner one: a soul murder. It was an inner feeling of deadness from which I suffered. Had I really wanted to write the book in the first place? Without an answer to this question, I lacked a clear motive for the crime. Why had I killed my own project? Was it, in fact, "my" project? Who was "I" after all?

Several months before the book fiasco had come to a head, I had sent some of my work to the writer Hal Zina Bennett, who worked as an independent writing consultant. I had long admired Hal's books. There was something intimate and trustworthy in his authorial voice. The integrity of his work in the consciousness field impressed me. I also knew that as a child, Hal had been an introvert, preferring solitary walks in the woods to parties or sports. He had imaginary friends and a pronounced psychic sensitivity to his natural and social environment, evidenced, for example, by his ability to immerse himself so completely in his natural surroundings that, as Hal writes, the "birds and other wildlife no longer noticed me and would go about their business as if I wasn't there."[1] He evinced a similar ability in social situations, easily picking up on the unspoken (and otherwise unexpressed) feelings and thoughts of others. In short, we had a lot in common, so I hoped Hal might help.

But by the time Hal's lengthy response arrived, my self-confidence was at its lowest. After scanning his report (a balanced and sensitive appreciation of my strengths and weaknesses as a writer), I quickly filed it away like an unwelcome guest.

It was this letter that I now held in my hand. For the first time I read it over carefully, several times. There was one sentence in particular that got under my skin: "You're an excellent writer overall, but it's almost as if there isn't any author there."

"Now what does *that* mean?" I muttered aloud, feeling hurt and insulted. Then the truth sank in. I realized what Hal was getting at. Oddly, I didn't put much of myself—my feelings, ideas, and experiences—into my writing. In rereading some of my essays, I noticed they had a stilted, almost disembodied quality.

It was as if I went out of my way to avoid revealing myself. I hid behind the protective shield of abstract ideas and big words like a frightened boy cowering beneath his bed.

This was the elusive smoking gun. After sifting through all the evidence, I now knew why I had killed my own book project. The answer was, it wasn't truly *my* project, after all.

Who was I, really? And who was the mischievous creature that had sabotaged "my" book? The unknown self had to be met.

I booked a place in a writing workshop Hal was giving in two months in Chicago, not far from where I'd attended graduate school. In a way, I realized, I would be returning to the real scene of the crime.

Around the Medicine Wheel

Hal's workshop was held in a storefront dance studio located on a quiet, shady, tree-lined street. After Hal and his wife, Susan, arrived, several of us pitched in to help set up. After arranging folding chairs in a circle, we put out the snacks, along with paper plates and cups, in the back room. There were cookies and grapes, herb teas and bottled water for refreshments. Gradually, the other participants began to arrive.

In the meantime, Hal walked about the room performing the Native American ritual of smudging, or purifying the atmosphere, by burning some fragrant sage and waving the smoke all around with a feather. Then he asked everyone to take a seat. I sat on the side of the circle opposite Hal and Susan. As I looked around the room, I could barely contain my astonishment. Apart from Hal, I was the only male.

I knew that I had to come to terms with my intuitive, feminine side, and here she was, in spades. Eves galore! Well, as they say, you get what you need.

Susan laughed as she saw me noticing my "predicament." She joked that she and Hal didn't tell me beforehand because they were afraid I might back out. It was unusual, she added. Usually the mix was more even. The room buzzed with comments.

"Yeah, where's all the men?" I heard someone shout above

the din. This was followed by an amen chorus of nods and murmurs of agreement all around.

"I can't speak for them, but I'm here," I replied, a bit defensively.

That seemed to satisfy everyone, more or less. At least for the moment.

After Hal formally introduced Susan and himself, he explained that the circle in which we were sitting was no ordinary circle but a Native American medicine wheel. (Many tribes have medicine wheels, but Hal referred specifically to the Zuni version.[2]) Each direction of the wheel—North, East, South, West (and above and below)—has a special meaning and is associated with a specific animal and the qualities or powers it represents. These powers, Hal explained, are at work in the universe, and in us. The work of each helps to balance the whole. Without consciously realizing it, each of us had selected a place on the wheel that corresponded to the very lesson we needed to learn.

In the Zuni interpretation of the medicine wheel, the Badger—a tenacious, single-minded fighter when threatened—is the guardian of the south, where I had chosen to sit. I faced north, whose guardian is Mountain Lion. According to Hal, Mountain Lion is the link to all the other forces in the spiritual and physical realms, and is thus the custodian of cosmic knowledge. Life is a balancing act between these two poles: the particular and the universal, the personal and the transcendent, the earthy and the ethereal.

This made sense to me. Anyone sensitive to the sea of unseen forces surrounding us knows how easy it is to lose touch with our identity. I have always felt like a psychic sponge soaking up the atmosphere. Since I knew what others wanted of me even if they didn't say so out loud, it was too easy to give it to them and lose sight of my own needs. Swimming in the sea, our individuality becomes frightening, a burden or a threat. Too much self-absorption, though, and we risk isolation from the whole.

After Hal completed his introductory remarks, I was in for the second shock of the day. In my naïveté, I had not realized that we were not simply going to discuss writing. We were going to write. Even worse, we would have to read our writing aloud to the group. I could feel my resolve collapse. What could I do?

I felt like sprinting out of the room all the way back to my hotel, and grabbing the first cab to the airport. I didn't, though. Somehow I did the exercises, scribbling a few lines here and there. I was terribly self-conscious writing in front of others. Luckily, I hadn't yet had to read anything aloud. My stomach was doing flip-flops.

None of this was Hal's fault. His calm, centered demeanor (and the flat Midwestern twang I detected in his voice) was reassuring. Nevertheless, to me it was like having a gun put to my head and being told I had to sing and dance on the spot.

Then, thankfully, our lunch break arrived. Before anyone could say a word to me, I bolted out the door and almost sprinted down the block. I ducked around a corner and found a cozy little Japanese restaurant where I nursed a bottle of beer and enjoyed a plate of crispy vegetable tempura. I tried to collect my thoughts. My energies still sagged. I felt like a rag doll. Or like I'd run a marathon. And I had another day and a half to go.

The rest of the afternoon passed in a blur. Somehow I muddled through. At last we finished for the day and I headed back to my hotel. I was bone tired. So I dialed up room service and ordered a hamburger and salad for dinner. After watching part of a *Star Trek* movie, I fell asleep around 9:30 P.M. (quite early for me). Then, sometime in the middle of the night, I had a nightmare. From my notes:

> I'm standing in the midst of an open green field surrounded by tall deciduous and pine trees. The sky is smoky grey, all cloudy, and the air is preternaturally still. Nothing is moving inside the park. It feels like the proverbial calm before the storm. Suddenly, the stillness is broken and I feel a great gust of wind blowing all about my body. It almost knocks me over. Off in the distance I can see an enormous funnel cloud churning up trees and spewing them out in all directions, like a giant weed

whacker. I'm so petrified I can't move my legs. Like the trees, I'm glued to the spot—a goner for sure! Finally, however, I find my legs are carrying me away from the approaching tornado. I'm running toward a massive building that is only partly above ground. I find myself in an underground corridor. Everywhere soldiers in uniform are striding about calmly and purposefully. I wonder why no one seems worried about the twister. A helpful soldier directs me to the central control room, where I find the officers in charge standing before control panels loaded with video screens, dials, gauges, and buttons. They are monitoring the tornado. Nothing to worry about, some-one reassures me. It's just a military experiment.

The next morning, I broke the ice by sharing my dream with the group. Hal asked me what I thought it meant, and I replied that I wasn't sure. On reflection later, I saw that the twister sym-bolized the wild forces of my inner nature (intuition and creativ-ity) that frightened me so. These forces had a secret entente with my rational side, symbolized by the military command. There wasn't anything to fear; it was all still me, and "I" (or a larger aspect of my self) was still in charge, if only unconsciously (as symbolized by the underground installation).

I guess the dream did allay my fears somewhat because I felt more relaxed and less self-conscious on the second day. My writing began to flow. Hal was indeed giving us useful tech-niques for "opening inward" (which was the title of the work-shop).

Later that day we did an exercise that combined guided visu-alization with writing. We were to imagine a meeting with our "inner critic," a personification of the inner forces that would stand in our way and try to block our development. Hal explained that this critic, whom we might have to confront, or at least get to know, could also turn out to be a most important teacher. We then had to write an account of our dialogue.

So I imagined I was in my favorite imaginary writing spot, a cozy office overlooking the lake on one side and the ocean on the other. I made the fantasy as vivid as I could. I heard seagulls crying. I felt the breeze blowing from the lakeside and inhaled the spicy aroma of the pine trees. I sat in a comfy chair in the middle of the bookcase-lined room, sunlight streaming in, and poured two generous glasses of cabernet, one for me and one for the critic.

I waited. And waited. And I waited some more.

No one showed up. The critic's seat remained empty! How could an inner invitation go unanswered? I was all set to dialogue, and then—nothing.

When I explained what happened to the group, several people remarked on the sensuous quality of the scene. But I was fixated on the no-show aspect. Why hadn't my critic at least had the decency to RSVP? If visualizations were no different from fantasies, why hadn't I been able to conjure up a partner? Something else was going on.

Hal appeared to be listening attentively to my story and the others' comments, his chin resting in his left hand. He seemed to be sinking somewhere deep inside himself. At last, emerging from this secret inner well, he looked at me and nodded.

"You know," he said thoughtfully, "I think the Void is your teacher. It happens that way some times with some people. The Mystery itself comes directly to a person."

Was the empty chair in fact filled with the Great Emptiness? Was I already in contact and didn't know it?

On the flight back from Chicago, I felt satisfied that I had at least begun to face my fears and open to the unknown. I also had a lot of tantalizing, unanswered questions.

Opening Inward—a Crack

During the few days I spent at the writer's workshop, I managed to resist the temptation to read a newspaper or watch the TV news. I did not want to be distracted by trivia or the events of the day. For a change, I gave my full attention to my inner world of dreams and my writing. It felt good.

Thus on my arrival home, I was hit full force by the media

feeding frenzy surrounding the suicides of the members of the Heaven's Gate cult. They had believed that a UFO hidden in the tail of the Hale-Bopp comet was going to transport their souls to some better, less sleazy venue than Earth. The TV endlessly showed the corpses, dressed in their purple shrouds and Nike sneakers, being removed from the Rancho Santa Fe mansion. Then there were the tapes of the cult's leader, Marshall Herff Applewhite, explaining in his pinched nasal twang why it was so important to overcome "the *vee-hi-cle*" (i.e., body).

The *what*? Where had I heard that before? It sounded eerily familiar—the weird obsession with UFOs as tour buses to heaven, the whole bizarre business.

Finally it dawned on me. I rifled through my files and found the clipping.

In August 1994, Cynthia and I were staying at the lake in Maine. I was browsing an issue of a local weekly when I came across an interview with two strange characters. They called themselves Rick and Song (they didn't believe in last names) and referred to their bodies as "vehicles." They both wore the eerie, blissed-out grins of Followers. They said they'd come to Maine on a "recruiting mission," in search for others, like themselves, who were prepared "to step beyond this primitive planet to a higher level."

It was obvious from the tone of the article that the reporter was doing this as a lark. She figured she had a couple of harmless loons on her hands, and it would make great copy. Her sophisticated urban readers could congratulate themselves on being so—well, sophisticated. But I became agitated as I read the piece. The photo of the pair was disturbing. The smiles got me. I felt something dreadful in the pit of my stomach. I was furious at the reporter for treating the whole thing as a joke.

"If you're so upset, why don't you call the reporter?" Cynthia suggested.

"And say what?" I replied irritably. That I have a gut feeling that these two "goofballs" are dangerous? I'd be the reporter's next victim of ridicule.

So I never telephoned the reporter. I guess I was just a coward (or prudent). Instead, in a white heat of inspiration (fueled by an equal mixture of anger and dread), I wrote an article on the spiritual dangers of giving in to an unthinking literalism and giving away one's power to authorities. (A magazine subsequently published the piece.)

Had Rick and Song's 1994 recruiting mission to Maine borne fruit? The thought now haunted me. I recognized Song's picture among a photo gallery of the victims published in a national newsmagazine. But not Rick. I wondered what had happened to him.

(A subsequent follow-up piece stated that an ex-cult member, one "Rkk" [Rick?], was among the few to "miss" the rendezvous with Hale-Bopp. Rkk had quit the group in 1996 because, even after more than twenty years, he still could not control his "vehicle." Alas, he still wanted sex. But Rkk confessed that, had he been at Rancho Santa Fe, he would have gladly joined his comrades in beaming up to the mothership.)

Following on the heels of the workshop, the cult suicides led me to admit that I often had intimations about death. It was not the first time (and wouldn't be the last). Indeed, not long afterward, I was sitting in a doctor's office when a well-dressed, distinguished-looking gentleman with a foreign accent engaged me in conversation.

"Excuse me," he said. "Are you by any chance a civil engineer?"

I glanced up from my magazine and quickly sized up my interlocutor. It was an odd question for a stranger to ask a stranger. Yet he didn't look the kooky type.

"No," I replied cautiously. "Actually, I teach philosophy. My main interest, however, is parapsychology—what used to be called psychical research."

The man's face lit up and he became very animated. He explained to me that he sometimes had "impressions" about people, and he had received such about me. But now he was excited to hear that I was a philosophy professor, and that I was receptive to the paranormal. He proceeded to tell me about his education in Argentina and his earlier interests in religion and philosophy (he had become a successful businessman).

"Spinoza was one of my favorite philosophers," he added.

"Really? One of my professors in college—my advisor, in fact—wrote a book on Spinoza," I recalled. "And I did an independent study on Spinoza with him."

I hadn't thought of this professor (his name was Robert J. McShea) in years. Lots of warm memories of afternoon conferences in his brownstone office debating fine points of theory suddenly came flooding back. Bob had had quite a colorful life. He had farmed in upstate New York for a while, then returned to Cornell University to get his doctorate when he was well into middle age.

That night, when I returned home, I was glancing at the college alumni magazine that had just arrived in the mail. There, in the obituaries, was Bob's death notice.

Apart from all the death notices, there were other sequels to the workshop as well.

Not long after I'd returned from Chicago, I had an uncanny dream. I was a pinpoint of awareness floating in a black void when I heard a voice say, "You worry a lot, don't you?" This was a rhetorical question. The voice knew damn well that I am a worrywart. I was not being upbraided, however. There wasn't a hint of judgment in this remark. I could only sense tremendous understanding and compassion in the voice. I was so shaken that I immediately awoke. I realized that I was being gently prodded to examine this long-ingrained neurotic habit.

Was the voice I heard in this black void my mysterious teacher, the Void?

Several weeks later, I had another dream that seemed like a follow-up to my tornado dream. I stood in an open field in a parklike setting. The dusky sky was smoky grey. An individual standing next to me pointed at the sky. I looked up. Floating inside a nebula-like gaseous cloud was an enormous crystalline city of light. The colors of the cloud were the most delicate, ethereal pastels I had ever seen: sumptuous purples, pinks, oranges, and reds. The light of the city towers shone through the clouds.

I awoke with a gasp, the dream trailing into waking reality. What was it? What had I just glimpsed?

In his groundbreaking book on the near-death experience, *Life After Life* (1975), Dr. Raymond Moody Jr. reported no cases of individuals describing images of the traditional "heaven." However, two years later, in his follow-up study, *Reflections on Life After Life,* Dr. Moody amended his initial findings. It turned out there were indeed those who had been afforded glimpses of magnificent "cities of light."[3] One of Moody's subjects described it thus: "Off in the distance . . . I could see a city. There were buildings—separate buildings. They were gleaming, bright. There was sparkling water, fountains . . . a city of light I guess would be the way to say it. . . . It was wonderful."[4]

"Motifs of paradise topography are the most constant features of Western otherworld journey narration," writes Dr. Carol Zaleski, a professor of religion at Smith College who has made one of the most comprehensive scholarly studies of the NDE to date.[5] She continues: "It is no surprise, then, to find that near-death narratives recall the pastoral meadows, formal gardens, seraphic choirs, life-giving trees and fountains, spacious courts, golden gates, and shining walled cities of biblical and early Christian revelation."[6] Perceiving a realm of subtle illumination pervaded by colors of indescribable beauty and perfection, Zaleski adds, is another common element of this type of heavenly apparition.

Had I briefly visited heaven? My pastel-colored cloud nebula, the park setting, and the crystal city echoed familiar heavenly themes. The word "home" did cross my mind after the dream, as I struggled to express my feelings. Of course, I was not near death at the time of my dream; I was merely asleep (and perhaps under stress). But many other individuals not suffering extreme physical situations have also reported experiencing various elements of the classical NDE—for example, the out-of-body experience, meeting with dead relatives, having a life review, or encountering an intelligent, compassionate Being of Light—in dream, waking vision, or meditation.[7] Thus close proximity to death may be a sufficient, but not necessary prerequisite for such episodes. Psychological stress, engaging in a meditative discipline, or even serendipity may also act as triggers.

Yet calling my city in the clouds "heaven" begs the real question. For what is "heaven," anyway? It is certainly not a physical place, though the heavenly imagery is robustly sensuous. That imagery functions as a cognitive bridge to nonphysical energies whose essential nature is largely beyond our conscious grasp. These energies (or energy-consciousnesses) are highly structured and cooperative, forming a cluster. Hence the symbolic image of a city, through which such energies are translated, channeled, and experienced, much as a step-down transformer reduces a higher voltage to a lower, more manageable level. (The city, of course, was invented with the rise of agricultural civilization, circa 8000 B.C.E., and is thus a culturally and historically conditioned concept. Such an image would make no sense, say, to a prehistoric human, who, if they were to "visit heaven," would not, I venture, glimpse such a sight.) Who, or what, then, are the many that, paradoxically, are also one?

That is the great unknown. I have not been back to the cloud city (though I may have visited its environs: the park—see chapter 7). However, the feeling of standing in the meadow at dusk and gazing up into the evening sky to behold the shining crystal towers has remained with me. "Home," "Source," and "Self" are words I have used to make (some) sense of the vision. Ultimately, all such labels are inadequate and unsatisfying, except as temporary markers pointing the way to a greater reality. I felt I was being shown that I had a "higher calling." But, if so, a calling to what? How would I get there (wherever "there" was)? I did not have the answers to these questions.

The more I opened myself to the Mystery, the more vulnerable I felt. I knew I had to wrestle with my fears of the unknown, just as I had to wrestle with the stark emptiness of the computer screen page each time I sat down to write. It was the same void. I sensed that my demons were also my greatest helpers, and that the things I tended to avoid were the very things I most needed—indeed wanted—to embrace. Still, it was hard. I had questions.

Then, in yet another of those splendidly serendipitous coincidences I had almost come to expect, one of my students introduced me to a real live goblin.

Goblins Away!

Silvia, as I'll call her, was a native of a small village in Ecuador. Her family had moved to the United States when she was only fourteen. A pretty blonde who was always impeccably dressed, Silvia was a business major, a budding corporate CEO. She worked hard and earned good grades. Her manner was quiet and serious, if somewhat reserved. Although she seldom spoke out in class, she did well on the exams. Silvia seemed to keep to herself. I seldom observed her chatting with the other members of her class.

Which is why Silvia surprised me when one day after class she asked if she could tell me about her Exceptional Human Experience: a scary encounter.

"It was—how do you say—a goblin," Silvia said in her softly accented English. Her head was cocked to one side, in a gesture that reminded me of my dog when he's on alert.

"A goblin, sure," I replied cautiously, not knowing what to expect.

It had happened when Silvia was ten years old and living in Ecuador. She had heard about goblins from friends and family, and was curious about them. What were they? What did they look like? What did they do? But whenever she approached an adult with her questions, they would clam up, telling her that she was too young to be asking about such things. But she suspected that they were just too scared to talk about the goblins.

Silvia had an older cousin, Diane. At seventeen, Diane was mainly interested in boys. There was going to be a carnival festival. Everyone in the village was looking forward to the event, especially boy-crazy Diane. She was making plans to go to the local beach with her older brothers, where they were going to meet up with some other friends and party.

So Diane became furious when she learned that her parents

had arranged with Silvia's parents for the two families to spend the festival together in Silvia's house. No beach partying for her! Diane stalked off in a huff and holed up in Silvia's bedroom, where she sulked. She was followed by her two sisters, a younger brother, and Silvia.

After the group had been in the bedroom only a short time, Diane heard some strange noises coming from outside the window. She thought it might be one of her older brothers trying to get her attention. She had been very angry with them for not siding with her against their parents. So Diane asked Silvia to go to the window to see what her brother wanted. But when Silvia opened the window, there was no one there.

About five minutes or so had passed when Diane suddenly screamed. "There is someone standing in the door," she cried. "I don't know who it is, but it's scaring me!"

Both sets of parents came running into the bedroom to see what was the matter. No one except Diane saw the frightening figure standing in the doorway, however. She described the apparition to Silvia, and Silvia told Diane's mother.

"My God," she exclaimed, "Diane is seeing a goblin!"

Diane now became hysterical. She screamed that the goblin was moving toward her. So the family made a circle around Diane to protect her. Then she fainted. Several minutes later, she awoke and told her parents that she just wanted to go to sleep. The bizarre episode seemed to be at an end.

But when Diane awoke the following morning, she saw the goblin. Now it began a conversation with her, which Diane related to Silvia. The goblin said it had been following Diane around for a year, watching her. It was in love with her and wanted her for its wife! The creature promised to make her happy, to give her riches and jewels.

"I'll give you anything you want," it pleaded. "If only you let me get closer to you, and talk to me whenever I feel alone."

Diane was now petrified. The family tried all sorts of ruses to banish the lovesick goblin. They bathed Diane with holy water at the local Catholic Church. They adorned her with rosaries and crucifixes. Her grandfather even gave her his pistol and instructed her to shoot at the goblin when no one else was around. But it was no use. The goblin wouldn't budge. It threatened to take Diane away—against her will, if necessary.

For weeks, the goblin bullied and frightened Diane, sending her and her family into an exhausting emotional tailspin. Although it never followed through on its threats to kidnap her, it refused to give up terrorizing her. Everyone was in a tizzy.

Finally, Diane snapped. She was frustrated and angry at the goblin and how he was upsetting her family and friends. So she started yelling at the creature, screaming at the top of her lungs, "the most horrible things that even animals wouldn't want to hear because they were very offensive," as Silvia described the tirade.

Diane reported to all present in her living room that her words were apparently having an effect: "It's working," she said, "because it's crying."

Then, to everyone's amazement, they all heard a loud slap land on Diane's face. Seconds later, her right cheek turned beet red.

At the same moment, a crow somehow flew into the living room.

Diane started to cry, but she heard a voice calling her. This "sweet voice" instructed her to leave the house. She obeyed, and the rest of the family followed her outside. What they now saw in the night sky made them all kneel down in a gesture of adoration—all except for Diane, who was still walking ahead and gazing skyward.

"Mother, do you see the light coming from the sky?" Diane cried.

They all beheld the dazzling light. Then, suddenly, the light was transformed.

"There He is!" Diane exclaimed.

The brilliant light in the sky had become Jesus on the cross. Everyone knelt. The families wept and prayed. Diane heard Jesus scold the goblin for its behavior. Then she saw Him take the goblin and grind it into a powder, which he poured into a small box. He instructed Diane not to be afraid and reassured her that she would never see the goblin again. Then the apparition in the sky vanished.

"The next day," Silvia said, "everybody went to church to pray to God and to thank Him for what He had done the night before."

A grateful Diane finally got to go to the beach. Though the carnival had been over for weeks, Diane's family decided it wasn't too late to celebrate.

The Light at the End of the Tunnel

When I first heard Silvia's story, I wasn't sure what to make of it. I realized that a skeptic would say that Diane was merely a sulky teenager hungry for attention, and used folklore about goblins as a scaffold for constructing her tale. Or else, she was hysterical and hallucinating. After all, only Diane saw the goblin.

However, this wouldn't explain either the noises heard outside the bedroom window before the first episode or the slap on Diane's cheek, which all present heard and saw (at least its result). Diane had first thought that the noise was one of her brothers throwing rocks to get her attention. Many poltergeist hauntings have begun with people hearing the sound of gravel being thrown against the house or on top of the roof.

I also realized that the poltergeist hypothesis wasn't necessarily inconsistent with a psychological explanation, either. When I was ten years old, I had read a book called *The Haunted Mind* by Nandor Fodor, M.D., a psychoanalyst and psychical researcher.[8] I knew that Fodor had argued that the paranormal events surrounding poltergeist hauntings, such as dinner plates mysteriously flying across rooms, result from an unconscious use of psychokinetic powers (of mind over matter) by sexually frustrated teenagers. There are no "external entities" involved. According to this model, Diane's "demon lover" was only her own subconscious.

To an extent, this hypothesis fit. Diane was a boy-crazy seventeen-year-old who had been kept from having a wild time at the beach. What with pent-up feelings of sexual frustration and anger over her parents' decision, this mix could easily turn combustible. Even the paranormal slap on the cheek could be explained as something essentially self-induced. After all, disturbed people do sometimes harm themselves—or others—to get attention. For example, in the so-called Munchausen-by-Proxy syndrome, a mother will make her own child ill in order to bask in the afterglow of attention showered on the sick child. And self-mutilation among teenagers (as well as teenage suicide) is not unknown.

The problem with this hypothesis is that it fit some of the facts, but not others. Instead of trying to force the experience to fit the interpretation, I decided to look at the phenomenon as a natural process. What I saw was not mental pathology (with paranormal window dressing), but a healthy transformation.

Diane had been a whiny, sulky teenager. She was a passive type who allowed herself to be bossed around by her parents and terrorized by her goblin Lothario. The turning point in the story came when she got up the gumption to declare, "Enough is enough!" and sent her ghostly suitor packing. The bullying stopped when Diane decided to take charge of her own destiny. That's when the evil goblin died.

Or did it? Moreover, was it really evil?

Who or what was Mr. Goblin?

The more I thought about it, the more convinced I became that Silvia had provided me with an important missing piece of the whole fear puzzle. Maybe more.

The dramatic ending in which all present (including Silvia) bore witness to the heavenly apparition shares certain features in common with many religious visions, episodes of cosmic awareness, NDEs, and even UFO encounters. The key element is the splendorous Light beheld by all, just before it transmogrified into Jesus on the cross.

For example, Tom Sawyer is a former bicycle racer and construction worker who suffered cardiac arrest when his chest was crushed beneath his pickup truck, which fell on him as he was attempting a repair. At the core of his NDE, Sawyer says that he glimpsed a mere speck of light that "was brighter than a million billion carbon arcs, or welder's torches, anything you can possibly compare it to."[9] Many NDErs also report experiencing a blissful merging with an all-loving Being of Light (more on this merging aspect later).

Richard Maurice Bucke, the nineteenth-century Canadian psychiatrist and author of the classic study of mysticism, *Cosmic Consciousness,* described his own taste of cosmic awareness as a sense of being wrapped within a "flame-colored cloud."[10]

Jacques Vallee is the famed UFO researcher who served as the real-life model for the character of the French UFO investigator played by François Truffaut in Steven Spielberg's 1978 film *Close Encounters of the Third Kind.* He says that many eyewitnesses to UFO events will not even see a spaceship or other "craft," but instead behold an unusually bright light or odd pattern of lights. He is convinced that this supernal luminosity is the primary reality behind not only the UFO phenomenon but also all religious experiences. Like a chameleon, it alters its appearance and behavior to suit the needs and expectations of its environment (and perhaps its own intentions). So in France, the "aliens" tend to behave like rational Cartesian, peace-loving tourists. In the United States, they appear as science-fiction monsters, and in South America, they act like *machos* spoiling for a fight.[11] Some witnesses see spaceships; others see Jesus or Mary; while still others frolic with wee folk in the fairy hills. But the Light is the thing.

Phyllis Atwater is a veteran NDE researcher who has undergone three near-death episodes. Her findings about the Light echo the speculations of Dr. Vallee. According to her studies, whenever NDErs challenged the angels, God, or other religious-type figures they encountered in their experience to reveal their true appearance, "the image would dissolve into light or suddenly burst into a massive sun-like sphere."[12]

It struck me that if the Light can appear as Jesus, a UFO, or a fairy, why not as a goblin? Was this Light the author, director, and producer of Diane's scary movie? Had it played the roles of both villain and savior? Silvia's story did have the feel of a psychodrama. If so, the Light was a damn shrewd psychologist. It had great insight into Diane's level of maturity and it deployed powerful techniques for accelerating her development. The goblin was hardly an agent of evil. Perhaps it was Diane's best friend.

Silvia herself seemed to understand this. When the ten-year-old had initially quizzed the adults about goblins, most warned her that a goblin was one of the worst things that a person could experience. But a few people were more circumspect. They noted that, despite the terrifying aspects of such encounters, people often changed for the better. A shy person would become more outgoing, a timid person less fearful and more courageous. He or she could become "a completely different person," Silvia noted.

This reminded me of something I'd read about the NDE. Psychologist Kenneth Ring, who has been studying the NDE scientifically for over twenty-five years, observes that one of the lasting aftereffects of an encounter with the Light is a greatly enhanced self-esteem. NDErs become less passive and less willing to give away their power to others. "NDErs like themselves more," notes Dr. Ring.[13] As one of his interviewees confessed, "I think I used to be a very superficial person, always breaking my butt to please or be accepted or to be liked. Now I just don't give a damn anymore. It's really a delicious feeling."[14] Another subject's typical comment: "I was easily intimidated. . . . I'm not like that anymore. . . . I have more confidence in myself."[15]

Now a heretical thought tiptoed across my mind.

What if the fear barrier exists only to be broken? What if the universe, or nature, wants—no, *needs*—us to be the unique individuals we all are, or could become? Could our official religions and spiritual philosophies have distorted so fundamental a truth?

The Truth Is in Here

Most of our official traditions are rooted in the teaching that the ego, the sense of ourselves as a distinct individual and center of authority, is evil, the source of all evil, or at least the main roadblock along the spiritual path. Saint Augustine said so explicitly. Freedom, he said, is the freedom to go wrong. Submission to outside authority is the ticket. Eve refused to obey blindly, so she and Adam were exiled (and cursed). The same goes for the old Devil who got expelled from heaven for similar reasons.

In the Eastern traditions, one is encouraged to give one's power away to a guru. Attachment to the little self supposedly stands in the way of realizing the Great Self. According to Joseph Campbell, the student *(chela)* must "submit absolutely to the teacher (guru)" and "any criticism disqualifies you for the guru's instruction."[16]

But what if such teachings say more about the psychological needs of teachers (and the political needs of institutions) than about the metaphysical needs of the cosmos? What if, by being and becoming ourselves, we each bring an irreplaceable piece of the puzzle to the table? What if there's a hole in the whole without us? Maybe what we're afraid of is just how important we are and what our responsibility is.

It's far easier to play dumb, helpless, or the worthless "sinner." Often we prefer living with the fear to accepting our responsibilities. Sometimes, no matter what our reason tells us, the need to believe that others know (or are) better can prove irresistible.

When I was young, I had a friend I'll call Ralph. Ralph was a big kid. At eleven, he already stood over six feet tall. Even Ralph's mother used to tease him about being the Jolly Green Giant. No shrinking violet in the ego department, Ralph was the acknowledged leader of our little band of two. We usually played over at his house, which I didn't mind because Ralph had neat toys (a big slot car setup and table hockey), and his Mom was sweet and always served us Cokes and Ring Dings for snacks.

Ralph enjoyed boasting about how his father knew the president of France and the King of Saudi Arabia. Which was probably the truth because his dad was a big oil company executive. As a result, Ralph got to travel around. He was always going off to far away exotic venues, like California, where he visited exciting places like Disneyland and Universal Studios—heaven for kids. I'd never even flown on an airplane before. But at least I got to hear Ralph's traveler's tales. I lived vicariously through his big adventures.

Whatever game we played (which he usually decided), Ralph almost always won. Then someone gave him an antique hand-carved ivory chess set for his birthday. Ralph asked me if I knew how to play, which I did. So whenever I visited, the chessboard would come out. Trouble was, although I was only a self-taught player, I beat Ralph every time. I had read a few chess books, so I knew openings and some strategies. I wasn't any great shakes, mind you, just good enough to beat a novice. You could almost see the steam pouring out of Ralph's ears when I won. He'd always ask for a rematch, but would lose again.

One day after school, my mother dropped me off at Ralph's house to play. Ralph's mom greeted me at the door and told me to go up to Ralph's room. Ralph was sitting hunched over his desk, writing in a spiral-bound notebook.

"Look at this," he said, showing me the pages.

I couldn't believe it. There was line after line of incomprehensible hieroglyphics, like a combination of Chinese and ancient Egyptian, neatly printed upside down and backward. Then he showed me several more notebooks, all filled with the same odd gibberish. It was like finding a library from the lost continent of Atlantis.

"They're my diaries," Ralph confided in a serious tone. Evidently he had a key code hidden away somewhere. He also implied cryptically that the diaries contained some sort of "secret knowledge," not privy to the eyes of ordinary mortals. Then he put the books away in a drawer and declared he would never discuss them again.

At first I marveled at Ralph's industry. It didn't take a psychology degree to see that Ralph was just trying to regain the upper hand in our relationship. I'd finally beaten him at something, and he couldn't stand it. Now he was getting his revenge.

But even as I knew all this, part of me was dying to know: What could he possibly have to say in all those books about his life? I could write my thoughts of the day on an index card. I couldn't help wondering whether he had "secret knowledge." Ralph always seemed so sure of himself. It nagged at me. Despite my better judgment, I even thought a few times about searching for the codebook when Ralph was out of the room.

Ralph had successfully constellated a very potent, very dangerous archetype: the Man of Knowledge. This icon can easily overwhelm good sense and reason. It whispers seductively of masters who have all the answers. These Great Ones are privy to the cosmic secrets, the highest wisdom. They may have access to invisible Mahatmas hidden away in the Himalayas or be custodians of a lost tradition that stretches back to ancient Egypt, or perhaps even Atlantis. In the presence of the Man of Knowledge—the Answer Man—we feel small and insignificant. We cling to fear and call it devotion while the Answer Man greedily pockets those golden chunks of our slivered selves that we have foolishly thrown away in our mad rush to erase our egos and surrender our individuality.

Whenever we minimize ourselves, disown our potential, and ignore our EHEs to pay homage to someone else's visions, we betray our one true calling, namely, to develop our own sensitivity and share its fruits with those who would "eat." This was one of the important lessons I learned from *Black Elk Speaks.*

Black Elk was only nine years old when the Six Grandfathers summoned him to the Great Lodge in the sky for instruction. Two braves with spears bearing tips of lightning flew down from the Great Lodge to issue the invitation. A little cloud swooped down from the sky and ferried Black Elk, in his spirit form, to his destination, and his destiny. Then he had his Great Vision. For seven years, the boy did not speak of his great vision with anyone. During this time, he was beset by seemingly irrational fears. He was afraid to be alone. He was afraid of the thunder. He was afraid of his own shadow. Sometimes it seemed as if the very birds were mocking him: "Crows would see me and shout to each other as though they were making fun of me: 'Behold him! Behold him!'"[17]

Then when he was seventeen, Black Elk finally told his

vision to an old medicine man named Black Road. Black Road explained to Black Elk that if he wanted to be free of his fear, he had to share his vision with the rest of his tribe. That's exactly what the Six Grandfathers—the powers of the universe—had wanted. His "compelling fear" was a result of bottling up his inner truth and denying the gifts he'd been given. When Black Elk told his vision, his fear vanished. By heeding the advice of Black Road and revealing himself, he healed himself, and became a healer of others.

Of course, I also knew from my own (sometimes painful) experience that it's important to use sound judgment and good old-fashioned common sense when it comes to sharing one's EHEs, and even the fact of one's sensitivity.

The Australian NDE researcher, sociologist Cherie Sutherland, tells the revealing story of a woman she calls Shana.[18] At twenty-three, Shana was a nursing student in England when she entered a hospital for a "routine" operation. On the operating table she suddenly went into anaphylactic shock—an allergic reaction to the anesthesia. This was followed by three full cardiac arrests. During her third heart attack, she had an NDE.

Shana floated out of her physical body through the top of her head. The thought of dying did not frighten her. Simultaneously, she saw her mother anxiously pacing the hospital corridor and her worried father back in Australia. She observed with detachment as the doctors worked feverishly to save her. Then she found herself "in this golden world" of light, with "all these beings, angels, angelic luminous beings and this feeling of *total love*." Suddenly, Shana slammed back into her body. She was in tremendous physical pain, and also in psychological shock. What had happened? She was perplexed.

Like Black Elk, Shana did not speak of her experience for years. Five years later, while attending a Buddhist meditation retreat, she decided to open up. Everyone listened attentively as she told her story. At first Shana felt relieved. But then several people told her that she must be mistaken. She could not have left her body through the top of her head, for only great saints and gurus who have practiced for many years can perform that particular feat. Shana felt confused and humiliated. She knew what she had experienced, even if it did not match the expectations or beliefs of others.

"I didn't talk about it until much, much later." She added wisely, "And I was very careful who I talked to."

As we learn to face our fears and embrace the inevitable changes brought about by exploring the More, we must maintain a bit of left-brained shrewdness. We have to realize that not everyone is going to welcome such change in us. Indeed, as the physicist David Bohm said, all old-fashioned systems (a system is a set of connected things or parts) resist fundamental change.[19] A jellyfish, a government bureaucracy, or a religion— it's all the same. Systems will let you tinker with them here and there around the edges (usually only if their survival depends on it), but they don't like you to monkey with their innards. They resist change like healthy cells automatically repel viral or bacterial invaders. And make no mistake: religions are systems. Otherwise they wouldn't claim to have all the answers.[20]

So we can't be too naïve about what we're doing when we develop our sensitivity. To some, it will be very threatening. Sharing our gifts is good, but indiscriminate sharing is rooted in a dangerous kind of false innocence.

This is what the poet Robert Bly refers to as the problem of "giving away the gold," after an episode in a fairy tale from the Brothers Grimm called "The Devil's Sooty Brother."[21] In the story, a depressed and grief-stricken ex-soldier spends many years in the service of the Devil, tending his fire and sweeping the ashes out of Old Nick's house. At long last, the retired soldier is granted his freedom, along with payment for his services: a sorry sack of ashes. But as he climbs out of Hell, the soldier's ashes are transmuted into gold. His first stop is a village inn, where he makes the mistake of showing the dishonest innkeeper his treasure. Naturally, the devious landlord steals the gold, and the soldier has to go to Hell and back to reclaim his worth.

Shana had made the mistake of showing her gold (her experience) to the wrong audience. It threatened their belief system, so they robbed Shana of her self-worth. Robbed her blind. Like the ex-soldier in the fairy tale, it took her years to recover. I, too, had been naïve at times in this way, and, like Silvia's sister Diane, I could be too passive.

But I also knew that I possessed at least some measure of Silvia's stubborn independence and insatiable curiosity. Her story of the goblin had helped me to see that I was at least moving in the right direction. I was more determined than ever to follow the trail, wherever it led. I resolved to face my fears, including my legitimate fear of ridicule and rejection. Black Elk's example weighed heavily on my mind.

Black Elk had been afraid to tell others what he experienced when he was a little boy and the animals spoke to him, and then later, when he visited the Six Grandfathers and had his great vision. But as Black Elk explained to John Neihardt, this silence and self-doubt only made matters worse. The fear intensified, nearly driving him crazy. What was inside was supposed to be cultivated and expressed. As Jesus says in the Gnostic Gospel of Thomas: "If you bring forth what is within you, what you bring forth will save you. If you do not bring forth what is within you, what you do not bring forth will destroy you."[22]

"Everyone's life aim," declares my friend, the EHE researcher Rhea White, "should be not simply to maintain the status quo, but to expand both inner and outer boundaries."[23] Ironically, as we've seen, it's precisely this expansion that not only promises the greatest rewards, but also ignites the greatest fears.

Yet, as all EHErs know deep in their hearts, it's impossible to stand still. Either you're growing or you're shrinking: There's no in-between. The hope of running in place is strictly an illusion. Maybe you can do it on your treadmill, but machines aren't real life. Once the Source has touched you, once you've opened up to your own natural sensitivity, there's no choice but to accept the invitation. If you refuse, the result will be an unforgiving and unremitting assault by what Black Elk called "the compelling fear."

The goblins will get you if you don't watch out.

The writer Hermann Hesse says, "We create gods and struggle with them, and they bless us."[24] Our gods are projections of our highest ideals—our best, truest, most complete selves. Similarly, out of our (largely unconscious) fears, we manufacture our demons and devils—our goblins—and struggle with them, too. We are a haunted lot. But if we are lucky, the goblins also bless us in the end. The crows mocked Black Elk until he opened up to his own inner value and purpose, and shared his vision.

It would be easy to dismiss these mischievous creatures as evil. After all, they threaten our stability and ridicule our notions of right and wrong. Yet sometimes this rigorous self-questioning (to be distinguished from paralyzing self-doubt) is just what the doctor ordered. Never mind that, for the patient, it's often a bitter pill to swallow. Take your medicine. Open up. The goblins can help you with that.

I now knew that I had to be on the lookout for an opening—a portal to the More, a doorway to change.

What I got was a gateway.

6

Through a Gateway, Lightly

Changes are the epitome of Unknowns—the greatest of fear generators.
—Robert A. Monroe, *Ultimate Journey* (1994)

If you are not prepared to step through the doorway of change, you can't grow with the learning process.
—Joseph McMoneagle, *Mind Trek* (1993)

"But Becoming *What* I Do Not Know"

I felt as if I'd been dropped inside a labyrinth, built with invisible walls. One minute I was happily strolling along in the clear. Next, I was flat on my backside, gazing up at the sky. Walls I thought to be barriers served as guardrails gently guiding me to yet another opening in the crumbling edifice of my old beliefs. I sensed certain patterns in this process of disillusionment, readjustment, or whatever one wishes to call it, though I could not say what they were.

I'd experience a series of dreams, coincidences, or inner "knowings," all related and highly meaningful, apparently heading toward a conclusion. Then—nothing, as if a joke had been told with the punch line omitted. At times, then, I seemed to be flowing smoothly along a specific path. Yet, if pressed, I would have admitted I hadn't the slightest idea as to my direction: north or south, east or west, up or down. I kept my eyes peeled for clues, signs—or maybe even a helping hand.

Then, by "chance," I came across a book that gave me some encouragement. It was *One White Crow* by Dr. J. Norman Emerson and George McMullen.

Dr. Emerson had been an eminent, if (by his own admission) fairly conventional scholar. Revered as the "father of Canadian archaeology," he was senior archaeologist and professor of anthropology at the University of Toronto. He was also the founding vice president and a past president of the Canadian Archaeological Association. No mean honors! Dr. Emerson, in short, had a fine career and a splendid reputation.

Then one day the professor discovered that his friend, George McMullen, could psychometrize objects. Simply by holding some ancient coins in his hands, George could gather details about their past—things Dr. Emerson didn't know but that subsequently checked out. From that time on, George collaborated with Dr. Emerson in his field research, providing on-site guidance and other information that was accurate, in Dr. Emerson's scientific estimation, about eighty percent of the time.

Dr. Emerson also courageously published and presented papers about "intuitive archaeology" at meetings of learned societies. But privately, the professor knew even more, for he had begun having psychic experiences. Mostly, these were helpful synchronicities that he could not write off as coincidences. The line between him and his work, the subject and object of research, became increasingly blurred. The professor had become part of his own inquiry and was changing in unpredictable ways. As he freely admitted (in an unpublished paper), sometimes it felt more like magic than science:

> I am not the same person who began these studies
> two and a half years ago. Each passing day seems to have

its impact and to initiate change. I very much sense that I am part of a situation and/or events which are part of a process or state of becoming—yet becoming just what I do not clearly see. The state of change is almost too fast and complex to grasp in a tangible, organized way.

Many things have happened which have almost daily urged me on in my pursuit. Much as I have endeavoured to follow a policy of go slow and take it easy, the whole matter seems to snowball and develop at an ever-increasing rate. There is something mysterious working behind the scenes that I cannot grasp and define, nor yet can I dismiss.

Events have proceeded forward in such a manner that I have developed a daily attitude of anticipation and expectancy—what will happen today that will help develop the program? A phone call? A letter? A new person that I will meet? An old friend with a relevant story to tell me? A challenging article? A new book that presents knowledge that is helpful? Something like this does happen almost daily.

Such events, as I have suggested, appear to be more than just coincidental and also seem to form a pattern. This raises the question . . . What is the ultimate purpose, the real priority, the possible and foreseeable end of this work? I am really no closer to an answer, for I seem— even myself—to be involved in a process of "becoming." But becoming *what* I do not know.[1]

Dr. Emerson had described my own predicament to a T. I, too, was bewildered. I, too, felt the process was taking me somewhere, all right. But exactly where—and how and why—was a mystery. Most of the time, the best I could do was hang on for the ride.

Kaito's Gifts

More and more, I was burdened with shadowy presentiments of death. For example, one night I dreamt that someone blew up an entire block of a nearby town. The downtown buildings had been reduced to piles of rubble. The scene resembled a war zone. It was realistic and matter-of-fact, as if I were watching a television news report.

The following evening on the actual TV news, the anchor-man reported that an entire neighborhood in a town near Mexico City had been leveled by an explosion in a fireworks factory. Pictures showed that the site resembled a war zone.

One morning, I went into a spontaneous reverie as I lay in bed. Behind the velvety blackness of my closed eyelids, I saw the word TRIP spelled out in large block letters of swirling luminescent colors—red, green, orange, and purple. The letters looked like candy canes. Suddenly the T fell over on its side like a drunken sailor, leaving only the letters RIP standing. Instantly, I knew that someone would soon be taking a final trip, to rest in peace. A day or so later, I received word that my great-uncle had died.

Not long afterward, I dreamt I visited the house of a distant cousin, Benny, whom I hadn't seen or spoken to in years. His house was packed with boisterous party-goers. Strangely, Benny wasn't there. Several days later, I learned that he died the day that I had this dream.

All this death business was starting to spook me. I needed someone who could give me some perspective on my wanderings in the labyrinth. So I visited a psychic friend who gave me a "reading." Among other things, she informed me that I had a helpful "spirit guide" named Arthur. She added that I would soon receive some confirmation of this.

I had forgotten all about Arthur when, several days later, I flipped on the car radio only to hear an advertisement that made reference to King Arthur slaying a dragon. (I hadn't heard the ad before this.) Neat coincidence, I mused. But so what?

The next day I was discussing the concept of love in one of my classes. I briefly thought of introducing the Arthurian romances as an example, but somehow I got sidetracked. Then Jerry, one of my favorite students that semester, raised his hand.

"Did you just say King Arthur?" he asked, looking befuddled.

I was dumbstruck. I just stared at Jerry, unable to respond.

"No, I didn't," I finally managed to say, "but I sure was thinking about him!"

More and more I began to understand that the wall separating the private and public spheres is largely a social convention. In truth, this wall is more like a semipermeable membrane. Telepathy, sympathy, synchronicity, or call it what you will, began occurring with increasing frequency. At times, it was unnerving.

One morning, I was working in my college office, trying to make sense of a recent dream. I had dreamt that I was being operated on by two shadowy beings. One of them held me down while the other wielded a strange, horseshoe-shaped device with a crystal tip—like a pair of calipers—to mark off a spot on my shoulder. Then, with a power drill in hand, he proceeded to drill right through my shoulder. Oddly, I felt no pain. At the same time, in my mind's eye, I was shown a blueprint for what the two mysterious shadow beings were doing: They were replacing all of my bones with interlocking metal bars.

Through research I discovered that some individuals on the verge of becoming tribal shamans have vivid, sometimes horrifying, visions or dreams of being rebuilt from the inside out—so-called bone dreams. What follows is a description of such an experience as recorded by that great student of shamanism, the Romanian scholar Mircea Eliade:

> For example, a Yakut shaman, Sofron Zatayev, states that as a rule the future shaman "dies" and lies in the yurt for three days without eating or drinking. Formerly the candidate went through the ceremony three times, in which he was cut to pieces. Another shaman, Pyotr Ivanov, gives further details. The candidate's limbs are removed and disjointed with an iron hook; the bones are cleaned, the flesh scraped, the body fluids thrown away, and the eyes torn from their sockets. After this operation *all the bones are gathered up and fastened with iron* [italics mine].[2]

The "bone dream" was clearly a symbol of a transformation of awareness—cutting to the bare bones, so to speak—and the similarity to my dream was startling. Was I tapping into another archetype? Was I in store for that kind of change?

Just then I was startled by a knock on my office door.

"Come in," I announced, as I put my journal aside.

The door opened. My visitor was Kaito, a quiet Japanese student who sat behind Jerry in the philosophy class. I motioned for him to come in and sit down.

Kaito told me that he had come to this country to study English. But what he wanted to talk about was Socrates' guardian angel—his *daimon,* the mysterious divine voice that had spoken to him since childhood, protecting and prophetically warning him of potential danger ahead.

"I think I also have a *daimon,*" Kaito confessed somewhat sheepishly. Even as a young boy, he indicated that he had seen and heard things that others did not—ghosts. (Eventually, he would tell me the story of his boyhood encounter with the spirit of the murdered man in the park kiosk that I recounted in chapter 4.)

"The other world is out there, on the other side of the door," Kaito stated matter-of-factly, gesturing at my office door. "Spirits knock. You can choose to open or not. It's up to you."

"Yes, I believe that," I said.

"I think maybe it runs in my family," Kaito continued. Then he told me a story about his mother, who still lives in their small village in Japan. One day she was out walking. Passing by a neighbor's house, she was suddenly overcome with intense feelings of shame and anguish. She did not believe that these feelings were hers. Something told her that they belonged to the people who lived in the house, whom she did not know well. A horrible thing happened there, she said to herself with a shiver. As she hurried home, she felt as if she were fleeing the presence of Evil itself.

Later she learned what had happened. The man who owned the house, a shopkeeper, had taken out a high-interest loan with the Japanese mafia *(Yakuza)* to prop up his failing business. When he couldn't repay the loan, he was found hanging from the rafters in the house. His son, who ran a construction business, vanished without a trace, Jimmy Hoffa style. The rest of the family left town soon after.

Having told me about his mother, Kaito was now ready to tell me his story.

"One day I was taking a nap," Kaito began. "Before I awoke I felt someone on my body. This one was holding my arm, not letting me move. So I thought that I needed to struggle with this one." This being took the form of a white shadow that had a female shape. Somehow Kaito knew that this shadow was the spirit guide whose voice he had heard ever since he was a little boy, informing and instructing him. But now, for the first time, he was seeing her and feeling her powerful presence.

They communicated telepathically, he said.

"I asked her why she was on my body and holding my arms," Kaito continued. "She told me that she was holding my body because I might abuse my power or skills to do selfish favors. Also, she warned me if I abused my power, it would take over and control me. So, I asked her, 'If I have control over myself, what will happen to me?' She said, 'You may keep your power.' Then I said, 'How am I going to do that?' And she said, 'Have good morals!' I accepted that because it seemed to me that I had no choice. Just like, 'Take it or leave it.' Then she disappeared."

A look of relief washed over Kaito's face. "I don't know," he mused, shaking his head. "It's strange. Maybe I am a shaman." Then, grinning, he wagged his finger at me.

"Maybe *you* are a shaman!" Kaito exclaimed gleefully.

I was speechless, though I knew Kaito would have no idea why.

"But, you know," he added seriously, shaking his head, "it's a big responsibility."

"You won't believe this," I finally managed to say after a long pause. "But just before you came in this morning, I was sitting here working on a dream I'd had recently. It was about us all being shamans now."

Suddenly, all the pieces fell into place. Then Kaito said goodbye, leaving me to my musings. I now knew why the shadow beings were holding me down (just as Kaito's spirit guide had done to him), and why they were drilling my shoulder, of all places.

Why, then, the shoulder? The shoulder, after all, is a prime symbol of doing one's duty, of stepping up to the plate. The Greek Titan Atlas is shown carrying the globe on his shoulders. In ordinary conversation, we speak of individuals who shoulder (or fail to shoulder) their responsibilities, or of an acquaintance with stooped shoulders who seems, like Atlas, to be bearing the weight of the world.

Mircea Eliade also suggests a specific association of the shoulder with shamanism. He reads the ancient Greek myth of Pelops (in which a missing shoulder plays a prominent role) as a symbolic tale of shamanic initiation, illustrating the shamanic process of death and resurrection (as well as the dismemberment–bone reconstruction motif).[3]

As for the myth: You will recall that Tantalus, Pelops's father, killed his son Pelops, dismembered him, and then served the remains to the gods for dinner. The Olympians caught on to Tantalus's perverse deception, but not before one of the gods (just who is in dispute) inadvertently nibbled a bit of "Pelops stew"—a shoulder. So when the gods restored Pelops to life (Tantalus, of course, was punished severely in the underworld for his perfidy), they had to fashion for Pelops a new shoulder—a prosthesis—made of ivory.[4]

Pelops, brought back to life and changed "in his bones," so to speak, had new responsibilities to shoulder. Just as Kaito understood, enlarging our awareness, increasing our sensitivity is a huge burden. Are we up to the task? Today we are all called upon to play our part. No longer can "magic" be left in the hands of a select few—an esoteric or priestly elite. We must all learn to become healers. We must all reestablish our link to the whole and experience ourselves as part of everything, connected by the invisible bonds. For everything is depending on us. The stakes couldn't be higher.

A few days passed uneventfully. One morning there was another knock on my office door. It was Kaito. After exchanging greetings, he shyly handed me two gifts he had purchased during a recent visit home to his village in Japan. He explained that his mother had insisted that he repay me for the "kindness" of listening to his stories.

First I opened a small box. It contained a wooden plaque bearing the comically fierce visage of a beady-eyed, long-nosed, red-faced demon. Kaito explained that this was no ordinary monster. It was the image of a local deity who acts as the guardian of wisdom. One must wrestle with the god to obtain his treasure (as all true philosophers know so well).

As I unfurled what I thought was a poster, Kaito informed me that it was a Japanese calendar for the coming year. I couldn't take my eyes off the front cover. It was a delicate painting of a peaceful scene, with lots of blank space in the Zen style. Three long-eared, snow-white rabbits (or hares) lazed about, looking rather satisfied. I felt a jolt, reminded of my rabbit dream of years before and the three white baby bunnies nestled in the womb of the kitchen sink.

But the rabbits in the calendar were no infants. They were mature adults.

I stared at the painting. Clearly, I was being sent a message. Only what was it?

After recovering my composure, I broke the silence by thanking Kaito for his gifts. Then I explained vaguely that the rabbits held a special significance for me.

"Oh, yeah?" he asked rhetorically. "In the Chinese Zodiac, this is the year of the rabbit."

I was relieved when Kaito then said good-bye. Alone once more, I sank back into my chair to ponder the meaning of the message.

"Ripeness is all," as Shakespeare said. Clearly, the time for *something* had come. An auspicious moment had arrived. A process set in motion almost twenty years before, when I first had the telepathic rabbit dream, was reaching fruition. My three baby rabbits were all grown up now. I figured this meant that the time was ripe for me to make a move. Now I just had to figure out what that move was.

Harder still, now I would have to trust my intuition to be my guide.

Maiden Voyage

Several months later, I received some welcome news: I had been awarded a modest research grant. It was not all the money I'd requested, but at least it would give me the impetus to begin work on my new research project: the philosopher as shaman.

In my grant proposal, I'd said that creative thoughts spring from the depths—not from old-time religious "faith" or the unquestioning acceptance of beliefs delivered by external authorities, but from one's own Exceptional Human Experiences. Real philosophy is inspired. It is also unafraid of boldly investigating the mysterious sources of that inspiration, even if they seem to defy rational comprehension. After all, how can our understanding grow if it isn't stretched? To dismiss outright or ignore the nonrational basis of intellect is the epitome of narrow-minded, bone-headed stupidity. . . .

All of which sounded fine as academic rhetoric. But as Nietzsche declared, the true philosopher must be willing to be his own guinea pig, his own experiment. Abstract theory is not enough. So I knew I had to go to the Source myself. Nothing less would do.

I now knew what I had to do. I contacted The Monroe Institute (TMI), a nonprofit research and educational center nestled in the foothills of the Blue Ridge Mountains in Virginia, and enrolled in its famed six-day Gateway Voyage program. I'd wanted to do this for years, but kept putting it off. It was as if some part of me knew that I wasn't ready. Now I was getting the green light.

I had long admired the late founder of TMI, Robert A. Monroe. He was a most reasonable man who, starting in the late 1950s, found himself caught up in a most unreasonable situation. Bob Monroe was a straight-laced, successful radio and television executive and entrepreneur who began, quite involuntarily and much to his initial horror, to leave his physical body whenever he tried to take a nap or fall asleep.

Nothing like this had ever happened to him before. He possessed no frame of reference to understand the out-of-body (OBE) phenomenon. Fearing that he might be suffering from a brain tumor or some other physical or mental malady, Monroe sought the counsel of physicians and psychiatrists. After receiving repeated assurances of his health and stability, he began to calm down enough to want to investigate his wild talent.

A doctor friend suggested he visit an ashram in India to study with yogis, some of whom, according to the doctor, deliberately try to induce OBEs. This was news to Monroe, yet he balked at the suggestion. He could not see himself abandoning his critical reason and apprenticing himself to gurus. His own solution would have to be palatable to his modern, Western mind-set. There could be no relinquishing of personal autonomy, no "erasing" of individual ego, no silencing of nagging left-brain questions.

After verifying for himself that his OBE episodes were real (a lengthy process he described in 1971 in his first book, *Journeys Out of the Body*[5]) and even subjecting himself to independent scientific study by parapsychologists, Monroe took another tack. He used some of his own money to set up a research and development division of one of his privately owned companies (the early forerunner of TMI).

Monroe and his engineers expanded his earlier work with special sound patterns that could facilitate sleep and sleep-learning. They created the now famous (patented) audio process called Hemi-Sync (hemispheric synchronization), which enables the right (intuitive) and left (rational) cerebral hemispheres of the brain to work together. They discovered that such harmonious, balanced, whole brain-wave patterns or states of awareness ("Focus Levels" in Monroe's nomenclature) are conducive not only to OBEs, but also to a host of other beneficial peak, visionary, and revelatory-type EHEs.

Bob Monroe would eventually lecture on OBEs at venues as diverse as the Esalen Institute and the Smithsonian. TMI would receive international recognition—in the pages of the staid *Wall Street Journal,* no less. Institute professionals and independent researchers alike would publish numerous scientific papers supporting or confirming the efficacy of the Hemi-Sync process in altering brain states and facilitating EHEs.[6]

Yet it was not the technology or the aura of scientific respectability that had always impressed me about Monroe's work. From the time I had picked up a dog-eared copy of *Journeys Out of the Body* on the dusty back shelves of a secondhand bookstore in the late 1970s, I was taken with Monroe's refusal to worship any sacred cows. There were no old-time religious or spiritual dogmas, no a priori limits set to inquiry. Monroe was a pragmatic explorer of an open reality, not an Answerist constructing yet another closed system of beliefs. His mantra was: Here are the tools; go check it out for yourself. The following quote, from his third and last book, *Ultimate Journey*, is vintage Monroe:

> What we need to do, whether in- or out-of-body, is to ignore or tear down the No Trespassing signs, the taboos, the notice that says Holy of Holies, the distortions of time and translation, the soft black holes of euphoria, the mysticisms, the myths, the fantasies of an eternal father or mother image, and then take a good look with our acquired and growing left brain. Nothing is sacred to the point where it should not be investigated or put under inquiry.[7]

Bob Monroe spoke my language. Now I realized it was high time that I got acquainted with his. In other words, I had no choice but to check it out for myself.

CHEC-in Time

On a hot, humid Friday in late August of 2000, I drove the seven or so hours from New Jersey to Virginia on boring interstates. My immediate destination was a Holiday Inn in Charlottesville. The program was not scheduled to begin until Saturday afternoon, but I wanted to be as fresh and rested as possible for the inner journey that lay ahead.

On a mountainous section of I-64 near Charlottesville, I stopped at a scenic overlook to stretch my stiff legs. It was a magnificent view. A grey mist hugged the verdant earth in the valley below. A white farmhouse, the lone outpost of human activity, sat on the banks of a meandering stream. This pastoral scene could have been from a hundred years ago. It was a place out of time.

I recalled my last experience of such pacific timelessness, years before. I had lolled about for hours under a tree on the grassy banks of Coniston Water in the Lake District of northern England. I watched white puffy clouds float by. I was serenaded by bleating sheep in the pasture. Nothing, it seemed, had changed for centuries. It could have been medieval times.

Once again, I felt myself in a timeless abode. But what was I feeling? Was it a pang of longing for a simple, rural life that I have never lived? Or nostalgia, perhaps for a lost time and place but not of this life?

Later that night, in my drab hotel room, I fell into a fitful sleep. I dreamed I was a time-traveling explorer who visits a bizarre post-apocalyptic world of the future. In this nightmare scenario (of *Mad Max* meets *Jurassic Park*), the remnants of the human race, armed with the dregs of their technological dystopia, are forced to battle with resurrected dinosaurs to survive.

At one point, I'm behind the wheel of a battered Jeep, ferrying a friend to a trading post for supplies. I feel the wind in my face and the bumps in the uneven dirt road as we drive on its dusty, potholed surface. Suddenly, the vehicle mysteriously picks up speed. I'm not in control. We're sent careening down the road in a roller-coaster ride and it feels as if the truck could lift off and fly into the air at any moment.

Next I am in darkness, the void. Although I can feel my physical body in the bed, I'm also inside the vision unfolding in the velvety blackness before my closed eyelids. I'm still moving very fast, hurtling like an Olympic bobsled racer along the inside of a winding tunnel-track composed of a lattice-like structure of colored lights. It is a web of different colored neon tubes—red, green, orange, and blue—glowing brightly in the dark. The image is vivid, sharp, crystal clear. The sensation of flying through the tunnel is all too frighteningly real, like an amusement park thrill ride. Then the scene fades out.

The next morning, after a brisk walk and a shower, I headed downstairs to the hotel restaurant, famished. I was in no hurry, as I didn't have to be at the Institute for hours. As the waitress filled my coffee cup for the fourth time, I pondered my dream.

My nightmare world was a place out of time, past and future scrambled together. Yet it was no blissful Happy Valley paradise. This seemed to serve as a warning that I would once again have to face fears that were holding me back—the fear of things from the past (resurrected dinosaurs) as well as the fear of the future (chaos, conflict, and change). Above all, I'd have to come to terms with the dread of losing control (the wild ride over the outback road and the aborted tunnel flight).

I wondered whether by ending my flight through the tunnel I had cut short an out-of-body experience—something I'd been seeking. I had to admit that I've never been fond of amusement park rides.

Well, it looked to me like I might be in for a bumpy ride over the next six days. My bluff had been called. It was put up or shut up time. It's tough to break out of old patterns.

Could I do it now?

The pastoral landscape surrounding the Institute was even more gorgeous than the scene that had moved me on the highway lookout. I felt the energies of the place supporting the work and consciousness of all those who visited or worked at the Institute.

I made my way inside and was warmly greeted by one of the staff. The comfortable, knotty-pine paneled interior of the center reminded me of a rustic Maine log cabin. I was shown to my room and my CHEC unit, in which I would be spending most of the next week, listening to Hemi-Sync tapes over headphones and sleeping. Bob Monroe adored acronyms: CHEC stands for Controlled Holistic Environmental Chamber; essentially, it is a narrow bunk bed designed as a sensory deprivation chamber, complete with heavy black curtains and soundproof walls. Many have likened it to a Pullman berth.

Since I had arrived early, Lee, one of the trainers, poked his head into my room and introduced himself. He invited me to do my intake interview before I unpacked. I agreed, and we adjourned to a small lounge area in the front of the building.

"What do you hope to get out of this experience?" Lee asked.

I explained that although I had enjoyed spontaneous psychic and mystical-type experiences since early childhood, I wanted a more controlled way of entering into these states. I told Lee that I'd already worked with some of the Hemi-Sync tapes at home.

Lee nodded. "Well, you've come to the right place," he declared. "This is the only true Western Mystery school."

I could tell that Lee was speaking here from deep personal experience, from what he had obtained from his own work at TMI. I could tell that he knew I had more in mind than I was saying.

"I sort of feel like I've reached a creative dead end," I blurted out. "My teaching and writing have become dry and dusty and unsatisfying. I'm in a rut. A big rut."

Lee nodded. He understood. We talked a bit more about my background. He seemed certain that I would find the program both beneficial and enjoyable.

Still, I wondered: Do I have what it takes to climb out of the rut?

The Laugh's on Me (or, The Eyes Have It)

The first few tape exercises of the program introduced the early signpost states of altered consciousness, which Monroe labeled Focus 10 and Focus 12. Focus 10 is described as "body asleep/mind awake," the baseline state of relaxed alertness that is a prerequisite for further exploration. Focus 12 is the first step toward "expanded awareness" of dimensions beyond the purely physical. (The numbers were emotionally neutral, arbitrary conventions Monroe introduced in order to distinguish identifiably different states of awareness without getting caught up in loaded associations with older spiritual and religious vocabularies.) I had already worked with the Hemi-Sync tapes at home, but this was different.

During one of the early Focus 10 exercises, I had the impression that I owned two sets of hands and feet, each set being slightly out of phase with the other. I felt my second set of hands as not quite in the same position as my (physical) hands, which were placed palms down on the bed at my sides. This sensation was at once strange, yet completely natural (and not at all unpleasant). My whole body (or was it bodies?) felt tingly, as if electrified.

In another Focus 10 exercise, I had the impression of my "second" left (nonphysical or subtle energy) arm reaching out and opening the door of a wooden cabinet. This felt like a physical action. Then in my mind's eye, I saw what looked like a pirate's treasure map that I had evidently pulled out of the chest. It showed an island in the middle of a large football-shaped lake surrounded by land on all four sides. On the far right was an asterisk accompanied by the legend, "You are here," marking my present location on the mainland. I somehow knew that the central island was my destination.

Was this a symbolic map of my inner journey? Later, as I stared at the rough sketch of the map I had made in my journal, I realized that it was shaped like a human eye. "Eye," of course, could also be a play on the pronoun "I." So here "I" was, staring into the depths, and who was staring back at me? None other than myself. Or rather, it was some unknown, hidden part of me. Perhaps this was the inner eye of subtle perception, the expanded awareness promised by Focus 12.

In another session, I was surprised to see a balding, middle-aged man floating in the black void, wearing a slightly goofy-looking angel's costume (white robe, wings, and all). This cheesy outfit looked like it had been rented at a costume shop. Then I realized with a start that the "angel" looked familiar. It was none other than Bob Monroe.

I sensed amusement on the part of "Angel Bob." I felt him

shrugging mentally, as if to say, "Well, it's your vision, but I'm no angel!"

Then he communicated with me, telepathically.

"Trust the process," he said.

I asked "Bob" if he could give me evidence that it was him and not simply my fantasy or a projection of some sort of Jungian Wise Man figure.

"It's too soon for that; it would be distracting," replied the figure. Then he indicated that he had to leave, and the scene dissolved.

Afterwards I recorded the incident in my notebook. But I was still skeptical that I had encountered an aspect of Bob Monroe's postmortem personality. This, despite the fact that several months before I knew that I would be attending the Gateway I had dreamed of meeting Bob Monroe.

In the dream, I walk into a lecture because it's advertised as being given by Bob Monroe. Since I know he's dead, I raise my hand and ask him how it's possible that he's here giving a lecture. He responds with a complicated explanation (it sounded plausible at the time) involving "time loops." I'm astonished that he calls me by name. When I ask him about this, Monroe chuckles warmly and tells me that, yes, he knows very well who I am. In fact, he adds, he "checks in" on me from time to time.

Although the Bob Monroe in my dream felt like a real presence (and someone who knew him reassured me that my experience was valid), even after my encounter with "Angel Bob" at the Gateway I was not prepared to accept that it was "really" him. Trust (in myself and in the process) did not come easily.

Perhaps this was because many of my fellow Voyagers reported detailed visions in which they felt themselves to be at the center of action in a densely plotted, three-dimensional scenario, whereas my own fragmentary and fleeting mind's-eye impressions felt like viewing faded snapshots in someone else's photo album. I yearned to perceive more, and better. I couldn't help comparing myself to the others and feeling frustrated when, on my own strict accounting, I saw myself coming up short.

In a later Focus 10 session, I issued an invitation to my non-physical guides to reveal themselves and to help me understand the purpose of my life. In response, I received several fragmentary impressions that made no sense to me, and then came this: the eerie sound of the echoing laughter of many voices.

Immediately after the session ended, I grabbed my notebook and scribbled down the phrase, "an Olympian laugh." There was something . . . well, not exactly inhuman, but rather nonhuman, about that laughter. It felt as if the gods were looking down from the top of Mount Olympus and having a jolly good time at my (or our) expense—not sadistically, mind you. A wise, compassionate, and, above all, divinely humorous wit was at work.

As an answer to my request, however, I found this Olympian laughter puzzling, and I still felt frustrated over the lack of improvement in the clarity and quality of my inner vision. So that evening, I corralled Karen, one of the trainers, and explained my predicament. She listened patiently as I poured out my self-doubt.

"You know," Karen offered, "sometimes the Higher Self acts like a parent who refuses to give in to a child's tantrum. It will not reinforce old patterns by rewarding unproductive demands."

"You mean, I keep asking for clarity of vision, so I get an aural message instead?"

Karen's eyes twinkled. She smiled warmly and nodded. "What does the laughter mean to you?" she asked.

"Lighten up," I replied without a moment's hesitation. This answer surprised me. I hadn't thought of it until I'd said it. Then it seemed obvious. Humor offers a higher, godlike perspective. If you can laugh at yourself, and your situation, then you're free.

"You are receiving validation," Karen added. "Only it may not be the kind you want or expect. It's like, you're being offered a rose, but you say, 'No, I want the lily.'"

Was I acting like a spoiled child, demanding "my way or the highway"?

"You know," she counseled, "as you do the exercises try to recall a time in your life when you were having fun. Play with it. Don't treat it as work."

I nodded my understanding and thanked Karen for her good advice. Truth was, I still didn't get it. I couldn't help treating the workshop as something I would be graded in. Humor and play were interesting concepts—nothing more.

Sometimes I have to get hit on the head. Hard, even.

The Three Weird Sisters Enter a House of Mourning

Working in Focus 12 (the state of expanded awareness) seemed to trigger many synchronistic events. For example, one afternoon at lunch I found myself seated next to Jon, an optometrist from California with a wickedly dry sense of humor. (When we met he explained that his wife thought him crazy for spending a week at the Institute, "to lay in a box listening to humming.") Jon was making a joke about the Wizard of Oz when I remembered that during a tape exercise that very morning I had been given a pair of shoes that were supposed to help me fly. It reminded me of Dorothy and the magical ruby slippers. There were numerous other such "coincidences."

Next we were introduced to Focus 15. The trainers were surprisingly mum about Focus 15 in our pre-tape briefing. This was unusual, and it lent an air of mystery to the proceedings. About all we were told was that Focus 15 is officially referred to as the state of "No Time" (though, in fact, as others have noted, this name is slightly misleading, as Focus 15 is a state in which all times—past, present, and future—are accessible).

As I moved into Focus 15 along with the tape, I momentarily felt myself pooling out in all directions at once, like water on a flat tabletop. Then it felt as if I were tumbling in slow motion, head over heels, like an astronaut in deep space. It was very quiet and peaceful.

Then I briefly glimpsed three women. They were wearing shawls, and they had their backs turned toward me, so that I couldn't see their faces. In silence, and bent over in grief, they entered the front door of a large house—a house of mourning. I sensed that these women were sisters, and that someone close to them had died.

The image made no sense to me. It was not a memory. It didn't feel like a fragment from a "past life." When I mentioned it in the debriefing, however, I heard my own voice catch as I described the scene to the group. Karen must have heard the raw emotion.

"I think there's something more for you in there," she indicated gently.

All I could do was wordlessly nod my agreement. I could not speak. It felt as if I had swallowed a hot coal that burned a hole through the center of my being.

By lunchtime, the hot coal had become a nameless dread burrowing in the pit of my stomach. For the first time at the Gateway, I felt emotionally fragile. Anxiety, my old enemy, had returned. I was on the verge of a panic attack.

Lee, the trainer who had done my intake interview, must have sensed my discomfort. At lunch, he brought his tray over to my booth, where I was sitting alone, feeling on edge. Forced to make small talk, I was distracted from my inner turmoil. I felt a bit better.

Later that afternoon, we resumed the exercises. Alone in my CHEC unit, waiting for the next tape to begin, my mind raced. Slowly the mood music playing over the loudspeaker entered the penumbra of my awareness. It was a hauntingly familiar, bittersweet melody. Then I recognized the music. It was a fragment from one of my favorite pieces, Dvorak's *New World* symphony. Specifically, it was the section where the composer had included themes from the old African-American spiritual, "Going Home."

Going Home. *Home!*

The senseless fog of dread lifted, leaving behind the dewy residue of its essence: grief. Tears ran down my cheeks, accompanied by sobs. I realized now that the sorrow of the three sisters was my own. I was grieving for myself, for the lost parts of myself, for all the parts I had mislaid or abandoned over the years. This included the humorous, playful, joyous parts that had become inconvenient or useless; the intuitive, sensitive, and imaginative parts that I had to ignore in order to make myself safe and successful and acceptable to others. Sadly, that was my fate.

But it was not my fate to suffer alone and in isolation. It was also the fate of our "civilized" culture. The three sisters belong to us all. They are the *Moirae*, the Three Fates of the ancient Greeks, or the exiled triple goddess of old: Virgin, Mother, and Crone—our rejected feminine side, the Eve principle. Call it what you will.

The panic subsided like a passing storm. In its place was a tender, poignant sense of loss. Everything was as it had to be, and yet, in the words of the *I Ching*, the Taoist book of wisdom, "No blame." It didn't have to stay that way, after all. I still had a choice. My sadness, tinged with a sense of sweet vulnerability, was bearable. I felt looser, freer.

Would this feeling of freedom last? What would come next?

Enter (and Leave) Laughing

The climax of the workshop was our introduction to the state Monroe labeled Focus 21. He described Focus 21 as "the edge" or interface between the physical and nonphysical energy systems. It is the bridge from Here to There. But within these broad parameters, the individual's experience of each Focus Level will be uniquely his own. The principle that the observed is relative to the observer is always operative.

In my first voyage to Focus 21, I felt like I was entering an enormous, brightly lit movie soundstage, like a cavernous set from a Stanley Kubrick film. Everything in the enormous room (floor, walls, ceiling) was brilliant white. The set was nearly empty, with a solitary couch, club chair, and coffee table (also white) in the middle of the floor. Seated in the chair was a mysterious, dark-haired woman. She held up her right hand in greeting. All about her familiar figures rushed by to make brief cameo appearances, including Woody Allen, John Cleese, and even Wile E. Coyote of the old Roadrunner cartoon.

I was mystified by this celebrity parade, and I couldn't square the description of Focus 21 as a "bridge" to other energy systems with my own ridiculous Hollywood extravaganza. I was disappointed. Had I even managed to get to 21?

At lunch, I buttonholed Lee once again. "Do you think it's possible to distinguish between what one subjectively experiences and what is 'objectively real' in the Focus Levels?" I asked.

Lee put down his fork and paused for a moment before he spoke. "I think what you came here for is a feeling experience," he said thoughtfully, seeming to change the subject. "As a child, you experienced *real* magic."

"True," I acknowledged. I knew from the start that things are not what they seem. To me there was never any doubt that, in the words of the Gateway affirmation, "we are more than our physical bodies." The ballerina had taught me that long ago.

"And now you have to know that you can experience your emotions and survive," Lee added. It was not about metaphysics or epistemology. I had already taken those courses—and passed them (with flying colors).

At last I got it.

Shakespeare said, "All the world's a stage," and so it is. In my Focus 21 experience, I had been afforded both a glimpse of the stage, stripped down to its bare essentials, as well as the staging area for what lay behind (or beyond) the curtain. Eve herself (the mysterious female) had welcomed me to the party. The figures I'd glimpsed were not accidental walk-ons. I realized now that they were comedians—clowns and tricksters all. (Coyote, of course, was a trickster figure in many Native American cultures.) This troupe was there to teach me a lesson.

Lee was right.

Well, I had already survived fear.

There was only one thing left. Were the gods still laughing?

The culminating exercise of the Gateway was a tape called "Superflow."

Inside my CHEC unit, I put on my headphones and flicked the ready light switch to signal the trainers that I was on board and ready to go. Usually they played ethereal meditative music to set the mood for the exercise, but the jumpy dance tune coming over the headphones was hardly meditative stuff—it was . . . the Macarena!

As I rolled in laughter, I heard the familiar voice of Bob Monroe and the soothing sounds of ocean surf in my headphones. But this time the surf was more than a mere symbol of peaceful relaxation. I felt as though I had indeed plunged headlong into the cosmic surf, riding wave after wave of surging nonphysical energies. Although I was completely aware of my physical surroundings in the CHEC unit, it was as if part of me were simultaneously detached. This "other me" was rocketing along on invisible energy currents in deep space, speeding up and down like a roller-coaster ride. It was a smooth, effortless joy of total freedom. I was engulfed by continuous waves of ecstasy. Starbursts exploded in my hands and feet. Images zoomed in and out of my awareness like shooting stars. A chalice was put to my lips, and I drank. Grapes were put to my mouth, and I ate. An artist's easel and paints stood on a deserted ocean beach, gulls flying overhead, ready and waiting for a willing creator to create. I was welcomed by a man and woman to a strangely familiar log cabin set deep in a tranquil wood. Their German shepherd dog, a playful Cerberus, guide of souls, ran to greet me.

So much more happened than I could take in, and more was taken in than I could say.

Finally, too soon, the fun was over. I was back.

Or was I?

On the way to the dining room, I felt I was floating a few inches above the floor, so ecstatic was I. Happier than Scrooge on Christmas morning. An idiot's wide silly grin was plastered on my face that I could not have suppressed even if I'd tried. I was like the cat that had swallowed not just the canary, but the whole cage. I kept my eyes glued to the floor as I walked. I couldn't look anyone in the eye. Not yet, anyway.

Standing ahead of me in line at the salad bar was Patricia. She had come to the Gateway with her husband, Sam. She'd paid for Sam's admission; it was her birthday present to him. But, standing there in line, I felt like a kid at my own birthday party.

Just then, Patricia turned to face me. Our eyes met. We just knew.

We both exploded into hearty, uncontrollable belly laughs. I laughed so hard it hurt. Tears streamed down my cheeks. I placed my hand on Patricia's shoulder in acknowledgment of our shared journey. Nothing else needed to be said. I had my confirmation. We had been There, all right, and it was pure joy.

Sauntering through the Doorway of Change

Our (materialist) cultural common sense tells us that life sucks, then you die. Our everyday experiences seem to confirm the wisdom of popular cynicism. There are the countless hurts, large and small, given and received. There is the gratuitous rudeness, the crude competition of bloated, fragile egos fighting for superior position at every turn, from the highway and super-market aisle to corporate boardrooms and school classrooms. Not to mention the inevitable losses and betrayals of time and failing bodies, folding relationships and foolish choices. Ignorance, pain, and mistrust seem to stalk us at every turn. You would have to be an idiot not to know that the world is shit.

Through clenched teeth and contrived smiles, grim "religious" folk preach about "Love" and "Grace." But their hellish belief in a tormenting, judgmental deity and their own daily actions belie their words. They, too, keep their powder dry.

Piety is puffery.

Then there are the serious, hardworking "spiritual" people. Even as they boast of their own "egolessness" and "compassion," they look down their noses in elite disdain at the unwashed, unenlightened multitudes who lack the necessary esoteric skills (or the right karma, or the right spiritual practice, or the right guru) to become perfect.

Violence and aggression take many forms.

But what if they're all wet? What if joy, delight, and playfulness are not self-indulgent therapies for the unsophisticated, the unsaved, and the uninitiated? What if these experiences express an important insight into the true nature of reality?

Two of my favorite TV programs from childhood were silly kids' shows called *Wonderama* and *Just for Fun*. Lately I have come to suspect that recovering and nourishing our childlike sense of wonder and fun may cut closer to the metaphysical bone than all the science (and philosophy) texts, Bible verses, and yoga sutras put together.

Could it be that Eve's playful curiosity is the best clue we have?

Widespread acceptance of this insight might put conventional wisdom in all its current forms out of business. Perhaps it's time for the lot of them to file for Chapter Eleven.

Would that be such a bad thing?

7

A Fountain Not Made
by the Hands of Men

Let it be known there is a fountain
That was not made by the hands of men
　　　　　　—from "Ripple," song by The Grateful Dead
　　　　　　(words by Robert Hunter, music by Jerry Garcia)

Dead?—I say. There is no death. Only a change of worlds.
　　　　　　—Chief Seattle, cited in *Pumpkin Seed Point:*
　　　　　　Being within the Hopi by Frank Waters (1969)

Wallowing in the Trough of Despond

All waves have both crests and troughs. Waves of change are
no exception. It's part of nature's cyclical rhythm that highs are
followed by lows, seasons of activity by seasons of rest. Without
winter, there could be no spring. That's the universal pattern.

Nevertheless, I was still shaken when, not long after my
return from Virginia, I found myself slipping into the murky
waters of a deep blue funk.

164

What had happened?

Often I was too tired to meditate. When I did, I would often fall asleep or "click out" (Monroe's term for the odd sense of blacking out during a Hemi-Sync exercise). The daily routines of commuting and teaching proved to be more draining than ever. The peace and exhilaration of my Gateway Voyage were melting away like ice cubes on a hot griddle.

A psychic friend weighed in with his opinion that my Gateway experience had been a mirage rather than a real oasis in the desert. To him, the whole thing was a sham. Another friend, hearing of my plight, gently advised me "not to push the river." She reminded me that everything must develop in its own time. Trust the process, she counseled.

I understood, but I also yearned for some sort of confirmation. In plain terms, I was hoping for a sign. I needed some sort of encouragement from the universe.

One day, heading home from the college, I was stuck in bumper-to-bumper traffic on the expressway. Cursing my bad luck and irritated, I glanced at the license plate of the SUV in front of me. Framing the plate was one of those brackets that car dealers use to advertise their dealerships.

"WE CARE," it proclaimed. On the bottom of the bracket was the name of the car dealership: "MONROE."

I felt a familiar shiver. For the moment I even forgot that I was miserable, stuck in rush-hour traffic. I'd never heard of a local dealership by that name. But I had, of course, heard of a certain out-of-body explorer by the name of Monroe.

I'd wanted a sign. So I got one. Well, at least the universe had kept its sense of humor.

More Signs and Portents

There may have been another, darker reason for my moodiness, for I was experiencing ominous foreshadowings of death.

This had happened before, as I mentioned. But this time it was different.

Beginning in October of 2000, these episodes occurred

periodically, over a span of months. They stirred urgency and unease within me. Much more than the death of a single individual was involved. Of this I became certain.

On several occasions during meditation, I found myself accosted by shadowy figures issuing vague warnings that "time was running out." Once, an inner guide figure, an elderly Native American woman that I had encountered during my Gateway (and in an earlier dream), grabbed me by the hand, insisting that I accompany her.

"Hurry," she implored, "there's little time."

Time for what? "Am I going to die soon, Grandmother?" I asked.

"No, not you," she replied tersely.

That shook me. There was something about her reply that told me that there were many deaths to be expected. I wrote in my journal, ". . . something much larger or bigger [than my death or that of a single individual]; an event or something."

In another meditation, I found myself in a dark chamber walking past an ancient Egyptian sarcophagus when I heard someone shout a warning: "Danger!"

Then one night I had three disturbing dreams in a row. In the first dream, I sat across from a man who claimed to be Adolf Hitler. In fact, he looked nothing like Hitler. Yet he radiated an intense, sadistic brutality. He had no conscience. Next to me sat another man who was busy filling a large capsule with poison. He gleefully explained that there was enough poison in that one capsule to kill an entire building full of people. Cold shivers cascaded down my spine. I felt I was in the presence of evil.

In the second dream, I was in a large building when everyone suddenly had to evacuate because the structure was collapsing. As I awoke, I experienced a puzzling vision. I saw a map of the East Coast of the United States. Off New Jersey, in the Atlantic Ocean, a marker indicated "Persian submarines."

Not long after this, I dreamt I was at the college when someone burst into my office. This person informed me that a TWA flight had crashed nearby, killing all aboard. He urged me to make a public announcement of the tragedy, but I was too upset to do so.

Initially, I tried to read these frightening dreams and visions symbolically, as references to my inner processes. Maybe, I reasoned, these images were calling attention to my darker aspects and fears, to what Carl Jung called the Shadow.

I knew, for example, that the Death card in the major arcana of the Tarot often has another, subtler meaning than literal death. "The death card strikes fear in the hearts of most people when it should be welcomed," writes Tarot expert Rosemary Ellen Guiley. "It is not an evil card. It is a card of change, of transformation."[1]

On the other hand, if these were dire warnings or premonitions, then what? Premonitions of what? Airplane crashes? Collapsing buildings? Lunatic mass murderers from Egypt and Iran? Whom would I tell? What would I say? Who would believe me?

I could not completely ignore my disturbing feelings, but I swept them under the rug, at least for the time being. I'll deal with them at some point, I promised.

The Lighter Side of the Trough

It wasn't all doom and gloom in the months following my Gateway. Indeed, I had several encouraging experiences that told me I was on the right path.

One night, for example, I had a dream about a small lizard and some turtles. One of the turtles was chasing the lizard over a rocky landscape. But the plucky lizard was too fast and outran the slow-moving turtle. When I awoke, I was puzzled. The dream didn't mean anything to me. It read more like a fragment of a folk tale than a personal dream. So I put it aside and forgot about it.

Several days later, I happened to pick up Richard Erdoes's book about the Sioux holy man Lame Deer (John Fire), *Lame Deer: Seeker of Visions,* which had lain unread on my bookshelves for many years. Lame Deer told Erdoes that, in the old days, before a child was born, a grandmother would make two little dolls, one in the shape of a lizard (for a boy) and one in the shape of a turtle (for a girl). These were guardian spirits, or good luck charms, meant to protect the baby against evil influences. They stood for strength and long life. The lizard "is very fast and hard to kill," explained Lame Deer.[2]

My library angel (or the synchronicity switchboard) was at it again.

On another occasion I was meditating when I found myself behind the wheel of a car zooming forward at terrific speed. Suddenly, I was coming up very fast behind another vehicle, a truck or bus. Panicking, I slammed on the brakes. This popped me right out of the meditation. Yet, for a few seconds afterwards, I still experienced a queasy sense of forward momentum, like when you get off an elevator and still feel you're moving.

Relaxing, I returned to my meditation. This time I was sitting at a round table with two other people when I began to experience an odd sensation. I was moving forward across the table, or part of me was sitting in the chair, while another part had popped out of my "body" and was flying toward the wall opposite the table. I realized with a start that I could no longer feel myself breathing. This scared me. I snapped back to waking awareness with a gasp, as if my breath had been taken away by a sucker punch to my gut.

This episode reminded me of the aborted racing/flying "dream" I'd had in the Holiday Inn, the night before my Gateway Voyage. Once again it seemed that I was on the verge of having a conscious out-of-body experience. If only I could master my fears, I figured I could move forward (or outward).

Whatever that might mean.

Return Engagement

In early April of 2001, Cynthia and I visited Maine during our spring break. As usual, the lake acted as a magic mirror, reflecting back to me the things I most needed to see inside me. One night I dreamt that a large ugly rat was creeping around the ground by my feet, evidently attracted by some rotting garbage. I was afraid it might bite me and I was relieved when it left me alone.

The next morning I awoke in a foul mood. At breakfast, I felt out of sorts and jittery, without knowing why. Then with a shudder, I remembered the rat dream. The message seemed clear: Leave your emotional garbage lying all about uncollected and you can expect to attract scavengers—nature's helpful recyclers.

Yet it wasn't enough just to interpret the dream. I felt I had to do something physical to banish the negative energies that hovered about me like a dark cloud. So I gathered some paper and plastic shopping bags and ambled up the hilly driveway to the dirt road beyond. I kept on walking all the way down to the paved road that runs the length of the cape.

I trudged along the shoulder of the cape road for an hour. The melting snow banks were receding into the woods, leaving behind their fresh winter deposits. But these were man-made, left by visitors, laborers, and, no doubt, local residents. Every few yards, I stooped to place another item in my swelling bags: Styrofoam coffee cups, beer cans, cigarette packs, fast-food cartons, and empty whiskey bottles. There was a kitchen knife, a surgical mask, and the bubble-wrap package from something called "The Jelly Future-Flex Ultimate Vibrator," which promised to send its user "straight into orbit" with its "powerful multi-speed dial control soft jelly exterior." A technological marvel.

I filled up two, three, then four bags with this junk. My arms ached from the heavy load. I lugged the trash two or three miles back to the house, where I placed the bags in larger plastic bags for disposal.

All the while I pondered the weirdness of my fellow human beings. How could anyone who enjoyed the beauty of this place despoil it so? Was it thoughtlessness or malice?

Then I realized with a start that the entire scenario, including my project of reclamation, could be viewed as a metaphor. Surely I had my own mental "garbage" to clean up. Whenever we avoid this task, out of laziness or fear, we act out our inner demons, polluting our environment. Mother Earth suffers when we avoid our personal responsibility. Was I moved to clean up the road because I was evading an inner housecleaning?

When we returned from our vacation, I received word that my research grant had been renewed. I immediately knew what I had to do: return to The Monroe Institute. I sensed that I was in this funk not because I'd gone too far, but because I hadn't gone far enough. I had to clean up my own act, as the rat dream implied.

The only question remained, Which program should I attend? I wanted to take the Guidelines workshop, which stressed inner self-knowledge. But Guidelines wasn't being offered during the only week in late August when I could attend. That left Lifeline.

What is Lifeline?

Bob Monroe described the genesis of the Lifeline program in his third and final book, *Ultimate Journey* (1994), published shortly after the passing of his beloved wife, Nancy, and only months before his own final out-of-body excursion.

Monroe found himself retrieving the souls of those deceased persons who hadn't yet accepted or understood their post-mortem condition. He brought them to a place where they were met by friends, relatives, or guides. In most cases, this destination was a peaceful parklike setting that he dubbed the Reception Center (or simply, the Park). However, in some cases, Monroe realized that these bewildered "lost souls" were actually dissociated aspects of his own larger identity, or what in *Ultimate Journey* he called the IT, or "I-There." This is the greater self "that each of us has [on the nonphysical side], containing all previous and present life personalities."[3] This whole self thus includes what is commonly referred to as "past lives" or "reincarnational personalities." But, as Monroe's definition tacitly implies, it also includes entities that might be called "co-incarnates": other members of one's I-There team that are living physical lives (in male and/or female form) during the same overall time period as oneself.

Thus Monroe developed the Lifeline program as a "service to those here in physical matter reality and service to those There who have made their transitions from the physical and who may benefit from assistance."[4] In seeking to help others, it may turn out that you are helping your (greater) self; but in seeking to heal yourself, you are also lightening the load for others.

Crossing the "Boggle Threshold"

Deciding to attend Lifeline seemed at first like a decision by default. But then I had a vivid dream that suggested it might be much more than that:

> I watch as a grieving man and his young daughter ride together in silence on a subway car. The little girl is crying softly. She is grieving over her mother's recent death. The man appears distraught but resigned. Then the scene shifts and I watch as the pair enters a coffee shop. They take seats opposite each other on two comfortable couches. As the man orders an espresso, the daughter curls up on her sofa and quickly falls asleep. An air of eager expectancy pervades the room. Suddenly, an attractive woman makes her entrance. She walks over to the man and they embrace warmly. I know that this is his dead wife, and that he was expecting to meet her here. Yet she looks every bit as alive, and as physical, as he does! As they talk quietly with each other, my attention shifts inward. I think about my own lost loved ones. I feel a wave of sadness, and also confusion. I wonder: Can contact with them really be this effortless, this easy?

This dream bugged me for days. It was so realistic and detailed that it felt like I was watching a movie—a good movie. I felt sorry for the man and his daughter. I also felt the husband and wife's joy as they were briefly reunited. So why was I so put out?

The dream forced me to confront my own limitations. I had reached what my friend, the EHE researcher Rhea White, calls "the boggle threshold." Even for those who accept the validity of certain EHEs (say, precognition or telepathy) there will come a point where one, in effect, declares, "Oh, no, I can't buy *that*."

"That" might refer to, say, UFOs or OBEs, or wherever one feels compelled to draw a line in the sand and beat a hasty retreat into the hard shell of self-protective skeptical denial.

For me, the idea of contacting or assisting "those who have made their transitions from the physical" apparently brought me to the edge of my "boggle threshold." I couldn't say why, but I felt resistance, almost like a magnetic repulsion. I had to admit that, like everyone else, I still harbored certain limiting beliefs. The dream was like a gauntlet thrown down before me.

Find your boggle threshold, I was being told—and cross it. Or else!

Grabbing the Lifeline

The Lifeline was held at the newly refurbished Roberts Mountain Retreat (RMR), at the summit of Roberts Mountain in Faber, Virginia. As I drove onto TMI grounds, past the Gate House and the Nancy Penn Center where my Gateway had been held the year before (almost to the very day), I was flooded with fond memories and warm feelings. It was great to be back.

A friendly staff member showed me to my CHEC unit in the new annex. It was a warm, comfortable room, complete with private bathroom. My roommate had not yet arrived, so I had my choice of bunks. After stowing my gear, I walked over to the main building (formerly the home of Bob and Nancy Monroe). A few other participants had already arrived and were chatting over snacks in the den. After introducing myself, I helped myself to a hot cup of coffee and a sandwich. As I listened in, the conversations flowed.

Gina and Miri, who had just introduced themselves to one another, were talking animatedly, excited by their discovery of an improbable connection. It turned out that Miri (who now lived in Alaska) had dated Gina's brother several years before, when she was attending college in California. Gina still lived in New Jersey, where her family was based. For me, this neat bit of synchronicity set the tone for the week.

As the other members of the group arrived (there would be fourteen in all), I realized something odd: I had no trouble recalling anyone's name. I'm not usually good with names, but I felt a rapport with these "strangers," some of whom, like Nora and Felippé, had journeyed a great way (Argentina and Spain, respectively) to attend Lifeline. It felt more like a reunion with dear old friends.

This mysterious sense of familiarity extended to the two veteran trainers, John and Carol. John's delightfully puckish humor was immediately apparent, and Carol's smile radiated a welcoming and reassuring warmth. She invited me into the spacious sunlit breakout room for my brief intake interview.

I had wound myself up beforehand wondering what to say, reflecting on my frustrations and fears, blockages and dark premonitions. But Carol's calm, centered demeanor proved contagious. I breathed a sigh of relief. I explained that I felt a little like a clumsy dancer tripping over my own feet.

Carol listened attentively, then she said that one of the aims of Lifeline is to help us uncover and examine our limiting beliefs, those fixed ideas about reality that may be hindering our development and keeping us from a fuller experience of life.

"That sounds like exactly what I need," I acknowledged.

Carol agreed.

Reset, Revisit, and Release

The first program exercises were given over to what in TMI parlance is called "resetting," or getting reacquainted with the various Focus Levels of consciousness to which we were introduced during our Gateway Voyage. According to brain-wave researchers, it's like riding a bicycle; once you learn, you never forget. Similarly, once the brain-mind has been educated on how to achieve the various altered states with the Hemi-Sync process, the pattern has been set. It's merely a matter of reinforcing the habit.

So our initial shakedown cruise in the CHEC unit was for resetting Focus 10 (the state of mind awake and alert/body asleep). I was delighted at how easily I entered the Focus Levels without "clicking out" or falling asleep. I saw several successive bursts of bright white light, like camera flashes. Then I glimpsed a mysterious figure in a hooded robe. He was wielding an axe, though I could not make out what he was cutting or chopping. I also felt a familiar discomfort: an annoying cramping sensation in my right leg (either my physical leg, or my nonphysical, energy-body leg—I couldn't tell which).

I had first noticed this puzzling cramp during my Gateway the previous year. I had asked Sharon, the massage therapist, whether she had any thoughts as to its origin.

"Hmmm," she mused. "Maybe you don't want to 'put your right foot forward'?"

In other words, I was resisting change. Which made sense. I remembered all those driving or flying dreams when I slammed on the brakes.

"You know," Sharon added, "you might experience some imagery when I work on that part of your body."

I did, in fact, have a brief impression of a dark place, like a cave, when she massaged my right leg. But the image faded quickly. I didn't make any sense of it.

Experiencing the leg cramp again, I resolved to ask about it in a future exercise. Perhaps I would get (or be ready to receive) a clearer answer.

The next morning at breakfast, I was seated next to John, one of the trainers. I was lost in my own thoughts when I over-heard him mentioning a strange figure wearing a hooded monk's robe. I recalled the robed monk I'd glimpsed in my meditation. I'd assumed this was only a symbol of "cutting myself off" from daily concerns. It just seemed too hokey to be anything else—as if it had come straight out of "spirit-guide" central casting.

"Wow, I saw him yesterday, too, during the Focus 10 reset!" I said eagerly.

"Ah, good, you know Zoltar, then," John said, grinning broadly.

"Zoltar? He has a name?"

It turned out that "Zoltar" was some character from a comic book or movie. At first I felt embarrassed at having missed the joke. But then I realized, joke or not, it was at least a funny coincidence. (John thought I was joking, too, until I told him of my vision.)

Later that morning we did a tape exercise that enabled us to work with healing energies. At one point we were encouraged to visualize our "Energy Bar Tool" (EBT), a mental device for focusing and accessing these energies. But every time I tried to imagine a glowing bar-shaped rod, as the tape instructions suggested, the bar would resolve itself into the shape of an hourglass resting on its side. In the narrow center of the hourglass, where the two ends met, was a glowing sphere. A sparkling energy-fluid, like twinkling stars in molten crystal, flowed from one end of the hourglass to the other, through the central sphere. It was beautiful, but strange. The EBT seemed to possess a mind of its own.

In the next exercise, a reset of Focus 12 (the state of expanded awareness), I decided to ask about my leg cramps, which were still bothering me on and off. I found myself in the darkest darkness. Slowly, I realized that I was inside a cave. I knew this was the same cave I'd briefly glimpsed during my massage the year before at the Gateway Voyage. The darkness now seemed to be pierced by a nearby light source—a torch, perhaps—and I could make out certain figures painted on the walls. Giraffes and other large animals. The pictures resembled the paintings discovered in Paleolithic caves.

My attention was drawn to the source of illumination. It turned out to be an illuminated globe, a glowing ball of yellow-white light. It had suddenly appeared out of nowhere, hovering in the midst of a band of humanoids, clearly startling them out of their wits. They were definitely not *Homo sapiens*. They were hairier, more apelike. The ape-people were grunting and pointing at the globe as they backed away in fear. I felt sorry for these poor, frightened creatures, yet I also felt a deep sense of kinship with one particular member of this timid group. Strangely, I identified with the pulsating globe of which they were all so afraid and which seemed to radiate compassion and wisdom.

I knew why this glowing sphere seemed familiar. It was the same light source that transected the sideways energy hourglass in the earlier exercise, when I couldn't get the energy bar tool (EBT) to do what I wanted it to.

But what did all this have to do with my leg cramp? Here I was still in the dark.

Next came the reset of Focus 15, the state of "no time." As usual, I experienced 15 as floating in thick darkness, a quiet muffled stillness. Then I found myself hovering above a wooded grove in wintertime, watching through bare branches as a group of people silently trudged through a clearing. I knew that they had just come from church, where the funeral service for the husband of the woman at the front of the group had been held. I felt her grief. Then I heard the word "Hon," whispered in my ear. It was my wife's voice. I was her husband, the man who had died. I was watching my own funeral. I felt guilty for leaving her. But she would get over it.

Afterwards I wondered whether this was truly a "past life." It had felt unusually vivid. The emotions were real and it certainly had a psychological validity. But was it only a symbol of the guilt I felt over leaving Cynthia for a week to come to Virginia? Or had my feelings in the present opened up a "time corridor" to another past existence in which I had experienced similar emotions? After all, if sensitives like Jane Roberts and Joe McMoneagle are right and all time is simultaneous, we should expect what Jane called "bleedthroughs" from what we regard as past to future—and from future to past. So was my ability to work through my guilt in this life helping that husband to work through his? The circumstantial details of the funeral scene were at least provocative. In this life, I don't attend church because I'm not a Christian. Nor does Cynthia ever call me "Hon."

I tried to tell myself that the scene had its own meaning, even if its factual truth couldn't be verified. (Details of names, dates, and place of death came later. I have yet to try and verify them, however.) Yet I couldn't trust my own perceptions.

Janet Stuns Me at Dinner

That night at dinner I found myself sitting opposite Janet. Soft-spoken but warm and friendly, she was easy to talk to. She reminded me of everyone's ideal aunt, or a kindly schoolteacher—hardly metaphysical. I could see her making you sit down for tea and cookies as soon as you walked through her front door. But Janet was a Reiki practitioner and a veteran out-of-body explorer who enjoyed surprising her son with her "unorthodox" visits to his home in faraway Japan.

Janet and I were chatting when her gaze took on a sparkle of intensity. She appeared to be looking over my right shoulder.

"Do you mind if I ask you a question?" Janet asked.

"No, not at all," I replied.

"Do you have any special relationship to American Indians?"

"Do I!" I cried. "Lately it seems I can't get interested in reading anything unless it's about Indians." However, I neglected to mention my many other experiences (synchronicities, dreams, and visions) involving Indians. Or the Indian "guide" I occasionally sensed hovering about me in my meditations. I wasn't sure I believed it myself. It all sounded too hokey—too New Agey—even to my ears.

"That makes sense," Janet stated matter-of-factly. "Because you have a guide figure, an Indian. He's standing right there"—indicating with a nod of her head the spot over my right shoulder where she'd been staring just a few moments before—"and he's wearing one of those chest plates. He's thin, forty-ish, and rather somber looking."

I was amazed. After dinner I showed Janet the Plains-style beaded Indian necklace I'd brought with me to the workshop as a kind of lucky charm. Janet was not surprised. I, on the other hand, was still in shock.

My limiting beliefs were wearing thin, showing signs of shriveling and cracking.

Then, in a valiant effort to preserve the status quo, my defenses stepped in. After all, I reasoned, perhaps Janet was "just" picking up telepathically on my obsession with Indians. (This is called Occam's Razor, the principle of method that says we should prefer the simpler explanation. A "lesser miracle"—like a medium reading the minds of the living—is even preferable to a "greater" one, such as the survival of bodily death.)

But was this really the simpler explanation? If Janet was "only" telepathic, she had to search through all my mental "files" for that one special bit of information. She also had to know how emotionally significant that datum might be for me—a brilliant act of psychological insight. And all of this had to be processed instantaneously, of course, on an unconscious level. A feat of supermental gymnastics in its own right.

As William James advised, we must not prematurely "close our accounts with reality." I was not ready to say what or who this Indian "guide" was. Maybe he was an aspect of my own larger multidimensional self, an entity whose outlines we can barely glimpse, or even imagine, and which challenges all our current concepts of human personality. Or maybe he was what he seemed, an independent entity—a friend.

Whatever he was, he was real, and I had perceived him. I could no longer dismiss my own experiences simply because they were mine.

Ari's Wall and Carol's Fountain

As the workshop got into high gear, we began our exploration of the Focus Levels associated with Lifeline work. These included Focus 23 (the area where the disoriented deceased and personality fragments are trapped), Focus 24–26 (the so-called Belief System Territories where the very religious and others with definite afterlife expectations tend to congregate), and Focus 27 (the area Monroe called the Park or Reception Center).

John and Carol emphasized that our goal was the exploration of vast new inner territories, not necessarily a retrieval of "lost souls" or missing parts of ourselves. They encouraged us to suspend our expectations and allow events to unfold in their own way in the moment. There would be plenty of opportunity later for analysis.

In an early excursion into Focus 23, I beheld a giant crystal sunflower. I felt myself pulled through the center of its head, which became a translucent tunnel. As I hurtled through the tunnel, I could make out faces looking in at me. Then a voice said, "You're helping just by being here." Next came a loud series of "thumps," like the sounds an airplane makes when encountering turbulence. Several times I got all choked up, though I could not say why. At one point I gasped. Then I arrived in a place filled with a dense grey mist, like foggy London in an old Sherlock Holmes movie.

In one of my first forays into the Belief System Territories (of Focus 24, 25, and 26), I felt myself opening a door. I sensed a vastness inside. I seemed to fly over adobe-like structures in an area that looked vaguely Southwestern. I sensed the hive-like activity of enormous, bizarre machines whizzing past me overhead like airplanes stacking up over an airport. Later I realized this was my symbolic way of perceiving those consciousness clusters that were so tightly ensnared in a rigid belief system— say, a religion—that they were trapped inside a lifeless mechanism that perpetually circled its real destination.

Could this be my fate? Was I so attached to certain beliefs that I would prefer the predictable (if decidedly claustrophobic) comfort of an insular illusion to an experience of an unknown reality?

Luckily, I wasn't the only one wrestling with such thoughts. Ari and his wife, Sara, were speech and feeding therapists from Brooklyn, New York, who did emotionally demanding early intervention work with babies born prematurely or with birth defects (such as cleft lip or palate), who had difficulties vocalizing, chewing, or swallowing. Ari had previously owned a successful computer consulting business, with most of his clientele coming from a list of top Wall Street investment firms and prominent banks. But one day he decided he'd "had enough of machines and wanted to work with people instead"—and also with healing energies of a more subtle kind. That's what originally brought him to The Monroe Institute, years before, to the Gateway program, and now, once again, on his (and Sara's) return trip.

This time around, however, Ari appeared to be running into obstacles in his meditations—though he didn't claim to view them that way. At least, not at first. Oddly, Ari's experiences never matched other people's reports of the Focus Levels. It was as if the rest of us had gone off to enjoy a cool swim in the lake, and Ari would come back complaining about how hot and dry it had been in the desert. Such discrepancies only seemed to amuse Ari, a born iconoclast. Then came the wall.

The wall was a mysterious structure that Ari kept bumping into as he journeyed into the higher Focus Levels. At our debriefings, he would describe his puzzlement at this turn of events. He didn't describe the wall itself, only its effect on him, and the questions he felt obliged to ask. Was it a barrier keeping him from going further? Was it a symbol of an inner blockage? Had he "hit the wall" of his own beliefs?

On an early journey to Focus 27 (the Park) I stopped off in Focus 26, one of the Belief System Territories. There I hovered above a stone building. At first I was disoriented, thinking I was viewing a vertical wall from an odd angle. Then I realized that the wall itself was angled. It belonged to a pyramid-like structure. Etched into the face of the wall were intricate, serpentine designs. Perhaps they were hieroglyphics. Their vibrant reddish color stood out against the sandy patina of the stone.

That's Ari's wall. I just "knew" this.

Following the exercise, we assembled in the carpeted breakout room for our debriefing.

"Hey, Ari, I think I saw your wall!" I excitedly announced as we all took our seats. Then I described what I had seen.

"That's it," Ari replied, his usual nonchalance offset by an impish grin.

Ari had had another encounter with his wall, but this time he discovered the wall was not an obstruction. Rather, it was a mystery he was meant to ponder. It would enhance his explorations.

I don't know if my momentary "presence" at Ari's wall had anything to do with his breakthrough. I do know that getting that confirmation from him bolstered my self-confidence. We had somehow shared this experience, and that may be as "real" as reality gets. Several people commented on the strong, if unspoken, link between the two of us. We even found ourselves wearing identical T-shirts one morning.

In a later trip to Focus 27, I arrived at the Park. Not perceiving much, I decided to let my imagination run wild. So I imagined myself standing near a bubbling water fountain surrounded by a circular stone walkway. All along the walkway were stone benches. In between the benches various paths radiated outward to different sections of the Park. It was a pleasant, peaceful little scene I'd managed to conjure up. I even sensed the presence of my Indian "guide."

During the breakout session, Carol happened to mention that she had participated in this exercise (which was not always the case). She reported that she'd gone to her own "special place" in Focus 27—a fountain.

I showed Carol the sketch I'd made of the fountain from my trip to the Park. "Yes, that's it, that's my fountain," she stated matter-of-factly. "I didn't see you there. But I was standing on the hill on the far side."

After this episode, I felt comfortable enough to ask her a question. "Do you think that Bob Monroe still 'visits' here on occasion? I know there are those who were close to him who are deeply skeptical of this notion." I told her about my dream in which I attended Monroe's lecture, and also of my humorous encounter with "Angel Bob."

"Funny you should ask," Carol replied. She explained that she had just finished writing an article in which she mentioned sensing Monroe's presence during a Gateway Outreach workshop she had recently given in Spain. Carol sensed things had changed.

In 1995, shortly after Bob's passing, Carol had a dream in which she saw Bob standing at the far end of a crowded bar. Excited to see her old friend and mentor, she made her way through the throng to greet him. Bob was pleased to see Carol, but after briefly acknowledging her, he shooed her away, explaining that he was far too busy to chat. He had to learn how to sing opera.

Carol laughed as she recalled this odd exchange. "I think this was Bob's way of contacting me," she said. She suggested their meeting was more than a "mere" dream, that it was Bob's spirit communicating with her. "Yet at the same time," she said, "he was letting me know that his focus was elsewhere, on new challenges." (Hence Bob's strange remark about studying opera.) Carol had the impression the situation had changed since her dream, however, and that Bob—or at least some portion of his nonphysical personality—was taking a more active interest in earthly affairs. His recent surprise "appearance" during her workshop in Spain had confirmed her impression.

"You know," she added, "this project [i.e., TMI] was pretty important to him."

As Carol went for a cup of tea, I recalled an incident that had slipped my mind. It was a dream in which I had glimpsed a funny-looking figure standing near a doorway, surrounded by admirers. As I approached this figure, I realized he was wearing a clown outfit—a white robe with oversized buttons, and big floppy shoes. He didn't say anything to me, but he looked familiar. Then I realized it was none other than Bob Monroe. What a silly dream, I'd thought afterwards.

Now, as I stood in what had been Bob Monroe's kitchen, it was as if I'd been struck by the proverbial thunderbolt out of the blue.

"*I, Pagliacci!*" I cried out, laughing. The opera with clowns!

Was this the confirmation "Angel Bob" had promised me at Gateway last year? It was difficult to ignore the evidence. Carol's and my dream had occurred years apart. We were strangers to each other then. I didn't even know why I'd brought up the subject with her to begin with, yet it all fit neatly together, like the last two pieces of a jigsaw puzzle.

Only who—or what—was the clever puzzle master?

Metaphysical Cross-Dressing (and Other Feelings of Inadequacy)

After my conversation with Carol, I mused about how easily we are seduced into believing that our "wispy" dreams are no more substantial than the effervescence of club soda. Or how reassuring it is to suppose that, even if nonphysical realms exist, only the "Ascended Masters" or the wise gurus have access to them. That way, we can avoid the tough questions and our own responsibility in creating our experience of reality.

Alas, if only it were so. But it is not.

This was brought home by a little experiment undertaken by Geoff, a member of our Lifeline crew. Geoff decided to see if he could communicate with Ann, another member of the group, during one of our excursions to Focus 27. So, without her prior knowledge, he decided to attempt to deliver a message to her while they were both There.

When the exercise was over, we met in the breakout room. Ann reported receiving Geoff's message, only she perceived it as coming from a trusted inner guide of long acquaintance—a beautiful woman in a blue dress.

Geoff's face turned red. We all had a good laugh at his expense.

Still, I think we all recognized that while the experiment had succeeded, it raised more questions than it answered—at least if you were open-minded about it. For it was tempting to conclude that Ann was more comfortable with the message coming from a trusted source, so she saw Geoff as her guide. But what if it was more complicated than that?

Perhaps, unbeknownst to Geoff, he is, at another level of reality, only one aspect of a nonphysical entity (Bob Monroe's I-There, or Jane Roberts's Source Self), another of whose personalities is Ann's Woman in the Blue Dress. It could be that Ann's perception is just as true as Geoff's. Maybe, in a sense, he is Ann's guide and just doesn't know it.

Physicists admit that light can be perceived as particles and continuous waves, depending on how it is measured. Philosophers like Hegel speak of grand "dialectical syntheses" of opposites. In truth, however, in our daily lives we all act as if such paradoxes, while interesting in theory, can safely be ignored in practice. The idea that we are simultaneously creating *and* discovering reality all the time is something we'd prefer to ignore. It's easier to abide by the old either/or dualisms—true or false, subjective or objective, imaginary or real, one or many. Remote viewer Joe McMoneagle says, "Through the tools of perception and cognition, we mold and shape our concept of reality and make reality what it is." Joe admits that for some people, "This is a scary concept."[5]

Scary? Try petrifying.

How can we overcome, or at least learn to control, this paralyzing fear?

John, one of our Lifeline trainers, suggested that we view fear as the emotional expression of an underlying "belief in our own inadequacy to deal with something (whatever that may be)." This formula offers hope; beliefs, after all, can change, and can be changed—if one is willing to listen to the voice of experience. The only way to challenge such a belief is to confront it head-on. You have to know that you can deal with it (whatever "it" is) after all. Even (or especially) if "it" happens to be expanding your concepts of reality and self.

Golden Retrievals

Even as I was enjoying some newfound flexibility in my consciousness muscles, I was still skeptical about the retrieval process. Others were reporting dramatic rescues, complete with names, dates, causes of death, and the like. Joan had recounted an emotional reunion with her recently deceased husband that choked us all up. Nora was gifted with a revelation about her older brother and his role in her life. (She had always felt inadequate next to him, but now she realized that he was only mirroring her own potential. What she had envied in him, she, in fact, was.) I was getting only tantalizing fragments.

Then we did another exercise in Focus 27. Although I did not experience being in the Park, I saw a little boy. He had dark hair and was perhaps five years old or so (I'm a notoriously bad judge of age). I asked him his name.

"It's Bobby," he replied. Bobby told me that he had died of leukemia.

After the exercise, Ann reported that she had rescued an eight-year-old Mexican boy in Focus 23 and brought him up to the Reception Center in Focus 27. The boy's name was Roberto, and he told Ann that he had died of leukemia.

Was Ann's Roberto my Bobby? I began to feel more confident.

In my next trip to Focus 27, I requested guidance. I felt the reassuring presence of my Indian friend (he refused to give me a name). Together we floated downward into the grey fog of Focus 23. There I had an idea. I imagined the two of us bathed in a cocoon of brilliant white light. Suddenly, like moths attracted to a flame, several figures emerged out of the mist and slowly, tentatively, moved toward us. I asked if anyone wished to accompany us to a better place. They all said yes! Now I just had to figure out how to get them there. Instantly, our cocoon of light began to swell to the size of a huge hot air balloon, surrounding the group. Then the Indian transformed himself into a great eagle. I grabbed its tail and it flew us up to Focus 27. Once safely inside the Park, a woman in her twenties thanked me. She told me her name was Celia. As the Indian led the group in the direction of the Reception Center, I asked him how I did, but all he did was look over his shoulder at me without comment.

The next morning we did a tape called "Vibe Flow." Following the preliminary relaxation exercises, I found myself floating in a black velvety void. Above me, I sensed a bright disk or sphere that was sending down rays of white light. Off in the distance, I saw an object that looked like a giant Ferris wheel. I recognized this as the symbolic "wheel of time" that I often glimpse when I visit Focus 15. (Although Bob Monroe called Focus 15 the state of "No-Time," it is a condition in which all times—past, present, and future—typically become available for exploration.)

Then the wheel of time was beneath me, resting flat on one side, like a roulette wheel, and I stood on its surface, near the center. Extending outward from the far edge of one of the wheel's spokes, out into the darkness, was a walkway. I made my way from the center of the wheel onto this walkway and kept going to the far end, where I stopped in front of a closed door colored like an abalone shell.

"What is this door?" I asked.

A voice replied, "This is the door to your heart."

I opened the door and walked through. In front and above me was an enormous pink rose. Soft, warm, healing pink light streamed down from the rose onto me. I was flooded with a bittersweet mix of joy and grief. Then, in the center of the room, I saw, or sensed, a crystal sphere set high up off the floor, like a diamond, by semicircular supports. The crystal pulsed on and off, alternating white and blue light. I recognized familiar faces of deceased relatives all around me. My mother was there, as were my aunt and my grandmother. I felt myself hoisted up, by a thousand hands, then placed inside a chalice. The hands raised the chalice up to the pulsating crystal, as if making a toast. Ribbons of love extended upward, from them to me, and downward, from me to them. Finally, I was given some personal information about my destiny, and also about our group.

Later, when I recounted this experience to the group, I felt the afterglow of that love and acceptance. I'll never forget that feeling. I was finding my boundaries—and moving beyond them, at last.

Moment of Revelation

Then came one of our final exercises. It was a tape with the momentous title of "Moment of Revelation." Oh, no, I moaned as the trainers introduced the tape. Talk about pressure! What if I don't get a revelation? Then, feeling like a greedy child, I was assaulted by a wave of guilt. After all, how could I expect more?

The tape was well guided. I flowed with the instructions and felt myself moving out, way out, to the edge of the known universe. There, in the blackness of deep space, a scene slowly unfolded. I was in the scene, and also observing it from the outside.

I found myself sitting in a nearly empty auditorium, like an old-fashioned movie house with a big screen or maybe a Broadway theater. A few other people occupied seats. The house lights were dim, and the heavy red velvet drapes that covered the screen or stage were closed. I couldn't tell if the curtain had just closed, or whether the show hadn't yet begun. Were we the first to arrive or the last to leave?

Then the scene faded. That was it. My Big Revelation.

As we moved back under the tape's guidance to normal waking consciousness, I was angry. I felt cheated. But as I sat in my CHEC unit making notes (futile gesture, I grumbled), I realized how dense I'd been. I laughed.

As the Bard said, "All the world's a stage." Now, had the stage show just ended, or was it about to begin? Both—or neither. This is infinity, after all.

In *Ultimate Journey,* Bob Monroe told of traveling to the furthest reaches of inner space, where he received his own revelation of the paradoxical infinite. He expressed it this way:

> *There is no beginning, there is no end,*
> > *There is only change.*
> *There is no teacher, there is no student,*
> > *There is only remembering.*
> *There is no good, there is no evil,*
> > *There is only expression.*
> *There is no union, there is no sharing,*
> > *There is only one.*
> *There is no joy, there is no sadness,*
> > *There is only love.*
> *There is no greater, there is no lesser,*
> > *There is only balance.*
> *There is no stasis, there is no entropy,*
> > *There is only motion.*
> *There is no wakefulness, there is no sleep,*
> > *There is only being.*
> *There is no limit, there is no chance,*
> > *There is only a plan.*

The plan was shown to me by cosmic intelligence in a way I could grasp. After all, how else do you explain infinity to a monkey? You use whatever crude gestures the monkey can understand. And we're the monkeys. The symbol was brilliant, economical, and humorous—a good example of what Bob called Non-Verbal Communication (NVC). And I had almost tossed it away like a useless candy bar wrapper.

Wait a minute, I thought. Why did I just say to myself, "How else do you explain infinity to a monkey?" This reminded me of something. What was it?

Then I remembered: in the cave, when I glimpsed that pulsating sideways hourglass and the ape-people scurrying away in fear. It was one of the first exercises we did at Lifeline. Could my theater image be connected to that? Had I come full circle?

You bet. I realized that the "sideways hourglass" was a familiar shape, after all: It is the lemniscate (from the Greek *lemniskos:* ribbon), the sideways figure eight that is the symbol for infinity. This, by the way, is the very same symbol that the venerable Dr. Zorba would write on the chalkboard during the introduction to each episode of the old *Ben Casey* TV show. Remember the series of symbols? "Man—Woman. Birth—Death. Infinity . . ."

No wonder my mother had seen Ben Casey come for her the night she died. Ben knew. And so did she. And now, at last, so did I.

Epilogue

Aftertime

To the Native people of the Americas, that world of the spirit is as everyday as eating and sleeping.
—Joseph Bruchac, *The Waters Between: A Novel of the Dawn Land* (1998)

Parapsychology is not even a science, but it may be on the route to revelation.
—Eileen Garrett, *Many Voices: The Autobiography of a Medium* (1969)

Fallout

A few days after I returned from the Lifeline workshop, the fall semester began. I was busy with registration and the rush of the first week, when everything is gloriously fresh and chaotic all at once. The faces of students still show nascent signs of interest and lectures are fun to deliver. I was finding the reentry process much smoother this time around. I felt energized, and I looked forward to continuing my inner journeys.

One morning, I woke up feeling unaccountably agitated and

anxious. I hadn't had any bad dreams I could recall, and there was nothing on my schedule that day that might prompt such feelings. So I brought a Hemi-Sync tape with me to work. I figured I'd have time before my 8:00 A.M. class to meditate. That would calm me down.

When I got to my office I put on my headphones and listened to the soothing sounds of the tape. Then I went to class. I did feel much better as I began my lecture. But about three quarters of the way through the hour, I suddenly felt like a punctured tire. There was nothing left. I plopped down on the edge of the desk (which I never do—I'm always pacing or writing on the board as I talk) and glanced at the clock. It was eight-forty—twenty minutes to go. I didn't think I could make it. So I finished up my remarks, and in an uncharacteristic gesture (and to the barely concealed delight of my students), I dismissed the class early. I was feeling worse by the minute as I retreated downstairs to my office. I thought I would just rest for a while and, I hoped, regain my stamina.

It was around 8:45 A.M. on Tuesday, September 11, 2001.

A scant few miles away over the clear Manhattan skies, the first of two airplanes was crashing into the twin towers of the World Trade Center.

Holed up in my office for more than an hour, I had no idea what was going on in the world. I emerged from my room into the busy hallway only to encounter a fellow professor who had just arrived on campus.

"Did you hear?" he asked, his voice trembling. "They attacked the World Trade Center and the Pentagon! We're at war!"

I couldn't absorb his words. They made no sense. I walked upstairs to the department office, where the radio was playing nonstop. So it was true. By this time, clouds of acrid yellow smoke filled the sky. It was from the fire. The towers had collapsed. It felt like a nightmare, unreal. We stood around in a group, half a dozen professors, shaking our heads in disbelief. Someone mentioned Pearl Harbor. We found out that all the tunnels and bridges were closed. The city was locked down. The phone lines were jammed. I couldn't call home and I couldn't get home. We didn't yet know how many people had died. I thought about them—thousands, we already suspected—who had suddenly, shockingly been obliterated. It was overwhelming.

Then it occurred to me: What about our Lifeline group (and all the Lifeliners out there)? Could we—I—do anything to help? At least it was a plan.

I returned to the solitude of my office. I took some deep breaths and tried to enter a meditative state. As I focused my intent on the twin towers, I was met with a hot furnace blast of emotion. I felt like a spinning top swept up in a tornado. I was helpless. Part of the problem, I knew, was my own distress. I couldn't relax. Later on, I realized I was in a mild state of shock. Hot rage had alternated with teary grief and cold, numbing disbelief. It was like riding a roller coaster. I hoped that others had met with more success.

Several days later, I communicated by email with members of our Lifeline group. They all told similar stories. There was just too much shock on both sides at first. But a few had managed to help, and the retrievals were still going on.

In late October, I received a handwritten note from George, one of our group. "Felt your presence at the W.T.C. site," he reported.

Had the strength of my intent enabled me to get through on some level anyway? As Bob Monroe often said, just because you can't remember it doesn't mean it didn't happen. So much, even in our nightly dreams, is beyond our ability to translate into terms the conscious mind can accept or even understand.

Questions Galore

As the initial trauma of the attack wore off, I was hounded by a number of disturbing questions. Was this the "big event" involving many deaths that I had been sensing—and dreading—for months? Could this have been the reason that "by chance" I found myself in Lifeline when I had wanted to take another workshop? Furthermore, how many others out there had experienced similar foreknowings? Were we somehow being prepared, on a collective level, for this horrific episode? Could anything have been done to prevent it had these warnings been taken seriously?

My students were consumed by questions as well. In several classes, there were heated debates about religion, for it was impossible to ignore the critical role that religion had played in the events of September 11. Some students argued that it was a cruel perversion of religion that led the attackers and their sympathizers to claim that they were doing "God's work." (In a bizarre twist, some prominent American religious "leaders" seemed to agree. They stated that God had removed his "protection" from the United States because we allow women to have abortions, don't force children to pray in public school, and recognize the civil rights of gays and lesbians.) But others pointed to the long, bloody, history of religious wars, intolerance, persecutions, and crusades as evidence of religion's complicity. They argued that even if religion was not the sole cause of social conflicts, it seemed impotent in the face of them.

I admitted to my students that the vengeful, egomaniacal "gods" of the fundamentalists always struck me as little more than childish revenge fantasies. If they existed, they would no more be worthy of worship than don Vito Corleone, General Custer, or Genghis Khan. Interesting literary characters, perhaps. Worthy of our (or anyone's) devotion? Not on your life. They're devils.

But the issue goes deeper than fundamentalism, deeper than rival theologies. I know I'll take a lot of heat for saying this, but there is something in *all* the "higher" religions of civilization that lends itself to fanaticism. That "something" is what I have called Answerism: the illusion that one can attain (or has already attained) Absolute Truth, and the consequent tendency to treat certain beliefs and authorities as sacred cows, beyond critical questioning. Answerism is the ultimate weapon of mass destruction, for it is inside us, inflating us with corrosive self-righteousness and immunizing us against deeper self-awareness. There is no greater source of corruption than the conceit that one can explain everything, once and for all.

Answerism is on the wane, but it is not going down without a fight. It is deeply afraid of the future. Like a star that burns brightest before it winks out, we see a resurgent religious fundamentalism, both here in America and abroad. Battle lines are being drawn.

As long ago as 1924, the English philosopher R. G. Collingwood declared that we would have to learn to become content with issuing a series of partial and infinitely revisable "interim reports" about reality. Fortunately, there are a growing number of individuals on the fringes of our religious and spiritual traditions who realize that no answer can ever be final or complete, and that it is the free play of consciousness itself that matters.

Inquiry, sparked by wonder, fired by curiosity, and freed from the arbitrary constraints of stale dogmas, will lead us to develop our own natural sensitivity in creative partnership with our rationality. So we will once again become close and inspired readers of Nature's great book—Eve herself—and the exquisitely intricate patterns of meaning woven therein.

We have no other choice.

Parapsychology en Route

Which is why, in the wake of 9/11, I began to feel more urgently than ever that official parapsychology is on the wrong track. Top psi researchers can still blithely dismiss anecdotal evidence (personal experiences) as not providing data worthy of scientific consideration. Their Holy Grail is proof in the laboratory through controlled experiments. For them, only EHEs that can be objectively measured and quantified are significant.

I have no doubt that useful things can be learned in a laboratory. I'm not against research or technical precision or technology. But if we continue to defer to Scientific Authority and its dictates, we will not learn to trust the data provided by our own experiences. Nor will we learn how to interpret that data, which is couched in the (to us) still arcane languages of Non-Verbal Communication (NVC). We will remain fledgling birds waiting anxiously in the nest with open beaks to be fed the sacred worms of Knowledge. In the meantime, we may starve to death.

I couldn't help wondering: What if everyone who had fore-knowledge of the September 11 events had trusted their perceptions and shared them with like-minded individuals? How many of us were there? Hundreds? Thousands? Tens of thousands? Millions, perhaps? Who knows? I refuse to believe that I am that unusual or special. Nor can I help speculating that if a mass network of people who knew how to spot and report an interesting psychic anecdote existed, those awful events might have been preventable.

Not having enough faith in ourselves may well be the ultimate intelligence failure.

Could this faith be what all the world "authorities"—political, religious, cultural, and social elites—are afraid of? What if democracy is only in its earliest infancy? The greatest revolutions in human history may lie ahead, as we embrace and nurture the evolution of our natural sensitivity.

"Being psychic is simply being more sensitive to the sea around us," writes Joe McMoneagle. "It's simply a method that allows for [an] additional sense of being."[1]

We all must learn how to swim in this sea of information and surf the waves of possibilities. Can it be done? Yes, it can. We are all natural sensitives. It is just a matter of recognizing and developing our abilities.

The philosopher Paul Feyerabend was suspicious of the privileged status that official science occupies in our culture. He insisted that "Laymen can and must supervise Science." He added that "it would not only be foolish *but downright irresponsible* to accept the judgment of scientists . . . without further examination"[2] (Feyerabend's italics). We must do even more. In effect, we must do an end run around official science and religion alike (and all the other officials). Science and religion have not lived up to their own principles. Both have allowed attachment to dogma (materialist metaphysics, statistical analysis) to dampen the spirit of scientific inquiry, which is unafraid to follow truth wherever it may lead. We must hold the feet of science to the fire of its own inner truth—whatever the cost.

As far back as 1972, the maverick psi researcher and transpersonal psychologist Dr. Charles Tart proposed a revolutionary "state-specific science of consciousness."[3] He asked his fellow scientists to relinquish their taboos against subjective self-reporting and anecdotal evidence. He invited his peers to enter into non-ordinary states of consciousness and study them from the inside, by experiencing them, instead of just observing events from the outside and quantifying the results.

These trained psychic explorers of inner space would then reflect on their experiences and compare notes to test the hypothesis that altered states of consciousness (Focus Levels) might yield insights into the existence of nonphysical realms. The lust for statistical proof would be replaced (or at least supplemented) with the exciting challenges of firsthand exploration.

With a few exceptions, Dr. Tart's proposal was not warmly received (at least on the official level) by his fellow scientists.[4] This, despite the fact that Dr. Tart had achieved widespread (if grudging) respect for his meticulous research and theoretical work. His colleagues were reluctant to modify or even suspend their assumptions—at least they didn't want to be seen doing so in public. If indeed they had had their own EHEs, most were reluctant to say so openly. They might go so far as to admit that an early anomalous experience in childhood (a dream, vision, or out-of-body episode) initially sparked their investigations. But they would not take the next logical step of making such inner experiences (and themselves) the focus of their inquiries. Unlike, say, archaeologist J. Norman Emerson, they could not bring themselves directly into their work. That would be "unscientific."

As my friend Steven Rosen notes, in parapsychology reason and intuition may be unified in theory, but in actual practice, they remain separate and far apart.[5]

I no longer believe we can afford to wait for these timid scientists to develop the backbone they need in order to break ranks with the most conservative elements of their own tradition. We must take matters into our own hands (and psyches). We laypersons must launch our own expeditions to the forbidden planets of consciousness.

Further Explorations

In the flurry of emails exchanged in the wake of September 11, I reestablished contact with Gina, one of my fellow Lifeliners. It was Gina who first suggested that we do some "partnered exploring" sessions. We would meditate on the same day and time, and attempt to "meet up" in the Focus Levels. Afterward, we would report our results (before reading our partner's report, of course) and compare notes via email.

I jumped at the chance—how could I not? I told Gina it was a great idea.

Sometimes our results were mystifying. It was almost as if Gina had taken a slow train to Boston and I'd hopped a red-eye to Chicago. But other times—well, listen to this:

During one session my tape player malfunctioned just as I was easing into Focus 10. Cursing and fumbling in the dark, I changed the batteries and began again. I was sure I wouldn't be able to relax. But no sooner had I closed my eyes than I received a vivid impression of a very thin woman with closely cropped dark hair. She looked distressed or confused. She also looked familiar. As for the rest of the session, it was fairly unremarkable. I must have "clicked out" because it seemed as if no time had passed before I was receiving the signal to return back to C1 (the state of normal waking consciousness).

I realized why the woman I'd glimpsed looked familiar: She reminded me of Kim Hunter, the actress. I remembered her playing the female ape-scientist opposite Roddy McDowell and Charlton Heston in *The Planet of the Apes*. I wondered why I'd thought of her? But it was such a minor thing. I hadn't yet told Gina that I'd struck out. No matter, I'd email her the next day.

On the way to work the next morning, I tuned the car radio

to the news and traffic report, and something caught my attention. Kim Hunter had died the previous day.

I couldn't believe what I was hearing.

When I arrived at my office, I turned on the computer and hurriedly dashed off an email to Gina. Later that same morning I received this reply:

> It is VERY interesting that you should mention Kim Hunter. One of the technicians here that works for me also moonlights as an actress in local theatre. She knew Kim Hunter from her New York theatre group. Doris (the tech) said, "Yesterday she [Kim Hunter] was on my mind and I [felt] I should write her a little note to say hello." This morning Doris got the news that she had passed. I said to Doris, funny that you should mention it to me, she MAY BE LOST [in Focus 23]. I told Doris that I would do a meditation at lunchtime to make sure she gets to the Reception Center [in Focus 27]. I also told Doris that she must have been very afraid when she passed, usually it's the fear that keep[s] a person wandering around in the "fog" [of Focus 23].

Sure enough, Gina went into meditation and found "a very frightened Kim" wandering around in the grey mist that many people experience as Focus 23. Gina moved Kim to the Reception Center in Focus 27 (the Park) where she was met by what Gina described as "a lively group of friends and family." She said that Kim appeared "very happy and expressed her thanks over and over."

Where will these new explorations lead? It is to be hoped to the yonder edge of further "boggle thresholds"—and far beyond.

Eve's Way: Paradise Renamed

Michael Grosso refers to anomalous experiences (EHEs) as "soulmaking" experiences because they enable us to know ourselves more deeply and to become ourselves more completely.

Living out of our EHEs means following our curiosity and not taming the wild impulse to question what we have been told. We must be courageous and irreverent—just like Mother Eve. We must listen to the forbidden voices of our inner selves and learn to trust our imagination, intuition, and creative inspiration. Becoming and remaining sensitive to the invisible bonds that link all forms of life, physical and nonphysical, is the one true aim of those who would live out of their EHEs.

Pioneering psychic explorers like Eileen Garrett,[6] Jane Roberts, and Bob Monroe have shown us that it is possible to develop our sensitivity without abandoning critical reason, and without falling back on shopworn dogmas.

Can we follow their brave lead?

What new theories of reality and self may come if we follow their example? What new philosophies will be born if we celebrate Eve as our hero instead of condemning her as our chief villain?

Many of the thoughtful sensitives and sensitive thinkers mentioned in this book have already provided important pieces of the puzzle. Carl Jung thought it likely that all the pieces would not be in place for at least another few hundred years. Perhaps he was right.

Yet we already know what the new views will *not* say.

They will not say that nature (and our own nature) is evil or sinful or fallen. They will not assume that the divine is apart from nature. (Indeed, any god who claims to be separate from nature is suffering from dissociative disorder, *Theologicus Ridiculous,* and is urged to seek immediate treatment.) They will not abhor the physical body or the feminine.

These new philosophies will not assume that life is a series of accidents. They will not dismiss cosmic meaning as a bad joke, a trick of perception, or the result of intellectual dishonesty or moral cowardice.

Nor will they hold that our individuality is an illusion or curse. Our uniqueness and our freedom will not be despised as burdens best surrendered to other humans, or as unwanted gifts returned, with a sigh of relief, to the cosmic All-Giver. They will not long for escape from the cruel karmic "wheel of rebirth." The left-brained rational ego will not be something to be "burned off" like a useless ugly wart but, rather, will be used as a booster rocket ignited by the fuel of EHEs into a creative expansion and cooperation with other, previously hidden and denied aspects of a larger selfhood.

These greater realities will be seen as intersecting and inter-penetrating even the most "mundane" moments and activities of everyday life, as well as the Earth on which we walk and the cells of our bodies.

In other words, whatever these new philosophies will be, they will be unlike all our conventional theories, religious or sci-entific, Western or Eastern.

Ironically, some of our best guides to the future are peoples we previously disparaged and discarded in the past: the native tribes of our American continent. As the Abenaki writer Joseph Bruchac observes, to these indigenous peoples the "world of the spirit is as everyday as eating and sleeping . . . It is a given. A gift like the gift of breath, which still remains the greatest mystery."[7] We should be grateful for this gift. We must accept it, humbly and sincerely, as the American Indians did.

We can't all be Indians, says the Sioux philosopher Vine Deloria Jr. in his famous manifesto, *God Is Red.* However, he adds, we can and must learn to think indigenously—if we hope to survive. What would this mean in practice?

According to Deloria, "It was not what [Indian] people believed to be true that was important but what they experi-enced as true."[8] The major world religions, he says, stress the adoption of fixed beliefs and practices: a universal gospel of sal-vation or enlightenment expressed in general formulas. The Indians' spiritual sensibility did not rest on such abstract notions, but was shaped by their particular (and changing) envi-ronment and their immediate relationship to the living family of consciousnesses that inhabited the world around them.

"Hence," concludes Deloria, for the Indian, "revelation was seen as a continuous process of adjustment to the natural sur-roundings and not as a specific message valid for all times and places."[9] The spirituality of the Indians was thus always a work in progress, an ongoing process of inquiry, and not a finished product.

In his essay on "Vision and Community," Deloria picks up on this theme of the pragmatic and questioning nature of the Indian spiritual way. He takes the established religious traditions to task for what I have called their Answerism. Not only do the great religions ask philosophical questions about the meaning, value, and ultimate purpose of human life; they grandiosely claim "to provide answers to these questions knowing full well that both questions and answers must come from honest and open participation in the world."[10]

In other words, the only thoughts worth thinking are those that arise out of contemplating our personal experience of the magic of nature's invisible bonds. According to the philosopher Schopenhauer, a thought not based in our individual experience and reasoning is like wearing a silly wax nose.[11] Lacking any organic relationship to the person's mind, it is only a put-on.

Thus what the Native Americans have to teach us is not undermined by their dwindling numbers, or even by the sad, violent history that the dominant society has foisted upon them. Their living legacy of a highly inquisitive and adaptable spiritual consciousness must be acknowledged and permitted to penetrate and color our awareness.

"Tribal religions do not claim to have answers to the larger questions of human life," writes Deloria. "But they do know various ways of asking the questions and this is their great strength and why they will ultimately have great influence in people's lives."[12]

By sowing the seeds of our philosophical reflections in the fertile soil of our psychic sensitivity, sympathy, or whatever one wishes to call this natural magic, we are making our way back to paradise—the inward source of truth. That has been the central argument of this book.

As we have seen, paradise is not a place or destination, but a "dialectical" way of being in the world. This just means that we hold a continuing conversation with reality in which the questions we ask invite "answers" in the form of exceptional experiences, experiences that in turn provoke further questions, and so on, in a never-ending, perhaps infinite, process of self-discovery and healing.

This is not merely a personal healing, however, as I have tried to show through my own example, but a reconciliation with others—indeed, with what the Sioux Indians call "all our relations" *(mitakuyé oyasin)*. These "others" include animals, plants, nonphysical teachers and friends, ancestors, family, our own past, and even the consciousness of planet Earth herself.

In order to accomplish this project of reconciliation, I have argued, we must triumph over our own individual fears, as well as overcome the obstacles in our beliefs that have been placed there, like clogged filters obstructing our perceptions, by the scientific, religious, and philosophical authorities of our culture. Not to mention the political, economic, and social elites who benefit from maintaining the ideological status quo.

Thus one of the key implications of my argument is that the cultivation of psychic sensibility is inextricably linked to a truly egalitarian democracy of spirit. I have suggested that the politics of the psychic, and of all exceptional human experience, cannot be overlooked or minimized if we wish to understand and transcend both the internal and external barriers to our further development and growth. Power is a concept that students of the psychic will have to take far more seriously in the future.

My quest has taken me very far afield from where I once expected to be. There have been many unexpected twists and turns, reversals and epiphanies, sorrows and joys, along the way. Yet this path has also led me to repair a relationship, broken off early in my childhood, to natural sources of wonder, wisdom, beauty, and truth both (and at once) inner and outer. I still have so many unanswered questions, and still hope to have so many more new experiences. But this is as it should be.

For many years, in many quarters, there has been a longing for, an eager anticipation of, a new world religion that would somehow overcome the defects and shortcomings of all the old myths and solve all our problems for us, once and for all.

What I have tried to show in this book is that the new religion—the new worldview—will be each individual's open-ended inquiry into their own experience of the great mystery, in gratitude and wonder, with no strings attached. When we embrace this quest, we make the future here and now.

We must not sit idly by and passively wait for the world to be remade for us. Such bright utopian hopes so easily fade into dark apocalyptic visions when disappointed (as history tells us they must). We cannot be rescued from ourselves.

Only when we elect to accept our personal responsibility and our innate psychic powers do we begin to make ourselves whole. Then we can trace the roots of our understanding to the magic of our lives, and to the magical life of the world.

That will truly be paradise.

Coda

It's springtime in Maine. We're at the lake again. The snow banks are beating a hasty retreat into the woods, and the thick crust of ice is melting off the surface of the lake. The air is perfumed with the sweet scent of decaying pine needles—Mother Nature's aromatherapy, free for the inhaling. I feel it in the air: Summer will be here in no time.

It's too soon yet to put up the hummingbird feeder. But it's not too early to think about what I might say to my old hummingbird teacher, if we should ever meet again.

Thank you. I am learning. I'll pass it on.

Endnotes

Prologue

1. See chapter 26 of Robert Graves's weird but wonderful work, *The White Goddess* (New York: Farrar, Straus and Giroux, 1966). The title of that chapter, by the way, is "Return of the Goddess." For my own earlier take on the return of the Goddess theme, see my essay, "From Darkness to Light: A Philosophical Musing on the Hanukkah Myth, the Return of the Goddess, and the End of Religion," in *Mythosphere* 1:4 (1999), pp. 463–506.

2. Albert Camus, *The Myth of Sisyphus: And Other Essays*, trans. Justin O'Brien (New York: Knopf, 1955), p. 37.

3. J. G. Frazer, *The Golden Bough: The Roots of Folklore and Religion* (New York: Avenel Books, 1981), p. 12.

4. Lewis Spence, *An Encyclopedia of Occultism* (New Hyde Park, N.Y.: University Books, 1960), p. 260.

5. Joseph Campbell with Bill Moyers, *The Power of Myth* (New York: Doubleday, 1988), p. 29.

6. Thomas Carlyle, *On Heroes, Hero-Worship and the Heroic in History*, ed. Carl Niemeyer (Lincoln: University of Nebraska Press, 1966), p. 54.

7. Joseph Campbell with Bill Moyers, *The Power of Myth* (New York: Doubleday, 1988), p. 71.

8. Willis Harman and Howard Rheingold, *Higher Creativity: Liberating the Unconscious for Breakthrough Insights* (Los Angeles: J. P. Tarcher, 1984), p. 76.

Chapter I

1. Bertrand Russell, "The Expanding Mental Universe," in Bertrand Russell, *Basic Writings: 1903–1959*, ed. Robert E. Egner and Lester E. Denonn (New York: Simon and Schuster, 1961), p. 398.

2. R. G. Collingwood, *Speculum Mentis or The Map of Knowledge* (Oxford: Clarendon Press, 1924), p. 35. The best critical introduction to Collingwood's thought remains Louis O. Mink, *Mind, History, and Dialectic: The Philosophy of R. G. Collingwood* (Bloomington: Indiana University Press, 1969).

3. David Bohm, *Wholeness and the Implicate Order* (Boston: Routledge and Kegan Paul, 1980), p. 55.

4. See C. N. Cochrane, *Christianity and Classical Culture* (Oxford: Oxford University Press, 1980), p. 418.

5. Edmund Gosse, *Father and Son* (New York: W. W. Norton, 1963).

6. For perspective on recent battles, see Claudia Johnson, *Stifled Laughter: One Woman's Story about Fighting Censorship* (Golden, Colo.: Fulcrum, 1994).

7. Hans Reichenbach, *The Rise of Scientific Philosophy* (Berkeley: University of California Press, 1951), p. 27.

8. As I discuss further on in the text, for certain reasons I prefer the term "sensitive" to "psychic"—and I believe that Ingo Swann does, too. Yet I persist calling him a "psychic" (and have used the term elsewhere in the book as well) for reasons of convenience. Too many people are familiar with the term, and to pretend it doesn't exist might be misleading.

9. Ingo Swann, "An Autobiographical Essay Regarding Psi and Exceptional Human Experiences," *Exceptional Human Experience* 15:2 (December 1994), pp. 160–171.

10. Swann's story of his involvement with parapsychology and, subsequently, the remote viewing project at SRI International can be found on his website: www.biomindsuperpowers.com. See also his books *Everybody's Guide to Natural ESP* (Los Angeles: J. P. Tarcher, 1991) and *Your Nostradamus Factor* (New York: Fireside, 1993). The other "must" reads for those interested in an accurate understanding of remote viewing are the four books by Joe McMoneagle: *Mind Trek* (1993), *The Ultimate Time Machine* (1998), *Remote Viewing Secrets* (2000), and *The Stargate Chronicles* (2002). All four are published by Hampton Roads.

11. Swann, "An Autobiographical Essay," p. 161.

12. Swann, *Your Nostradamus Factor*, p. 65.

13. Chief Luther Standing Bear, *My Indian Boyhood* (Lincoln, Nebr.: University of Nebraska Press, 1988), p. 13.

14. Bear Heart with Molly Larkin, *The Wind Is My Mother* (New York: Clarkson Potter, 1996), p. 4.

15. William James, *The Varieties of Religious Experience* (New York: Modern Library, 1936), p. 490.

16. Standing Bear, p. 13.

17. In a posthumously published essay, "How to Build a Universe That Doesn't Fall Apart Two Days Later," included as the introduction in a collection of short stories, *I Hope I Shall Arrive Soon,* edited by Mark Hurst and Paul Williams (New York: St. Martin's, 1985), p. 4.

18. Colin Wilson, *Mysteries* (New York: Putnam, 1978), pp. 269–270.

19. Brian Weiss, *Messages from the Masters* (New York: Warner Books, 2000), p. 229.

20. It was the late 1980s when I finally got hold of a reprint of Layard's original (1944) work. See John Layard, *The Lady of the Hare: A Study in the Healing Power of Dreams* (Boston: Shambhala, 1988).

21. Hal Zina Bennett, *Spirit Animals and the Wheel of Life: Earth-Centered Practices for Daily Living* (Charlottesville, Va.: Hampton Roads, 2000), p. 29.

22. Ibid.

23. Marie-Louise von Franz, *An Introduction to the Interpretation of Fairy Tales* (Dallas, Tex.: Spring, 1970), p. 90. See also: von Franz, *Archetypal Patterns in Fairy Tales* (Toronto: Inner City, 1997), p. 169.

24. Bennett, *Spirit Animals,* p. 77.

25. Edward S. Curtis, *Native American Wisdom* (Philadelphia, Penn.: Running Press, 1993), p. 30.

Chapter 2

1. Fray Diego Durán, *The Aztecs: The History of the Indies of New Spain,* trans. Doris Hayden and Fernando Horcasitas (New York: Orion, 1964), p. 94.

2. See: Ian Stevenson, *Twenty Cases Suggestive of Reincarnation,* 2d ed. (Charlottesville: University Press of Virginia, 1974). Recently, Dr. Stevenson's work has been popularized by the Philadelphia writer Carol Bowman in her two fascinating books, *Children's Past Lives* (New York: Bantam, 1997) and *Return from Heaven* (New York: HarperCollins, 2001); and also by Tom Shroder, an initially skeptical Washington, D.C., journalist who investigated Stevenson's work in his book *Old Souls* (New York: Simon and Schuster, 1999).

3. Michael Talbot, *Your Past Lives: A Reincarnation Handbook* (New York: Harmony Books, 1987), pp. 1–2.

4. Michael Talbot, *Mysticism and the New Physics,* 2d ed. (London: Arkana, 1992), p. 134.

5. John Neihardt, *Black Elk Speaks: Being the Life Story of a Holy Man of the Oglala Sioux* (New York: Washington Square Press, 1972), p. 205.

6. See, for example, her *Adventures in Consciousness* (Englewood Cliffs, N.J.: Prentice-Hall, 1975) and *Psychic Politics* (Englewood Cliffs, N.J.: Prentice-Hall, 1976). Psychologist Roger Woolger is one of the few past-life therapist/ researchers to have appreciated the distinctive originality of Jane Roberts's view of reincarnation and the way it departs from both the orthodoxy of Eastern traditions, and what Woolger himself describes as the "well-worn Theosophical platitudes" characteristic of Western adaptations (Roger Woolger, *Other Lives, Other Selves: A Jungian Psychotherapist Discovers Past Lives* [New York: Bantam, 1988], p. 60). As Woolger noted in an interview with (the now defunct) *Common Boundary* magazine in 1987, Jane Roberts's view is neither viciously cyclical (like the Eastern view) nor straightforwardly linear and progressive (like the evolutionary doctrine of Madame Blavatsky and other Western esoterics), but holographic ("On Past-Life Therapy: An Interview with Roger Woolger," *Common Boundary* 5:6 [November/December 1987]). According to Roberts, all time is simultaneous and the whole of the greater self is equally present, albeit in somewhat different permutations and combinations, in each "incarnation" or personality, all of which exist at once, or in what she called a "spacious present." Hence the possibility (which I mention in chapter 7) of what Roberts called "bleedthroughs," not only from "past" to "future" selves, but also from "future" to "past" lives.

7. Joseph Chilton Pearce, *Magical Child: Rediscovering Nature's Plan for Our Children* (New York: Bantam, 1980).

8. Joseph Chilton Pearce, *Spiritual Initiation and the Breakthrough of Consciousness: The Bond of Power* (Rochester, Vt.: Park Street Press, 2003), p. 105. (Originally published by Dutton in 1981 as *The Bond of Power.*)

9. Ibid.

10. Joseph Campbell, *Transformations of Myth through Time* (New York: Harper and Row, 1990), p. 183.

11. Ibid.

12. Layne Redmond, *When the Drummers Were Women: A Spiritual History of Rhythm* (New York: Three Rivers Press, 1997), pp. 152–153.

13. Ibid., p. 152.

14. For years this impression baffled me, in the sense that I could find no independent corroboration for this kind of experience. I didn't doubt what I'd felt, but it seemed that no one else shared such feelings. (I could even recall as a child

treating certain chairs in our house as living, sentient beings.) Then, years later, I came across the animism of Native Americans, which most commentators (both scientific and religious) derided as "primitive," "childish," and "superstitious." Yet here was the confirmation I'd sought. Thus, Bear Heart: "What Western society calls 'inanimate objects'—rocks, jewelry, clothing, even furniture and buildings—my people regard as living entities because there's energy within them that's alive. We call stones 'rock people'" (p. 82). In our culture, when you give up what you truly know for what other people tell you to believe, you become a sophisticated, thoughtful, mature adult. Sort of ass-backward, isn't it?

15. Ingo Swann, "Remote Viewing: The Real Story," www.biomindsuperpowers.com.

16. Bear Heart, p. 68.

17. Personal communication with author.

18. On the symbolism of moon and snake, see his exquisite discussion in *The Masks of God: Occidental Mythology* (New York: VikingPenguin, 1976), pp. 9–17. I first encountered Campbell's writings by accident, while I was doing research for my dissertation at Oxford University back in the mid-1980s (this was shortly before Campbell's death and the subsequent Bill Moyers PBS interviews that made him somewhat of a household name). If it hadn't been for that chance encounter, however, I might never have finished my dissertation. Campbell's scholarship opened up whole new vistas for me. When I returned from my six-month stay in England, I completely revised my dissertation and eventually finished it after many false starts. There is an additional irony, and a kind of synchronistic "might have been," at work here. Years later, I met a woman from the Chicago area who had known Campbell. She informed me that he was still giving occasional lectures at the Jung Institute in Evanston in the late 1970s and early 1980s—around the time that "Julie," the female acquaintance I mentioned in chapter 1, advised me to drop in on the Jung Institute. If I had only followed Julie's suggestion, I might have encountered Campbell in the flesh and been saved a number of trying years of labor. For my own take on Campbell's view of myth and religion, see my article "Was Joseph Campbell a Postmodernist?" *Journal of the American Academy of Religion* 114:2 (Summer 1996), pp. 395–417.

19. Arthur Edward Waite, *The Pictorial Key to the Tarot* (Blauvelt, N.Y.: Rudolf Steiner, 1971), p. 140. It's often difficult to tell if Waite means what he says or whether he's just playing his metaphysical cards very close to the vest in the manner of the old-style "I've-got-a-secret-and-you-don't" forms of Western occultism ("occult" means hidden). It's entirely possible, however, that he really does believe that the lobster symbolizes "the nameless and hideous tendency which is lower than the savage beast" (Ibid.). In the biblical tradition, of course, matter is separate from spirit, and (inspirited) humans are "higher" forms than the "mere" animals, over whom they rule. Thus our own "lower" aspects are negatively identified with animals. This theme was amplified in the mainstream schools of Western esotericism, which accepted the Platonic dualism of the (rational) soul and (passionate, sensuous) body. In his great dialogue, the *Phaedo,* Plato cites approvingly the doctrine of the Orphic cult that the body is a tomb in which the soul is imprisoned; the physical form being the cause of all evil (in the sense of wrongdoing as well as pain and suffering). And in the *Phaedrus* Plato compares the body to a "crooked, lumbering animal" that must be mastered by the imperial soul. But compare all of this with Native American teachings: "The white man seems to look upon all animal life as enemies," writes

Chief Luther Standing Bear, "while we looked upon them as friends and benefactors" (Standing Bear, p.13). And Bear Heart declares, "We didn't consider ourselves above or below nature—we considered ourselves a part of nature . . . and [we] considered all life forms as [our] relatives, even plants, trees, birds, and animals" (Bear Heart, pp. 164–165).

20. A. T. Mann, *The Elements of the Tarot* (Rockport, Mass.: Element, 1993), p. 62.

21. Ed McGaa (Eagle Man), *Mother Earth Spirituality* (San Francisco: Harper and Row, 1990).

22. Bear Heart, p. 128.

23. Jane Roberts, *The Seth Material* (Englewood Cliffs, N.J.: Prentice-Hall, 1970), pp. 23–32.

Chapter 3

1. See chapters 1 and 2 of Campbell's *The Masks of God: Occidental Mythology* (New York: VikingPenguin, 1976), pp. 3–95. One of the truly original thinkers about Genesis is the writer (and onetime seminarian) Daniel Quinn. Quinn has his own distinctive view of the historical content of the Adam and Eve story (somewhat different from mine). In addition, he has provided one of the most stinging indictments of the failures of civilization and its religions. See, for example, his novels *Ishmael* (New York: Bantam, 1992) and *The Story of B* (New York: Bantam, 1996), the nonfiction work *Beyond Civilization* (New York: Three Rivers Press, 1999), and the autobiographical *Providence: The Story of a Fifty-Year Vision Quest* (New York: Bantam, 1995). Even when I disagree with Quinn's particular conclusions, I never fail to find him provocative and illuminating.

2. Compare the Hindu-Buddhist imperative of "breaking the circle" (or cycle) of life with Black Elk's desire to "mend the sacred hoop (circle)." The word-denying/escaping aspects of Eastern views are often soft-peddled when marketed to Western audiences, and they are certainly less dreary and caustic than old doom and gloom Christian apocalyptics. But there's a world of difference between the metaphysical assumptions and outlook of all the "higher" religions and those of the American Indian tradition, which feels at home in all the worlds—including this one. Which is why when so-called psychic or mystical experiences are viewed through the interpretive lenses of the "higher" religions, the meaning of those experiences becomes distorted and rigidly fixed in ways that do not permit the full opening to transcendence (and further inquiry) they were meant to provide. See my article, "Parapsychology without Religion: 'Breaking the Circle' or Circling the Wagons?" *Journal of the American Society for Psychical Research* 93:3 (July 1999), pp. 259–279.

3. Bruno Bettelheim, *The Uses of Enchantment: The Meaning and Importance of Fairy Tales* (New York: Vintage, 1977), pp. 212, 299–303.

4. See Jung's essay, "The Philosophical Tree," in *Alchemical Studies*, trans. R. F. C. Hull, Bollingen Series XX (Princeton, N.J.: Princeton University Press, 1983), pp. 251–349.

5. Mark St. Pierre and Tilda Long Soldier, *Walking in the Sacred Manner: Healers, Dreamers, and Pipe Carriers—Medicine Women of the Plains Indians* (New York: Simon and Schuster, 1995), p. 17.

6. See, for example, his essay "Relativity, Relatedness, and Reality," in *Spirit and Reason: The Vine Deloria Jr. Reader* (Golden, Colo.: Fulcrum, 1999), pp. 32–39.

7. Bear Heart, pp. 69–70.

8. "Can you answer? Yes I can, but what would be the answer to the answer

man?" Line from "St. Stephen," a song by The Grateful Dead (words by Robert Hunter; music by Jerry Garcia).

9. Elaine Pagels, *The Origin of Satan* (New York: Random House, 1995), pp. 163–164.

10. Thomas S. Kuhn, *The Structure of Scientific Revolutions*, 2d ed. (Chicago: University of Chicago Press, 1970). I was introduced to Kuhn's work in 1978, when I was a college undergraduate, by one of my professors. But I accidentally stumbled across David Bohm's magnum opus, *Wholeness and the Implicate Order* (Boston: Routledge and Kegan Paul, 1980) a few years later. Then I was an unhappy graduate student perusing the shelves of a local bookstore in search of ideas more nourishing than what I was being fed in my classes. I spied the intriguing title on the spine of the book, and that was it.

11. The story of Bohr and Einstein comes from Bohm, who was originally Einstein's protégé. See David Bohm and F. David Peat, *Science, Order and Creativity* (New York: Bantam, 1987), pp. 84–87. Bohm spent most of his final years discussing the links between his unique holistic vision of the universe and his view of the obstacles to creative thinking, inquiry, and dialogue. See, for example, his *Unfolding Meaning* (London: Ark/Routledge, 1987) and *Thought as a System* (New York: Routledge, 1994).

12. Vine Deloria Jr., "If You Think about It, You Will See That It Is True," in *Spirit and Reason*, p. 46.

13. "Information may be the body of knowledge, but questioning is its soul." (R. G. Collingwood, *Speculum Mentis*, p. 78). For a contemporary perspective on the importance of questioning, see Sam Keen *Hymns to an Unknown God: Awakening the Spirit in Everyday Life* (New York: Bantam, 1994).

14. Russell Means with Marvin J. Wolf, *Where White Men Fear to Tread: The Autobiography of Russell Means* (New York: St. Martin's Press, 1995), p. 13.

15. Stephen LaBerge of the Stanford University Sleep Research Center is unquestionably the greatest authority on lucid dreams. See his *Lucid Dreaming: The Power of Being Awake and Aware in Your Dreams* (New York: Ballantine, 1986).

16. Joseph McMoneagle, *Mind Trek* (Norfolk, Va.: Hampton Roads, 1993), p. 103.

Chapter 4

1. Michael Grosso, *Soulmaking: Uncommon Paths to Self-Understanding* (Charlottesville, Va.: Hampton Roads, 1997), p. 48.

2. Ralph Blum, *The Book of Runes* (New York: St. Martin's Press, 1993), pp. 137–138.

3. Ed McGaa (Eagle Man), *Native Wisdom: Perceptions of the Natural Way* (Minneapolis, Minn.: Four Directions, 1995), p. 62.

4. S. M. Rosen, "Exceptional Human Experience 13: Kundalini Awakening in a Hypnagogic State," *Exceptional Human Experience* 10 (1992), p. 190.

5. Cited in Mishka Jambor, "The Mystery of Frightening Transcendent Experiences: A Rejoinder to Nancy Evans Bush and Christopher Bache," *Journal of Near-Death Studies* 16:2, p. 174.

6. This correspondence was subsequently published in Steven M. Rosen, *Science, Paradox, and the Moebius Principle: The Evolution of a "Transcultural" Approach to Wholeness* (Albany, N.Y.: SUNY Press, 1994).

7. Raymond A. Moody Jr., *Life After Life* (Harrisburg, Penn.: Stackpole Books, 1976).

8. I originally read Rhea's account of her NDE in an unpublished paper she sent me soon after we initially became acquainted in the early 1990s. But this

paper was subsequently published (in a revised form) as a guest editorial in the *Journal of Near-Death Studies* 16:3, (Spring 1998), pp. 181–204, under the title, "The Amplification and Integration of Near-Death and Other Exceptional Human Experiences by the Larger Cultural Context: An Autobiographical Case." I am here quoting from the published version of her account (so that the reader may refer to it), which is identical in its essentials to the unpublished version with which I was first familiar. This excerpt appears on pp. 182–183.

9. Susy Smith, *The Afterlife Codes: Searching for Evidence of the Survival of the Soul* (Charlottesville, Va.: Hampton Roads, 2000), pp. 98–99.

10. Arthur Schopenhauer, "On Various Subjects," in *Essays and Aphorisms*, selected and translated with an introduction by R. J. Hollingdale (New York: Penguin, 1970), p. 222.

11. Ibid.

12. Swann, *Remote Viewing*, chapter 54, p. 7.

13. C. P. Snow, *The Two Cultures and a Second Look: An Expanded Version of "The Two Cultures and the Scientific Revolution"* (London: Cambridge University Press, 1969).

14. For information on advertising's history I am indebted to "History of Advertising—In Brief," at www.mediaknowall.com/gcse/advertising/history.html.

15. J. B. Watson, "Psychology as the Behaviorist Views It," *Psychological Review* 20 (1913), pp. 158–177.

16. "Little Snow White," in *The Complete Grimm's Fairy Tales*, introduction by Padraic Colum, folkloristic commentary by Joseph Campbell (New York: Pantheon Books, 1974), pp. 249–258.

17. Robert Bly, *Iron John: A Book about Men* (Reading, Mass.: Addison-Wesley, 1990).

18. Marie-Louise von Franz, *An Introduction to the Interpretation of Fairy Tales* (Dallas, Tex.: Spring, 1970), p. 13.

19. Layard, *The Lady of the Hare*, pp. 224–226.

Chapter 5

1. Hal Zina Bennett, *Write from the Heart: Unleashing the Power of Your Creativity* (Novato, Calif.: New World Library, 2001), p. xviii.

2. See Hal Zina Bennett, *Zuni Fetishes: Using Native American Objects for Meditation, Reflection, and Insight* (San Francisco: HarperSanFrancisco, 1993).

3. Raymond A. Moody Jr., *Reflections on Life After Life* (New York: Bantam, 1978), p. 15. (The original Mockingbird Books edition was published in 1977.)

4. Moody, *Reflections*, p. 17.

5. Carol Zaleski, *Otherworld Journeys: Accounts of Near-Death Experience in Medieval and Modern Times* (New York: Oxford University Press, 1987), p. 134.

6. Ibid.

7. For an argument along these lines, see Michael Grosso, "Psi, Survival, and Transpersonal Psychology: Some Points of Mutual Support," *Journal of the American Society for Psychical Research* 94:3–4 (July–October 2000), pp. 101–129.

8. Nandor Fodor, *The Haunted Mind: A Psychoanalyst Looks at the Supernatural* (New York: NAL Signet, 1969).

9. Sidney Saylor Farr, *What Tom Sawyer Learned from Dying* (Norfolk, Va.: Hampton Roads, 1993), p. 27.

10. Richard Maurice Bucke, *Cosmic Consciousness: A Study in the Evolution of the Human Mind* (New York: E. P. Dutton, 1969), pp. 9–10.

11. Jacques Vallee, *Dimensions: A Casebook of Alien Contact* (Chicago: Contemporary Books, 1988).

12. P. M. H. Atwater, "Another Look: The Experience/The Experiencer," *Vital Signs* 17:4 (1998), p. 7.

13. Kenneth Ring, *Heading toward Omega: In Search of the Meaning of the Near-Death Experience* (New York: Quill, 1985), p. 102.

14. Ibid., p. 100.

15. Ibid.

16. Joseph Campbell with Michael Toms, *An Open Life: Joseph Campbell in Conversation with Michael Toms*, ed. John M. Maher and Dennie Briggs (New York: Larson, 1988), pp.73–75.

17. John Neihardt, *Black Elk Speaks*, p. 134.

18. Cherie Sutherland, *Within the Light* (New York: Bantam, 1995), pp. 179–185.

19. David Bohm, *Thought as a System*, pp. 22–23.

20. Which is why the history of the "higher" religions of civilization (both exoteric and esoteric) is a long, bloody story of sectarian schisms and conflicts and drives for total "purification." Of course, some religious systems are less permeable to outside influences than others (at least that's the way they see themselves). For example, holistic health expert Dr. Andrew Weil has commented in his monthly newsletter on the crusade against soy and soy products launched by evangelical Christians "who believe that soy is an unfit food because it isn't mentioned in the Bible" (*Andrew Weil's Self Healing* [March 2003], p.2). (And probably also because interest in health foods may lead to an unhealthy interest in self-healing and other forbidden "New Age" concepts. After all, bananas and computers aren't mentioned in the Bible, either, but you don't see fundamentalists launching crusades against them.)

21. Robert Bly with Michael Toms, "Male Naïveté and Giving the Gold Away," A *New Dimensions* radio interview with Robert Bly, program no. 2052 (1990).

22. Cited in Elaine Pagels, *The Gnostic Gospels* (New York: Vintage, 1981), p. 153.

23. Rhea A. White, "Exceptional Human Experiences and the Experiential Paradigm," in *Body, Mind, Spirit: Exploring the Parapsychology of Spirituality*, edited by Charles T. Tart (Charlottesville, Va.: Hampton Roads, 1997), p. 84.

24. Hermann Hesse, *Demian*, trans. M. Roloff and M. Lebeck (New York: Bantam, 1970), p. 102.

Chapter 6

1. Cited in George McMullen, *One White Crow* (Norfolk, Va.: Hampton Roads, 1994), p. 94. Here's another "almost synchronicity" that, much like my missing out on meeting Joseph Campbell in the flesh, might have saved me much subsequent anguish. In 1974, when I was a high school senior, several of the members of our anthropology class (along with our teacher) were invited by the American Anthropological Association to deliver papers at a symposium to be conducted at the association's annual meeting in Mexico City. (This was the first time that high school students participated in such a way.) We did indeed attend the meeting (some of our group even got to meet Dr. Margaret Mead, the famous anthropologist, who was on our flight from New York to Mexico City). But it somehow escaped my notice that one Dr. Norman Emerson would be delivering a paper entitled "Intuitive Archaeology: A Developing Approach" at the very same meeting. Had I attended that symposium and met Dr. Emerson—well, who knows?

2. Mircea Eliade, *Shamanism: Archaic Techniques of Ecstasy,* trans. Willard R. Trask, Bollingen Series LXXVI (Princeton, N.J.: Princeton University Press, 1964), p. 36.

3. Ibid., p. 66.

4. White, of course, is often the color of purity and rebirth (and also of death). But an ancient Greek legend said that while true dreams passed through gates of horn from their origin in the underworld on their way to the upper realm of humans, false dreams passed through gates of ivory (see Edith Hamilton, *Mythology* [New York: NAL Penguin, Inc., 1969], p. 40). Perhaps, then, the ivory shoulder of Pelops is also a tacit reference to the shaman's well-known trickster-like qualities.

5. Robert A. Monroe, *Journeys Out of the Body* (Garden City, N.Y.: Doubleday, 1971).

6. This literature is vast and ever expanding. The Institute has literally hundreds of papers in its files. A partial listing through 1994 may be found in the bibliography of Robert Monroe's third book, *Ultimate Journey.* But the literature has grown ever so much since then. For a basic survey of the uses of Hemi-Sync, see Ronald Russell (ed.), *Focusing the Whole Brain: Transforming Your Life with Hemispheric Synchronization* (Charlottesville, Va: Hampton Roads, 2004). The clearest, most accurate, and most succinct explanation of the Hemi-Sync process as it is used in Institute workshops may be found in a paper authored by TMI's research director, F. Holmes ("Skip") Atwater, entitled "The Hemi-Sync Process," (June 1999), published by The Monroe Institute (reprints available by request). Psychologist Todd Joseph Masluk recently published a comprehensive two-part study of the Hemi-Sync process and its role in facilitating Exceptional Human Experiences. See "Reports of Peak and Other Experiences during a Neurotechnology-Based Training Program," *Journal of the American Society for Psychical Research* 92:4 (October 1998), pp. 313–401, and 93:1 (January 1999), pp. 1–98.

7. Robert A. Monroe, *Ultimate Journey* (New York: Doubleday, 1994), p. 109.

Chapter 7

1. Rosemary Ellen Guiley, *The Mystical Tarot* (New York: Signet, 1991), p. 110.

2. Lame Deer/John Fire and Richard Erdoes, *Lame Deer: Seeker of Visions* (New York: Simon and Schuster, 1972), p. 135.

3. Monroe, *Ultimate Journey,* p. 273.

4. From "Welcome to *Lifeline,*" a flyer of The Monroe Institute.

5. McMoneagle, *Mind Trek,* p. 113.

Epilogue

1. McMoneagle, *Mind Trek,* p. 113.

2. Paul Feyerabend, *Science in a Free Society* (London: New Left Books, 1978), p. 96.

3. Charles T. Tart, "States of Consciousness and the State-Specific Sciences," *Science* 176:12 (June 1972), pp. 1203–1210. See his follow-up commentary, "On the Scientific Study of Other Worlds," in D. Weiner and R. Nelson (eds.), *Research in Parapsychology 1986* (Metuchen, N.J.: Scarecrow Press, 1987), p. 145.

4. See Chares T. Tart, "On the Scientific Study of Nonphysical Worlds," chapter 13 of Charles T. Tart (ed.), *Body, Mind, Spirit: Exploring the Parapsychology of Spirituality* (Charlottesville, Va.: Hampton Roads, 1997), p. 214.

5. See, for example, his brilliant 1984 essay "Parapsychology's 'Four Cultures': Can the Schism Be Mended?" reprinted as Chapter 10 of Steven M. Rosen, *Science, Paradox, and the Moebius Principle,* pp. 167–178.

6. The famous and esteemed Irish medium/sensitive Eileen Garrett

(1893–1970) had a most intellectually sophisticated understanding of her abilities. Although originally influenced by the Spiritualist movement (and though she allowed herself to be thoroughly studied by scientists and psychologists), she steadfastly refused to accommodate her experiences to any preconceived conceptual or theoretical categories. For example, she refused to subscribe to the belief that her "controls" (trance personalities) were either merely subconscious fragments of her own personality or the fully independent Spirit Guides that they themselves claimed to be. So she could accept neither the psychological reductionism of "scientific" psychology nor the naïve uncritical credulity of old-fashioned Spiritualist doctrine. And this left the door wide open to a genuine inquiry into the nature of the phenomenon—which is exactly what she intended. Mrs. Garrett went on to found the nonprofit Parapsychology Foundation in New York City, which, thanks to her prodigious influence and courageous example, remains a center of genuine inquiry to this day. See, for example, her riveting memoir, *Many Voices: The Autobiography of a Medium* (New York: Dell, 1969).

7. Joseph Bruchac, *The Waters Between: A Novel of the Dawn Land* (Hanover, N.H.: University Press of New England, 1998), p. xv.

8. Vine Deloria Jr., *God Is Red: A Native View of Religion,* 2d ed. (Golden, Colo.: Fulcrum, 1994), p. 67.

9. Ibid.

10. Vine Deloria Jr., "Vision and Community," chapter in Vine Deloria Jr., *For This Land: Writings on Religion in America,* ed. James Treat (New York: Routledge, 1999), p. 116.

11. Arthur Schopenhauer, "On Thinking for Yourself," chapter in Arthur Schopenhauer, *Essays and Aphorisms,* selected and translated with an introduction by R. J. Hollingdale (New York: Penguin, 1970), p. 91.

12. Deloria, "Vision and Community," p. 117.

Bibliography

Atwater, F. Holmes (1999). *The Hemi-Sync Process*. Faber, Va.: The Monroe Institute.

Atwater, P. M. H. (1998). "Another look: The experience/the experiencer." *Vital Signs* 17: 6–8.

Bear Heart with Larkin, Molly (1996). *The Wind Is My Mother*. New York: Clarkson Potter.

Bennett, Hal Zina (1993). *Zuni Fetishes: Using Native American Objects for Meditation, Reflection, and Insight*. San Francisco: HarperSanFrancisco.

——— (2000). *Spirit Animals and the Wheel of Life*. Charlottesville, Va.: Hampton Roads.

——— (2001). *Write from the Heart: Unleashing the Power of Your Creativity*. Novato, Calif.: New World Library.

Bettelheim, Bruno (1977). *The Uses of Enchantment: The Meaning and Importance of Fairy Tales*. New York: Vintage.

Blum, Ralph (1993). *The Book of Runes*. New York: St. Martin's Press.

Bly, Robert (1990). *Iron John: A Book about Men*. Reading, Mass.: Addison-Wesley.

Bly, Robert, with Michael Toms (1990). Male naïveté and giving the gold away: A New Dimensions radio interview with Robert Bly. Program no. 2052.

Bohm, David (1980). *Wholeness and the Implicate Order*. Boston: Routledge and Kegan Paul.

——— (1987). *Unfolding Meaning*. London: Ark/Routledge.

——— (1994). *Thought as a System*. New York: Routledge.

Bohm, David, and F. David Peat (1987). *Science, Order and Creativity*. New York: Bantam.

Bowman, Carol (1997). *Children's Past Lives.* New York: Bantam.

——— (2001). *Return from Heaven.* New York: HarperCollins.

Bruchac, Joseph (1998). *The Waters Between: A Novel of the Dawn Land.* Hanover, N.H.: University Press of New England.

Bucke, Richard Maurice (1969). *Cosmic Consciousness: A Study in the Evolution of the Human Mind.* New York: E. P. Dutton. (Original work published 1901.)

Campbell, Joseph (1976). *The Masks of God: Occidental Mythology.* New York: Viking Penguin.

——— (1990). *Transformations of Myth through Time.* New York: Harper and Row.

Campbell, Joseph, with Bill Moyers (1988). *The Power of Myth.* New York: Doubleday.

Campbell, Joseph, with Michael Toms (1988). *An Open Life: Joseph Campbell in Conversation with Michael Toms.* Ed. John M. Maher and Dennie Briggs. New York: Larson.

Camus, Albert (1955). *The Myth of Sisyphus: And Other Essays.* Trans. Justin O'Brien. New York: Knopf.

Cochrane, Charles Norris (1980). *Christianity and Classical Culture.* Oxford: Oxford University Press. (Original work published 1940.)

Collingwood, Robin George (1924). *Speculum Mentis.* Oxford: Clarendon Press.

The Complete Grimm's Fairy Tales (1974). New York: Pantheon.

Curtis, Edward S. (1993) *Native American Wisdom.* Philadephia, Penn.: Running Press.

Deloria, Vine Jr. (1994). *God Is Red: A Native View of Religion.* 2d ed. Golden, Colo.: Fulcrum.

——— (1999). *For This Land: Writings on Religion in America.* Ed. James Treat. New York: Routledge.

——— (1999). *Spirit and Reason: The Vine Deloria Jr. Reader.* Golden, Colo.: Fulcrum.

Dick, Philip K. (1985). *I Hope I Shall Arrive Soon.* Ed. Mark Hurst and Paul Williams. New York: Doubleday.

Durán, Fray Diego (1964). *The Aztecs: The History of the Indies of New Spain.* Trans. Doris Hayden and Fernando Horcasitas. New York: Orion.

Eliade, Mircea (1964). *Shamanism: Archaic Techniques of Ecstasy.* Trans. Willard V. Trask. Bollingen Series LXXVI. Princeton, N.J.: Princeton University Press.

Farr, Sidney Saylor (1993). *What Tom Sawyer Learned from Dying.* Norfolk, Va.: Hampton Roads.

Felser, Joseph M. (1996). Was Joseph Campbell a postmodernist? *Journal of the American Academy of Religion* 114: 395–417.

—— (1999a). From darkness to light: A philosophical musing on the hanukkah myth, the return of the goddess, and the end of religion. *Mythosphere* 1: 463–506.

—— (1999b). Parapsychology without religion: "Breaking the circle" or circling the wagons? *Journal of the American Society for Psychical Research* 93: 259–279.

Feyerabend, Paul (1978). *Science in a Free Society.* London: New Left Books.

Fodor, Nandor (1969). *The Haunted Mind: A Psychoanalyst Looks at the Supernatural.* New York: NAL Signet.

Franz, Marie-Louise von (1970). *An Introduction to the Interpretation of Fairy Tales.* Dallas, Tex.: Spring.

—— (1997). *Archetypal Patterns in Fairy Tales.* Toronto: Inner City.

Frazer, J. G. (1981). *The Golden Bough: The Roots of Folklore and Religion.* Two vols. in one. New York: Avanel. (Original work published in 1890.)

Garrett, Eileen J. (1969). *Many Voices: The Autobiography of a Medium.* New York: Dell.

Gosse, Edmund (1963). *Father and Son: A Study of Two Temperaments.* New York: W. W. Norton. (Original work published 1907.)

Graves, Robert (1966). *The White Goddess: A Historical Grammar of Poetic Myth.* 2nd ed. New York: Farrar, Straus and Giroux. (Original work published 1948.)

Grosso, Michael (1997). *Soulmaking: Uncommon Paths to Self-Understanding.* Charlottesville, Va.: Hampton Roads.

—— (2000). Psi, survival, and transpersonal psychology: Some points of mutual support. *Journal of the American Society for Psychical Research* 94: 3–4, 101–129.

Guiley, Rosemary Ellen (1991). *The Mystical Tarot.* New York: Signet.

Hamilton, Edith (1969). *Mythology.* New York: NAL Penguin, Inc. (Original work published in 1942, Boston: Little, Brown and Company.)

Harman, Willis, and Howard Rheingold (1984). *Higher Creativity: Liberating the Unconscious for Breakthrough Insights.* Los Angeles: J.P. Tarcher.

Hesse, Hermann (1970). *Demian.* Trans. M. Roloff and M. Lebeck. New York: Bantam.

Jambor, Mishka (1998). The mystery of frightening transcendent experiences: A rejoinder to Nancy Evans Bush and Christopher Bache. *Journal of Near-Death Studies* 16: 163–176.

James, William (1936). *The Varieties of Religious Experience.* New York: Modern Library. (Original work published in 1902.)

Johnson, Claudia (1994). *Stifled Laughter: One Woman's Story about Fighting Censorship.* Golden, Colo.: Fulcrum.

Jung, Carl G. (1965). *Memories, Dreams, Reflections.* 2d ed. Ed. Aniela Jaffé. Trans. Richard and Clara Winston. New York: Vintage.

——— (1983). *Alchemical Studies.* Trans. R. F. C. Hull. Bollingen Series XX. Princeton, N.J.: Princeton University Press.

Keen, Sam (1994). *Hymns to an Unknown God: Awakening the Spirit in Everyday Life.* New York: Bantam.

Kuhn, Thomas S. (1970). *The Structure of Scientific Revolutions.* 2d ed. Chicago: University of Chicago Press.

LaBerge, Stephen (1986). *Lucid Dreaming: The Power of Being Awake and Aware in Your Dreams.* New York: Ballantine.

Lame Deer/John Fire and Richard Erdoes (1972). *Lame Deer: Seeker of Visions.* New York: Simon and Schuster.

Layard, John (1988). *The Lady of the Hare: A Study in the Healing Power of Dreams.* Boston: Shambhala. (Original work published 1944.)

Mann, A. T. (1993). *The Elements of the Tarot.* Rockport, Mass.: Element.

Masluk, Todd Joseph (1998). Reports of peak- and other experiences during a neurotechnology-based training program. *Journal of the American Society for Psychical Research* 92: 313–401.

——— (1999). Reports of peak- and other experiences during a neurotechnology-based training program. *Journal of the American Society for Psychical Research* 93: 1–98.

McGaa, Ed (Eagle Man) (1990). *Mother Earth Spirituality.* San Francisco: Harper and Row.

——— (1995). *Native Wisdom: Perceptions of the Natural Way.* Minneapolis, Minn.: Four Directions.

McMoneagle, Joseph (1993). *Mind Trek.* Norfolk, Va.: Hampton Roads.

——— (1998). *The Ultimate Time Machine.* Charlottesville, Va.: Hampton Roads.

——— (2000). *Remote Viewing Secrets.* Charlottesville, Va.: Hampton Roads.

——— (2002). *The Stargate Chronicles.* Charlottesville, Va.: Hampton Roads.

McMullen, George (1994). *One White Crow.* Norfolk, Va.: Hampton Roads.

Means, Russell, with Marvin Wolf (1995). *Where White Men Fear to Tread: The Autobiography of Russell Means.* New York: St. Martin's Press.

Monroe, Robert A. (1971). *Journeys Out of the Body.* Garden City, N.Y.: Doubleday.

——— (1994). *Ultimate Journey.* New York: Doubleday.

Moody, Raymond A. Jr. (1976). *Life After Life.* Harrisburg, Penn.: Stackpole Books.

——— (1978). *Reflections on Life After Life.* New York: Bantam.

Neihardt, John (1972). *Black Elk Speaks: Being the Life Story of a Holy Man of the Oglala Sioux.* New York: Washington Square Press. (Original work published 1932.)

Pagels, Elaine (1981). *The Gnostic Gospels*. New York: Vintage.

—— (1995). *The Origin of Satan*. New York: Random House.

Pearce, Joseph Chilton (1980). *Magical Child: Rediscovering Nature's Plan for Our Children*. New York: Bantam.

—— (2003). *Spiritual Initiation and the Breakthrough of Consciousness: The Bond of Power*. Rochester, Vt.: Park Street Press.

Quinn, Daniel (1992). *Ishmael*. New York: Bantam.

—— (1995). *Providence: The Story of a Fifty-Year Vision Quest*. New York: Bantam.

—— (1996). *The Story of B*. New York: Bantam.

—— (1999). *Beyond Civilization*. New York: Random House.

Redmond, Layne (1997). *When the Drummers Were Women: A Spiritual History of Rhythm*. New York: Three Rivers Press.

Reichenbach, Hans (1951). *The Rise of Scientific Philosophy*. Berkeley: University of California Press.

Ring, Kenneth (1985). *Heading toward Omega: In Search of the Meaning of the Near-Death Experience*. New York: Quill.

Roberts, Jane (1970). *The Seth Material*. Englewood Cliffs, N.J.: Prentice-Hall.

—— (1975). *Adventures in Consciousness*. Englewood Cliffs, N.J.: Prentice-Hall.

—— (1976). *Psychic Politics*. Englewood Cliffs, N.J.: Prentice-Hall.

—— (1981). *The God of Jane: A Psychic Manifesto*. Englewood Cliffs, N.J.: Prentice-Hall.

Rosen, Steven M. (1992). Exceptional human experience 13: Kundalini awakening in a hypnagogic state. *Exceptional Human Experience* 10: 190.

—— (1994). *Science, Paradox, and the Moebius Principle: The Evolution of a "Transcultural" Approach to Wholeness*. Albany, N.Y.: SUNY Press.

Russell, Bertrand (1961). *Basic Writings: 1903–1959*. Ed. Robert E. Egner and Lester E. Denonn. New York: Simon and Schuster.

Russell, Ronald, ed. (2004). *Focusing the Whole Brain: Transforming Your Life with Hemisheric Synchronization*. Charlottesville, Va.: Hampton Roads.

St. Pierre, Mark, and Tilda Long Soldier (1995). *Walking in the Sacred Manner: Healers, Dreamers, and Pipe Carriers—Medicine Women of the Plains Indians*. New York: Simon and Schuster.

Schopenhauer, Arthur (1970). *Essays and Aphorisms*. Selected and translated with an introduction by R. J. Hollingdale. New York: Penguin.

Shroder, Tom (1999). *Old Souls*. New York: Simon and Schuster.

Smith, Susy (2000). *The Afterlife Codes: Searching for Evidence of the Survival of the Soul*. Charlottesville, Va.: Hampton Roads.

Snow, C. P. (1969). *The Two Cultures and a Second Look: An Expanded Version of "The Two Cultures and the Scientific Revolution."* London: Cambridge University Press.

Spence, Lewis (1960). *An Encyclopedia of Occultism.* New Hyde Park, N.Y.: University Books. (Original work published in 1920.)

Standing Bear, Chief Luther (1988). *My Indian Boyhood.* Lincoln, Nebr.: University of Nebraska Press. (Original work published 1931.)

Stevenson, Ian (1974). *Twenty Cases Suggestive of Reincarnation.* 2d ed. Charlottesville: University Press of Virginia.

Storm, Hyemeyohsts (1994). *Lightningbolt.* New York: Ballantine.

Sutherland, Cherie (1995). *Within the Light.* New York: Bantam.

Swann, Ingo (1991). *Everybody's Guide to Natural ESP.* Los Angeles: J. P. Tarcher.

———— (1993). *Your Nostradamus Factor.* New York: Fireside.

———— (1994). An autobiographical essay regarding psi and exceptional human experiences. *Exceptional Human Experience* 15, 160–171.

———— *Remote Viewing: The Real Story.* www.biomindsuperpowers.com.

Talbot, Michael (1987). *Your Past Lives: A Reincarnation Handbook.* New York: Harmony.

———— (1992). *Mysticism and the New Physics.* 2d ed. London: Arkana.

Tart, Charles T. (1972). States of consciousness and the state-specific sciences. *Science* 176: 1203–1210.

———— (1987). On the scientific study of other worlds. In D. Weiner and R. Nelson (eds.). *Research in Parapsychology 1986.* Metuchen, N.J.: Scarecrow Press.

Tart, Charles T., ed. (1997). *Body, Mind, Spirit: Exploring the Parapsychology of Spirituality.* Charlottesville, Va.: Hampton Roads.

Vallee, Jacques (1988). *Dimensions: A Casebook of Alien Contact.* Chicago: Contemporary Books.

Waite, Arthur Edward (1971). *The Pictorial Key to the Tarot.* Blauvelt, N.Y.: Rudolf Steiner.

Watson, J. B. (1913). Psychology as the behaviorist views it. *Psychological Review* 20: 158–177.

Weiss, Brian (2000). *Messages from the Masters.* New York: Warner Books.

White, Rhea A. (1998). The amplification and integration of near-death and other exceptional human experiences by the larger cultural context: An autobiographical case. *Journal of Near-Death Studies* 16: 181–204.

———— (1997). Exceptional human experiences and the experiential paradigm. In Charles T. Tart (ed). *Body, Mind, Spirit: Exploring the Parapsychology of Spirituality.* Charlottesville, Va.: Hampton Roads, pp 83–100.

Wilson, Colin (1978). *Mysteries.* New York: Putnam.

Woolger, Roger (1987). On past-life therapy: An interview with Roger Woolger. *Common Boundary* 5:7–9.

——— (1988). *Other Lives, Other Selves: A Jungian Psychotherapist Discovers Past Lives.* New York: Bantam.

Zaleski, Carol (1987). *Otherworld Journeys: Accounts of Near-Death Experience in Medieval and Modern Times.* New York: Oxford University Press.

Index

About the Author

Joseph M. Felser received his doctorate in philosophy from the University of Chicago. He has taught at various colleges in the New York City area and is presently on the faculty of Kingsborough Community College/CUNY in Brooklyn, New York. He is the author of numerous articles on religion, myth, parapsychology, and the paranormal. His essays and reviews have appeared in both scholarly journals and popular magazines, including *The Journal of the American Society for Psychical Research, Mythosphere,* and *The Anomalist.* For the past seven years he has served as an editorial advisor to Rhea A. White's groundbreaking journal, *Exceptional Human Experience.* He lives with his wife and their golden retriever in suburban New Jersey and spends most of his summers on Maine's majestic Sebago Lake, where he enjoys writing, swimming, walking, and watching the sun set over Douglas Mountain and the Saddleback Hills.

Dr. Felser is currently conducting research for his second book, a study of individuals who had premonitions of the 9/11 attack on America. For more information on this and other works by the author, please visit his web site: www.magicand reason.com.

Hampton Roads Publishing Company

. . . for the evolving human spirit

Hampton Roads Publishing Company
publishes books on a variety of subjects,
including metaphysics, health,
visionary fiction, and other related topics.

For a copy of our latest catalog, call toll-free
(800) 766-8009, or send your name and address to:

Hampton Roads Publishing Company, Inc.
1125 Stoney Ridge Road
Charlottesville, VA 22902

e-mail: hrpc@hrpub.com
www.hrpub.com